W9-BMG-693

A12901 739642

4/08

Withdrawn

I.C.C. LIBRARY

PENSION PUZZLES

PENSION PUZZLES
SOCIAL SECURITY
AND THE GREAT DEBATE

MELISSA HARDY AND LAWRENCE HAZELRIGG

I.C.C. LIBRARY

A Volume in the American Sociological Association's
Rose Series in Sociology

Russell Sage Foundation • New York

HD
7125
.H333
2007

Library of Congress Cataloging-in-Publication Data

Hardy, Melissa A., 1952–
    Pension puzzles : social security and the great debate / by Melissa Hardy & Lawrence Hazelrigg.
        p. cm.
    Includes bibliographical references and index.
    ISBN 978-0-87154-333-2
    1. Social security—United States—Finance. 2. Social security—United States. 3. Pension trusts—United States. 4. Privatization—United States. I. Hazelrigg, Lawrence. II. Title.

    HD7125.H333 2007
    368.4'300973—dc22

                                                        2006102838

Copyright © 2007 by American Sociological Association. All rights reserved. Printed in the United States of America. No part of this publication may be reproduced, stored in a retrieval system, or transmitted in any form or by any means, electronic, mechanical, photo-copying, recording, or otherwise, without the prior written permission of the publisher.

Reproduction by the United States Government in whole or in part is permitted for any purpose.

The paper used in this publication meets the minimum requirements of American National Standard for Information Sciences—Permanence of Paper for Printed Library Materials. ANSI Z39.48-1992.

Text design by Suzanne Nichols.

RUSSELL SAGE FOUNDATION
112 East 64th Street, New York, New York 10021
10 9 8 7 6 5 4 3 2 1

The Russell Sage Foundation

The Russell Sage Foundation, one of the oldest of America's general purpose foundations, was established in 1907 by Mrs. Margaret Olivia Sage for "the improvement of social and living conditions in the United States." The Foundation seeks to fulfill this mandate by fostering the development and dissemination of knowledge about the country's political, social, and economic problems. While the Foundation endeavors to assure the accuracy and objectivity of each book it publishes, the conclusions and interpretations in Russell Sage Foundation publications are those of the authors and not of the Foundation, its Trustees, or its staff. Publication by Russell Sage, therefore, does not imply Foundation endorsement.

BOARD OF TRUSTEES
Thomas D. Cook, Chair

Kenneth D. Brody	Jennifer L. Hochschild	Cora B. Marrett
Robert E. Denham	Kathleen Hall Jamieson	Richard H. Thaler
Christopher Edley, Jr.	Melvin J. Konner	Eric Wanner
John A. Ferejohn	Alan B. Krueger	Mary C. Waters
Larry V. Hedges		

EDITORS OF THE ROSE SERIES IN SOCIOLOGY

Douglas L. Anderton	Naomi Gerstel	Randall G. Stokes
Dan Clawson	Joya Misra	Robert Zussman

THE ROSE SERIES IN SOCIOLOGY EDITORIAL BOARD

Karen Barkey	Nicole P. Marwell	Rogelio Saenz
Frank D. Bean	Douglas McAdam	Michael Schwartz
Howard S. Becker	Mark Mizruchi	Rachel Sherman
Charles L. Bosk	Jan P. Nederveen Pieterse	Judith Stepan-Norris
Maxine Craig	Margaret K. Nelson	Ronald L. Taylor
Frank Dobbin	Katherine Shelley Newman	Kim Voss
Peter B. Evans	Francesca Polletta	Jerry G. Watts
Sally K. Gallagher	Harriet B. Presser	Julia C. Wrigley
Sharon Hays	Jyoti Puri	Robert Wuthnow
Pierrette Hondagneu-Sotelo	William G. Roy	Alford A. Young, Jr.
Miliann Kang	Deirdre Royster	

2/08 B&T 37.50

Previous Volumes in the Series

Forthcoming Titles

The Rose Series in Sociology

THE AMERICAN Sociological Association's Rose Series in Sociology publishes books that integrate knowledge and address controversies from a sociological perspective. Books in the Rose Series are at the forefront of sociological knowledge. They are lively and often involve timely and fundamental issues on significant social concerns. The series is intended for broad dissemination throughout sociology, across social science and other professional communities, and to policy audiences. The series was established in 1967 by a bequest to ASA from Arnold and Caroline Rose to support innovations in scholarly publishing.

DOUGLAS L. ANDERTON
DAN CLAWSON
NAOMI GERSTEL
JOYA MISRA
RANDALL G. STOKES
ROBERT ZUSSMAN

EDITORS

Contents

About the Authors

Melissa Hardy is director of the Gerontology Center and Distinguished Professor of Human Development and Family Studies, Sociology and Demography at The Pennsylvania State University.

Lawrence Hazelrigg is professor emeritus at Florida State University and adjunct professor of sociology at The Pennsylvania State University.

Preface

When we began writing this book, we faced an obvious question: Why another book about Social Security? As we wrote and rewrote sections and chapters, we struggled to keep our focus on a coherent response to that question. This book is not just about Social Security: it uses the case of Social Security to show readers that the current conflict over the future of this particular public program is really about something bigger. True, the conflict has overtly been mostly about the benefits, taxes, trust fund, and rules of eligibility that make up the Social Security program. But the real points of dispute are more fundamental and less arcane. We wrote this book mainly to rekindle a dialogue on these more fundamental questions. Our intended audience is the general but interested reader, anyone who is interested in current issues of social policy. This intent accounts for the fact that our presentation is sometimes rather conversational in style and tone. We do not avoid complex technical issues, but, where useful, translate them into simpler, more accessible language. We have been sensitive to the fact that such efforts of translation can neglect important nuances. Retrieving those nuances, also into more accessible language, has rendered some of our text very slow to the eye of professional policy analysts and social scientists. We were not writing for them. Our preference was to err toward being too elementary in detail and length of exposition, rather than to assume too much. As we acknowledge repeatedly, there are too many discussions already that attempt to persuade of this or that view by camouflaging with words and omissions. We have tried genuinely to avoid all such tricks, though we recognize that effort does not equate with success. We also recognize, however, that part of that difference is up to the reader. We ask the reader to work with us to understand the different arguments about Social Security, and the larger issues in which they are embedded, in their own terms before deciding whether he or she finds this or that particular argument the more persuasive.

As some readers will soon recognize, the book draws on many other authors. A large stable of footnotes (or, now, endnotes—a format requirement) pays much of the debt. For the missing notes also we apologize. Our intent has not been to claim anything that we have no right to claim as ours. We have lived long enough to realize that most ideas are recycled, often a great many times, sometimes in vocabulary or application that gives them the flavor of novelty (which is another way of saying that development is usually more important, at least quantitatively, than invention). Our wish and our struggle has been to enhance clarity of understanding of some issues that are actually quite complicated, and to do so in spite of and because of the many efforts to deflect attention away from the complications in order better to serve some ideological or political religious agenda.

Some acknowledgments cannot be omitted. First of all, each of us thanks the other for patience, forbearance, respect, and love; daughter, Katherine, for all her help and generosity; sons Greg and Chris, and grandchildren Chase, Sasha, Ella, Noah, and Sha Sha for encouragement and motivation; Suzanne Nichols for shepherding the manuscript through the publishing process with skill and patience; students over too many years who listened to our ideas and encouraged us to compose them as a book; colleagues who read different chapters, and several colleagues in particular—Douglas Anderton, Angela O'Rand, Debra Street, Pam Farley Short, the Rose Monograph Editorial Board, and anonymous reviewers—who read several versions and offered much good advice for improvements; Ann Shuey, who helped us keep track of bits and pieces that ultimately became a complete manuscript and who provided frequent doses of humor and enthusiasm; Helen Glenn Court for her expert copyediting; and Robert M. Ball, whose deep and abiding commitment to the Social Security program remains vital, inspiring, and cause of great admiration.

We are content with the fact that errors hereafter are ours.

Chapter 1

Introduction

I s ANY American adult still unaware of the crisis of Social Security—or, more generally, as the title of an article in *Forbes Magazine* declared, "the end of pensions" (Dan Ackman, "The End of Pensions," *Forbes.com*, May 11, 2005)? Certainly most adults who do not yet receive Social Security or private pension benefits hope to live long enough to need retirement income, and those who do surely expect those benefits to continue at current levels (and in some cases, Social Security among them, at inflation-adjusted levels). Add to those expectations the enormous clamor in recent years over the bankruptcy of Social Security and employer-sponsored pension plans, and surely anyone but the privately wealthy would be expressing profound concern about the fragility of their claims on future benefits. Granted, the clamor has often been what is sometimes called all heat and no light. Still, it seems odd that, as of February 2005, judging from a national survey by Princeton University's Survey Research Center, nearly one in ten adults aged fifty-five or older professed to follow news about Social Security "not at all closely" and to know nothing about sitting President G. W. Bush's proposal to privatize Social Security (Pew Research Center for the People and the Press 2005). Perhaps this ignorance was professed only because Bush's proposal was very short on specifics. Bush and his supporters had been working hard to make "the crisis of Social Security" a defining issue of his second administration, however, and the survey results suggested that more and more adults were beginning to pay attention—though it appeared that the more they heard about the Bush proposal, the less they liked it.

Adults in their forties or older, however, have already seen so-called problems with Social Security come and go as a series of adjustments addressed concerns about the program's sustainability. As its name implies, the prevailing view of Social Security has been an underlying confidence in the security of its promise. Each reincarnation of concern pits forecasts of economic catastrophe against equally insistent claims that the program is, on the whole, sound enough that some present-day tinkering with benefits and revenues will make it even better. That this tinkering cannot be accomplished in a routine fashion is one piece of the puzzle that captured our attention and inspired this book. Any attempt

1

at serious discussion of how Social Security could be tailored, gradually and on the margin, to address the challenges of the twenty-first century population it must serve produces a deluge of doomsday predictions, a flurry of dueling statistical reports, and a cacophony of voices claiming to tell the real story of Social Security. Perhaps many of us simply tune out, unless or until we are convinced that the latest so-called crisis differs in some significant way from previous ones.

Why is this great debate over "the problem of Social Security" still with us? After all, awareness of the financial issues facing Social Security has been explicit in public discourse for decades (see, for example, Samuelson 1958), yet the alternatives most hotly debated are those contested when the original legislation was developed (Orszag and Stiglitz 2001; Peterson 1996; Mitchell, Myers, and Young 1998; Munnell 2004a, 2004b, 2005; Munnell and Soto 2005). As pundit P. J. O'Rourke observed, with scant exaggeration, in May of 2005, "the president discovers a ticking time bomb that's been in plain sight for seventy years" ("Freedom, Responsibility . . . and What? Social Security Reform—an Explanation," *The Atlantic*, 295, p. 42). Lost in the hyperbole is that several solutions to the financing have been proposed, and at least a few of those would actually work, albeit with differing effects. If the problem is simply that Social Security will one day be paying out more money to beneficiaries than it is receiving in income, two basic options, or probably a blend of the two, suggest themselves: reconfigure and reduce benefits in some way for some future beneficiaries, or increase the revenue. As usual, however, the devil is in the details.[1] In this case, "fixing" Social Security creates a different sort of problem—because fixing it means continuing a program others want to replace. Within this context, the "great debate" over Social Security is really about something more than the future of this one program.

The future of Social Security has been caught up as a sort of demonstration project for particular political viewpoints, a litmus test of ideological postures in a much larger debate. As a result, fairly straightforward alternative solutions to the core technical-fiscal problem of Social Security have been shunted aside as inadequate or irresponsible or irrelevant. By July 2005, as the collection of programs known as Social Security celebrated its seventieth anniversary of successful operation—seventy years of success almost unparalleled in modern governmental programs—its future had been put into doubt.

The vulnerability of the program is not because the technical (that is, fiscal) problems cannot be solved. Rather, it is because the program has been redefined as the expression of a far graver problem—a moral problem and behind that an ethical problem—that present and future citizens must face. As the public has rediscovered the costs of security—national security (including defending ourselves against evil empires), health security (including the rising costs of insurance, care, medicine and fraud), financial security (including the costs of poor investment decisions, job loss, unanticipated market fluctuations and fraud, again), each citizen is also scrutinized for signs of moral hazard. We are asked to be vigilant in reporting those who would take advantage of our liberties, our economy, or our social services. To do so is to stand, according to some, as an ethical exemplar of the ideal actor of the twenty-first century. It is this fuel of moral debate, combined with customary, career-oriented ingenuity from politicians, public appetites for the sensational and the scandalous, and the mass media market's attempts to generate the greatest attention for its advertisers' dollar, that accounts for O'Rourke's apparently puzzled observation in *The Atlantic* in May 2005 that "the political side-taking on reforming Social Security is suddenly, urgently bitter" (p. 42).

Social Security in a Toxic Climate

Times have changed, no doubt. Yet, the ugliness of a culture of fear and loathing that acute observers documented during the 1970s did not wither from exposure. It survived partly because that culture is so deeply rooted, but also because some of those observers were so easily discredited in the eyes of mainstream America by leading spokespeople of that culture. Hunter Thompson, Ken Kesey, Tom Wolfe, and other critics reduced to caricatures at times seemed all but complicit in their own marginalization.[2] The culture of fear and loathing simply spread and strengthened.

What is the source of this fear and loathing? The question makes inadequate every answer that has been put forth. As long ago as 1965, Richard Hofstadter documented the prominent strain of paranoia in American political culture, citing examples from the nineteenth as well as the early twentieth century. Domestic politics in the United States seem to run on antagonisms. Real or imaginary, an enemy is identified— whether external, internal, or even better, a link to a dangerous outside world and covert attempts to undermine the moral character of American citizens. Politicians then seek to tar an opponent, who may not be appreciably different in ideology, with charges of being weak on the new greater evil, of being soft-hearted in the face of what they see as irresponsible behavior. Because media gives much greater play to negative stories (especially impending disaster stories), major media outlets feed on and deepen the focus on any new greater danger.[3] For politicians, this is a cheap road to campaign victory. Even though the monetary costs of media campaigning are exorbitant, the real substantive issues facing us can be successfully ignored as we engage the more emotionally charged concerns about moral decay and the evildoers of the world. These tactics have proved successful with majorities of the electorate.

The events of September 11, 2001, certainly added tinder to the fires of suspicion and xenophobia. But as Michael Barkun (2003) and others have amply documented, conspiracy theories, paranoia, xenophobia, and similar windows on the world have long been a major feature of American culture, ranging from the popular diversions of motion picture escapism to the rather more serious sorts of escapism in presidential and congressional politics. Scurrilous campaigning and stolen votes are not new charges in the political landscape of the twenty-first century; they were features of the nineteenth and twentieth centuries. The yellow journalism of the late nineteenth century polished a number of feints of wordplay that campaign managers later extended in inventive ways with new advertising tools, marketing, and focus groups. The Red Scare and the Palmer Raids of the 1920s, the Red Scare and McCarthyism of the 1950s, the Evil Empire and the Star Wars defense initiative of the 1980s, the Crescent Scare and assaults on the Bill of Rights during the first decade of the twenty-first century—these are but the most prominent instances of a long and troubled record.

The various descriptions by Hofstadter, Barkun, and others certainly call on easily recognizable experiences, but they do not provide explanation of why so much of U.S. history has been guided by forces of paranoia, xenophobia, and other emotions of a culture of fear and loathing. The moral debate surrounding Social Security has been peculiar to the United States. However, the great cross-class coalitions that called for, created, and then supported successful programs of the common good and public welfare (those of Social Security but also unemployment compensation, public education, public health care, and the like) have been unraveling elsewhere (see, for example, Mares 2003), and in national cultures that have not been as prone to the paranoid style Hofstadter described. The typical citizen of the United States or the United Kingdom or France or any number of other countries of the wealthy world has not been transformed into a character from the futuristic and dystopian novels of the twentieth century. Yet citizens of those countries, European as well as North American, have been relinquishing civil rights, directly or indirectly, little by little, and the assault continues. Do conscious citizens give up any of their hard-won civil rights unless they have become fearful? This was Hunter Thompson's question in 1971.

So again the question, now in slightly altered vocabulary: why the distrust, the suspicion, the xenophobia, the renewed infatuation with a fundamentalism of belief? Why have those cross-class coalitions been undermined so effectively that members of subordinated classes (the poor, the working class, lower middle classes, even the once-proud upper middle class) willingly subordinate their own interests of economic well-being to protect the culture from a diversity it both fears and despises? And how did the very real problems—that is, the technical problems of fiscal soundness—facing Social Security get caught up in such a quagmire?

This Book

Our aim in this book is to answer mainly the last of those questions, though the others will be pursued to the extent that they have been involved in framing what we call the great debate over Social Security. We do our best to give all major parties to that debate their due, fairly presenting the various positions and facts without reinforcing their exaggerations or deceptive claims. As the rest of this introduction should make clear, however, we too have a stake in the debate because we have a stake in how this society turns out for our and our neighbors' children, grandchildren, and great grandchildren; we do not attempt to hide our own sentiments, perspectives, and preferences. All has been written honestly and in good faith. We do not claim to know all the correct answers to all the questions asked, or even that we have asked all the correct questions; and those limits are only partly because the main questions and answers have to do with future conditions and actions, which we can only guess at. We also try to remind ourselves from time to time that intellectual pursuits are no insurance against fallibility even with respect to the "what is," much less the "what might yet be." This recognition tends to quiet any wish to tell others how to live their lives.

This book is indeed about the present and possible future conditions of Social Security and the general context that frames efforts to provide individuals some sort of insurance of income during their postemployment years. The central fact around which much of the discussion is organized, a fact on which virtually all parties to the debate agree, is that Social Security has been losing its fiscal soundness and, without some sort of correction, will face an increasingly severe shortfall in funds. Discussion of this fact, its causes and implications, and alternative proposed solutions will necessarily require our attention to several technical issues. These are technical in the sense that they have to do with the mechanics of the Social Security programs, risk management, saving and investment behavior, markets, the law of contract and property rights, government trust funds, and related matters.

Unfortunately, the political skirmishing that has taken place under the auspices of "fixing Social Security" in recent years has piled heaps upon heaps of deceptive, manipulative, often deliberately dishonest information on top of issues already poorly understood by the public—and in some instances, one suspects, by many of the politicians who have engaged in similar practices. Because bad information tends to drive good information out of the arena, our first task after this introductory discussion is excavation. We reclaim some terminology, try to describe as clearly and forthrightly as we can the main issues that have been subject to misleading presentation, and prepare a reasoned foundation for the subsequent chapters.

We do not for a minute believe that all of the information problems are due to deliberate dishonesty, manipulation, or deception. The debate over the future of Social Security involves genuine disagreements about a number of principles, and these disagreements are often forthrightly stated by proponents and opponents of this or that position regarding Social Security and related concerns. Some genuine differences are integral to the larger debate. Others are about best guess assumptions involved in technical issues—for example, assumptions about future rates of private saving, future rates of growth in wage rates and earnings income. Still others involve terms that carry with them certain underlying assumptions; when experts use them, it is—we assume—with the recognition that these assumptions are invoked, but need not be rehearsed because they form a taken-for-granted contextual understanding. Unfortunately, when these arguments are imported into speeches for mass consumption, the assumptions recede into the shadows. Because these terms are also everyday words, everyday meanings and these denser structures of meaning can get confused. *Welfare* and *efficiency* are two examples of terms that stand atop large literatures—within and across disciplines—that frame their meaning. The term *market*, on the other hand, can be more fundamentally misunderstood because in everyday conversation, it refers to a place, whereas the economic term invoked in phrases such as "best left to the market" refers to a process, to dynamic sets of relationships, not to a physical site. To play the market as a novice is to step into a stream to learn to swim: sometimes it's hard to know how much of your progress is due to your actions and how much is due to the current.

It also seems clear to us, however, that much of the recent talk has been deliberately deceptive, as the political climate of public discourse in the United States has grown increasingly sour, fractured, incoherent, and destructive. Much of the talk about the Social Security Trust Fund is a good example. Government officials who know, or ought to know, perfectly well the legal requirements and administrative procedures of a government trust fund instead offer images that are at best seriously misleading.

This work of clearing out some of the debris is initiated in chapter 2 and continued in chapter 3, where we attempt to clarify major concepts and perspectives underlying the technical issues of Social Security and its proposed alternatives. Although video and print media have dedicated significant chunks of space and time to the general issue, they frequently sacrifice clarity for brevity, paragraphs for sound bites, civility for volume. Describing the basics of the disagreement requires a better

understanding of federal budgets, historical trends, and routine accounting procedures than most people can claim. Rather than educate people
on these points, however, both sides of the debate focus on (and can be
faulted for) generating slogans rather than building comprehension. Our
goal is to provide a primer on these concepts, which means that (especially) these two chapters will require some effort to digest; in contrast,
those who already have this knowledge may find these chapters too
superficial. This book is not written for experts, however. It is written for
people who prefer to make their own decisions rather than rely on one
or another public figure to dictate where their interests lie and how they
can best pursue them.

Having accomplished some of that clarification,[4] we then turn, in
chapter 4, to the main arguments in favor of replacing Social Security
with a different program of postemployment income insurance and the
main arguments for the restoration of Social Security to fiscal health. Several important recent books have attempted to make the cases for or
against Social Security and alternative (privatized) programs. We draw
primarily on a list that is exemplified by Henry Aaron and Robert
Reischauer's *Countdown to Reform*, Dean Baker and Mark Weisbrot's
Social Security, Michael Graetz and Jerry Mashaw's *True Security*,
Sylvester Schieber and John Shoven's *The Real Deal*, and Max Skidmore's
Social Security and Its Enemies. We also rely on a large number of
papers included in the National Bureau of Economic Research working papers series, position papers sponsored by the National Academy
of Social Insurance, and briefs distributed by various research centers,
government agencies, and universities. All these, along with several articles published in scholarly journals, argue different, sometimes sharply
different positions in the technical debates. They proceed from different
starting points and reflect differing agendas. Whether one agrees or dis-
agrees, each of the works on which we primarily draw offers intelligently
considered arguments, and we try to give a fair hearing to all of the main
positions. A number of other important works—Robin Blackburn's
Banking on Death, Christoph Borgmann's *Social Security, Demographics,
and Risk,* and Jennifer Klein's *For All These Rights* come immediately to
mind—take a broader approach to the issue of the history and future of
pensions (the subtitle of Blackburn's volume), broader in both geographic scope and in historical detail of the development of different pension schemes than we intend in this small volume. We do draw on these
latter works occasionally, but our focus is principally on the U.S. case and
on the main points of its development since the Social Security Act of
1935 was enacted.

Many of the works on which we draw are authored by economists,
academic and professional. In fact, an emphasis on efficiency as well as
on cost-benefit types of analyses has guaranteed economists' positions of

particular authority in these and other policy debates. However, this fact is also recognition that much of the best analytic treatment of the technical issues involved in programs such as Social Security and its proposed alternatives has come from the component disciplines of economics. No doubt some of the writings of economists, like those from any other of the sciences, are remarkably sterile. But the best of economic analyses are insightful in ways that no other discipline has matched. It is sometimes said that the main economic models are unrealistic and demonstrably false. That is indeed the case. The would-be criticism betrays more than anything else a lack of understanding of how science works. The models are unrealistic and demonstrably false as descriptions, precisely because of the simplifying assumptions that are made to advance our understanding of underlying processes that, in the round, are enormously complex. A number of people, Charles Plott among them, have argued that these same unrealistic, demonstrably false models have been more productive of genuine insights into economic processes than any bundle of highly realistic, demonstrably accurate descriptions of observed outcomes or states of being.[5]

On the other hand, economists are prone, as are other scientists, to claim the mantle of value neutrality for their own analyses. That claim is worth no more for them than it is for others. Economists themselves have systematically studied it and have come to the conclusion we just stated. Victor Fuchs, Alan Krueger, and James Poterba (1998), for instance, analyzed data pertaining to economists at forty leading research universities in the United States regarding their preferences on policy issues, such as whether IRAs (that is, the existing investment program of individual retirement accounts) should be expanded, whether the cap on taxes paid on workers' wages into Social Security (that is, the FICA taxes) should be eliminated, and whether affirmative action should be eliminated. They concluded that variations in economists' preferences on these issues were correlated with their values as reflected in their preferences concerning the relative importance of individual responsibility versus social responsibility, the relative importance of economic efficiency versus economic equity or fairness, and the role of the federal government in income distribution.[6] The impact of values on policy preferences remained even after controlling for differences in the economists' political identifications and differences in their estimates of a number of technical matters (for example, the fraction of total net worth in the United States that is held by the richest 1 percent of U.S. households, the magnitude of the effect of Social Security (that is, FICA) taxes on the personal saving rate, the ratio of administrative costs for mandatory private saving accounts to the administrative costs of Social Security). For economists, too, values tend to trump knowledge and ignorance. That is, although the variation in the economists' estimates of those technical data was considerable, it did not correlate well with the difference in their policy positions.

The dominant dimension of the technical issues in the debate about Social Security is a contrast between what are called (sometimes misleadingly) market-based and government-based solutions to socioeconomic problems. The corresponding alternatives typically proposed to a fiscally challenged Social Security system are built around private-account investments in market securities—that is, mainly, corporate stocks and various kinds of bonds, both corporate and governmental. Because there has been much deception in discussions of market returns, we devote chapter 5 to a review of actual data on market returns, chiefly stock-market returns, with attention to issues of measurement and reporting as well as analysis. Markets being places of commerce, the "buyer beware" adage tells us that probably the vast majority of the deceptive information about rates of return on investments in corporate stocks has been motivated by interests much older than and now mostly indifferent to the Social Security debate. Too often, protagonists in the debate simply pick and choose among deceptions and popular misunderstandings already in circulation to sway public opinion toward their preferred solution or solutions to the problems Social Security faces.

It will be apparent throughout chapters 4 and 5 that politics is never far from the surface of the picture, even though the discussions focus primarily on various technical issues. This is partly because the line between what is technical and what is political is never as clear substantively as the boundaries of white space between and around the words might suggest. But it is also because, whatever one's views on technical issues, markets are stuffed with politics in the most fundamental sense; actors bring different resources of power to bear on market transactions and depend on prior definitions and enforcements of individual liberties and property rights. That means that government—politics as the regulation of conflicts over the distributions of goods, for example—is also always present, no matter how fierce one's pretense of being against government.

The debate over Social Security is necessarily about current problems and future solutions, and there is no escaping the fact that any decision regarding the future of Social Security, and postemployment income insurance more generally, will necessarily be achieved through political processes. We can do little in this book to combat the poisoned atmosphere of congressional, presidential, and judicial politics, or the rapidly eroding respect of the public for congressional, presidential, and judicial institutions. Perhaps on those fronts the most we can do is to remind members of the electorate, those who do not as well as those who do vote, that the electorate generally gets the officials, the government, it deserves.

We nevertheless pursue a variety of relevant political (or sociopolitical) issues in the Social Security debate in chapter 6, with some hope of furthering a balanced, insightful consideration of the inescapable relationships and mutual interdependencies between markets and governments. Part of our concern in the chapter is with the cross-class coalition forged during the 1930s, with Social Security as one of the most important programs to come out of that coalition of interests (see Klein 2003). One of the now mostly forgotten facts of that era was the resistance of business interests to agree to practices such as tax farming (government assigning to selected private firms the rights to taxes paid by the populace) which had long been regarded as invitation to political cronyism and financial corruption. Another all-too-often-forgotten fact about that coalition is that it was not merely a political expediency designed to win approval of a controversial policy among the electorate and among members of Congress. It was a coalition that in fact did cut across lines of class—that is, across what were gulfs of difference and disparity in basic economic, social, and political interests. It was also successful. It knitted together great divergences and made U.S. society the better for it. It was far from perfect, to be sure. But the accomplishment of that coalition was instrumental in the recovery of a society from collapse. Coalitions as broad and as deeply rooted as that one was are very difficult to achieve. Its destruction has contributed to the resurgence of material inequality in the United States (see, for example, Keister 2000) and arguably has had a hand in the American public's increased inability to identify a commonwealth of shared interests (see, for example, Lipset and Schneider 1987). U.S. society is probably quickly approaching a condition in which a similar broadly based coalition would be highly useful, if not necessary, in response to profound difficulties.

In chapter 6, we also examine Pew Research Center data on public attitudes about Social Security and the proposed private accounts initiative of the second G. W. Bush administration. Our aim is to gain some sense of the social as well as political and economic sources of support for different approaches to the problems facing Social Security. We do not argue that these survey data necessarily tell us about much more than today's mood. They do, however, still provide a benchmark against which to assess the connection, or lack of connection, between policy proposals and popular conceptions of the problems to which the proposals have been made.

As we observed earlier, when considering the set of technical (largely financial) issues involved in the politically declared crisis of Social Security one is struck by the thought that, given all the rancor and bad faith present in that declaration, something else must be going on. The motivations behind the repeated and often successful efforts of manipulation, deceptive information management, and smear-tactics must be about something larger and in some sense deeper than Social Security as such. We focus on this larger debate in chapter 7.

The character of the larger debate could be described as philosophical, generally in the looser sense of that word, and as ideological, generally in the stricter sense of the word, that is, the study of a system of ideas. The system and the philosophical principles involved in the debate are complex and thus involve many dimensions of human society. Our entry point into this complexity, which will also frame the bulk of our discussion of the larger debate, has to do with competing conceptions of the individual, both as a reality in itself and as both a component of and a counterpoint to society. In terms that are closer to the disagreements about the future of Social Security, it is a debate about the sort of person, the kind of social actor, that government and schools and churches should encourage American citizens of the twenty-first century to be, or to become.

Anyone who remembers reading Ralph Waldo Emerson's essay on self-reliance, first published in 1841, will have a good idea what much of this debate is about, even though circumstances today are surely not Emerson's. Encouraging people to become self-sufficient was a major preoccupation of leading figures of the mid-nineteenth century, as it had been in the eighteenth century. It is still with us early in the twenty-first century, having been rejuvenated by what several commentators have called the culture wars that preoccupy American society.

In the final chapter, we return to more general issues of income and wealth distributions, the role of government in reinforcing versus counteracting growing inequalities, and how the choice between a more resilient Social Security program and individualized accounts fits within this context. One aspect of repositioning the puzzle pieces is reconciling the fear and loathing component of U.S. culture with its emphasis on the power of individual agency. Although we fear the subversive influence of enemies in our midst, we also believe that we can overcome tremendous disadvantage, breakthrough barriers, and beat the odds—not just occasionally, but routinely. We all see ourselves as the exception and thus align ourselves with the interests of the groups we aspire to join. By reframing the American Dream as a rags-to-riches story, rather than as a poverty-to-middle class story, we prefer to view affluence as the outcome in need of protection.

Some Missing Context

Chapter 7 discusses some of the key contextual features of the Social Security debate, but other matters of context must be mostly assumed within the covers of this book. Otherwise, it would become a much larger work than the one we set out to write, and important matters of context would still have been neglected. Nevertheless, in the remainder of this introductory chapter we want to outline some of that missing content, especially a part that has been peculiarly missing from the explicit register of the Social Security debate. This is the enormous increase in the extent and depth of interdependence of the United States with other economies, governments, and cultures of the world. It is the context known as globalization, a process with a very long history that began to reach a comparable stage of development in the late nineteenth and early twentieth centuries (before the world wars intervened), and that has been accelerating very rapidly during the late years of the twentieth and early years of the twenty-first century. No doubt globalization has become a familiar word, a hot-button topic, indeed a topic of much, perhaps still growing controversy in many countries.

Few alive today can recall the experiences of cultures as different as Irish, Italian, Polish, or Yiddish rubbing against that of the mainstream white Anglo-Saxon Protestant during the 1880s or 1920s. In addition to the highly beneficial cross-fertilizations that occurred then, a number of often horrific conflicts were also sparked, leaving many victims of xenophobic, paranoid fears, and hatreds. Imagine, then, the consequences of the current round of globalization, bringing much more diverse cultures (Islamic, Chinese, Indian, and so on) into increasing competition, and increasingly effective competition, with the United States. Despite its greater internal diversities since the 1920s, America has remained peculiarly insular in its dominant attitudes toward an outside world. This outside world now knocks on the doors of our most honored institutions and declares itself at least as good, at least as moral, at least as worthy of respect for its traditions, however different they might be.

The debate about the future of Social Security has been mostly silent about globalization or its likely relevance for the future of such programs. That is a mistaken silence. Capital markets (that is, markets of credit and debit, of currency, of venture or investment money, and so on) have been international and cross-national for a long time, and now to such an extent that national boundaries mean less and less.[7] Labor markets are rapidly following suit. Consumption markets have long been international and cross-national. European countries and the United States draw heavily on raw materials and lightly processed materials from other countries, which in turn have become growing markets for finished goods shipped back to them. Now, however, production capacities—and decisions about what gets produced, by whom, with what technical skills, and for what purposes—have been rapidly internationalizing as well.

Enough has changed already that one recent observer's conclusion is as acutely sensitive to foreseeable future conditions as it is startling to observers who have been less attentive:

Today no one reasonably anticipates that the opportunity to live as they please will be secured automatically by the economic or political dynamics of a global market economy; and no one at all can have well-founded confidence that they will enjoy such an opportunity, if the economic or political dynamics of that economy fail to secure it for them. More disturbingly still, no set whatever of political, economic and social agents, up to and including the present human population of the entire globe, can reasonably assume that they have the effective power to ensure that outcome by any set of actions which they might conceivably perform. (Dunn 2000, 350)

What does any of this have to do with Social Security? First, begin with observation that funding programs such as Social Security is sensitive to the stability of employment tax bases. Much of what U.S. consumers purchase is produced in other countries, and the income-producing properties of that production process have therefore increasingly shifted to other countries—the attraction being not simply lower labor costs but also and increasingly the comparative advantages of production specialization. Loss of within-country production-based income also means lower relative wages and salaries that are taxable by federal, state, and local government agencies. These changes have only just begun.[8]

The issue of whether globalization, particularly in the form of treaties such as the North American Free Trade Agreement (NAFTA), has resulted to date in a net gain or a net loss of jobs in the United States is highly contentious. It is also a far more complicated matter than most commentators would lead us to believe, and the complications continue to make an unambiguous answer elusive. For one thing, there is the conceptual symmetry that is endemic to economic relationships: a sale is also a purchase, a consumption is also a production, and an export of labor demand in the form of a job is also the import of labor supply in the form of the good or service produced by the offshore labor power (and vice versa). To the uninitiated reader, this symmetry, which is in fact perfectly straightforward and soundly motivated, can be confusing, to the point that one might suspect trickery. There is no shortage of trickery, to be sure. If, for example, the off-shoring of jobs is unpopular with one's audience (whether in a school classroom or an electoral constituency)—and it typically is—then negative reactions can be diffused by shifting to the other view within the symmetry—the import of goods and services. The symmetry is real, however, not the result of sleight of hand, and if politicians or government officials were genuinely concerned about the welfare of citizens, they would further citizens' education, not exploit their confusion.

The only analysis, to our knowledge, that systematically estimates the effects of international trade on U.S. employment, with open sensitivity to the symmetries involved in imports and exports, is a recent study by economists of the Federal Reserve (Groshen, Hobijn, and McConnell 2005). Specifically, they estimated the number of "U.S. workers, at current wages, prices, and productivity levels, that would be needed to produce the goods and services imported" by the United States each year, from 1983 to 2003, and the number of U.S. jobs "needed to produce the goods and services exported" (4) by the United States during that period. The difference is the net effect of trade on U.S. employment.[9] In brief, the results indicate a net loss of jobs during the twenty years, but at an uneven rate. It was higher during the 1980s, lower during the 1990s, and from 1998 steadily and notably higher. By sector, the loss was heaviest in the manufacture of durable goods and then in the manufacture of nondurable goods. Trade in services has been slower to develop, but generally has seen a net gain in service jobs, though the rate of gain slowed persistently after 1997. From 1997 to 2003, the net number of jobs lost to trade averaged about 40,000 jobs a month. As a share of total U.S. employment, the net job loss was about 2.4 percent in 2003 (see figure 1.1).

The composition of the net loss is significant. Many of the lost jobs were in what had been relatively high-wage manufacturing employment. Many of the gained service jobs that partially offset the loss were in low-wage employment. Many that were not low-wage were contract-labor jobs, in which the worker is solely responsible for funding his or her own insurance needs (health and retirement, and so on), either by purchasing private insurance policies or by future funding from own-wealth accumulations. In any case, these patterns do not bode well for public programs that depend on taxes from employment wages and salaries. Forecasting is often based on past patterns, so a reasonable guess is that the trends will continue for some time (Appelbaum, Bernhardt, and Murnane 2003; Baumol, Blinder, and Wolff 2003).

Such data add to the rancor of political discourse, especially as election time approaches. It is mistaken, however, to tie the net job loss to any particular governmental administration, Republican or Democrat, regardless of whether the principals were enthusiastic, lukewarm, or antagonistic toward such instruments as NAFTA. Although certainly affected by such agreements, the economic forces displayed in such outcomes are of much longer and more powerful gestation. They operate increasingly independently of nation-state politics. They are not literally unstoppable—wars, plagues, and other catastrophic devastations can impede much—but they do have great momentum.

During the middle decades of the nineteenth century, a pair of authors offered a notably accurate description of changes then taking place through what amounted to a growing globalization of economic forces. Their vocabulary strikes today's reader as out of date, almost quaint; and the authors were perhaps a bit romantic in their enthusiasm. In the context of the 1830s and 1840s, the new major actors on the scene were

Figure 1.1   U.S. Job Loss Due to International Trade, as a Share of Payroll Employment, 1983 to 2003

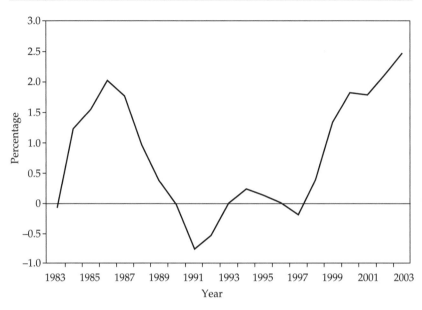

Source: Groshen, Hobijn, and McConnell 2005.

city-dwelling (that is, bourgeois) factory owners and investors who had overturned the values preferred by the old order society of aristocrats and peasants, based in the countryside and on land ownership. "The need of a constantly expanding market chases the bourgeoisie" (487)— these people of the city who care little for the land but much for profits—

> over the whole surface of the globe. It must nestle everywhere, settle everywhere, establish connections everywhere. The bourgeoisie has through its exploitation of the world market given a cosmopolitan character to production and consumption in every country. . . . It compels all nations, on pain of extinction, to adopt the bourgeois mode of production; it compels them to introduce what it calls civilization into their midst, i.e., to become bourgeois themselves. In one word, it creates a world after its own image. (Marx and Engels 1848/1976, 487–8)

And in this new world, they wrote, "all that is solid melts into air, all that is holy is profaned, and man is at last compelled to face with his sober senses his real conditions of life and his relations with his kind" (487). That process has continued during the past 150 years with such extraordinary effects that even those prescient authors would probably be astonished, were they to stop in for a visit today.[10] Were they naïve?

Even as a set of technical issues, the debate over Social Security is only one manifestation of some deep-seated changes surging through American society. As we have already announced, and will pursue further in chapters 7 and 8, the energy of the debate is drawn from some profound philosophical-ideological disagreements about the proper actor. That underlying level of the Social Security debate, as well as its specific technical dimensions, takes place within a dynamic context of political-economic forces that will shape whatever successes and failures emerge as resolutions. As nation-state boundaries increasingly lose their insulating properties, American citizens will probably learn that judgments about the proper actor continue to be forged primarily in market relations of exchange, with government officials, the citizen's agents in institutions of representative democracy, having diminished ability to modify those determinations even at the margin.

═ Chapter 2 ═

Words, Concepts, and
Principles in Contention

EVEN THOUGH as children we rehearse the sticks and stones mantra, we soon learn that words can be weapons. Propaganda is the weaponry in any war of words and, because words are the currency of all argument, the distinction between a difference of opinion and a distortion of fact is a particularly important boundary to recognize. This is especially true of technical terms, which can be used in deliberately confusing or misleading ways, but also of everyday language. Rhetoric, the discipline of using words to persuade, is not a new discipline. One of the "seven liberal arts" of the medieval European curriculum, before that a major feature of the body of Greek philosophy, rhetoric has had a lot of bad press, beginning with Plato, who thought it (along with poetics) a bewitchment of clear thinking and therefore dangerous. In fact, the notion of a language-use free of any techniques of persuasion is an illusion: it does not exist. Nor is rhetoric necessarily a bad thing. When someone says, "I promise (such and such)," for instance, that person is trying to persuade someone else of his or her sincerity and reliability in regard to what is promised. The sincerity and reliability may be genuine. When someone claims to be speaking the word of God, that person is trying to persuade someone else of the grave authority of what is being said. When a person invokes scientific fact, she or he is doing the same thing, though scientific fact proclaims itself to be open to challenge and empirical testing in ways that religious ideologies generally do not. The opportunity to persuade openly, such as when someone says "I promise," rests on trust and a respect for trust.

This chapter is a primer, in part because we review a number of basic terms, concepts, principles, and relationships, several of which have gotten caught up in the culture wars. In a sense, our aim is to reclaim terminology, recognizing that neither we, nor anyone else, can ever achieve words that are exactly neutral in this or that contested terrain. Major players in American political culture have become so adept at manipulating audiences by spin—slogans or phrases that have been carefully shaped, through trial-and-error tests on focus groups, to achieve desired effects—

that certain words have become badly stained. Foremost among these, undoubtedly, is liberal and liberalism, which once referred to liberty (supposedly a good thing) and meant openhandedness and generosity in one who gives (akin to the virtue of charity).

Our list is surely not complete. Some of the treatments are noticeably too brief and tread close to being overly simple. But space is always at a premium, as is a reader's attention, and we want to move quickly to the engagement between proponents and opponents of Social Security, relative to its alternatives, yet minimize the extra baggage that much of this terminology has collected.

Demographic Assumptions and Projections

Programs such as Social Security and employer-sponsored pension plans are transactions between present and future realities. Obviously the future realities are unknown and can only be guessed at. Some guesses are better than others, and much can depend on the difference. Many everyday activities are transactions between present and future realities— if I eat dessert tonight, I promise to walk an extra two miles tomorrow. But few of those transactions span more than a few days or weeks or months—to say nothing of decades, as in the case of planning for post-employment income security. And few involve as many complexly intertwined component relationships as long-term planning activity does. To engage in such planning, we must make estimations about our future income streams, stock of wealth, health conditions, consumption preferences, and life expectancies at successive ages. These estimations can indeed be made, but on the basis of categories of people (that is, life expectancies for a white woman with present earnings income of $47,000 a year, and so on), and the specific individual can usually best be located within the relevant category only by assuming that she or he is typical of that category (that is, has mean, median, and modal values on the relevant variables). Clearly there is room for error in that assumption.

Planning for an individual, therefore, must take place within some population of individuals. Indeed, that necessary context is a good deal more complicated than the description would indicate. First, we can question whether there may be other information (or relevant variables) we should be using to define the most appropriate population category, because we will use that category as the basis for generating a given person's estimations. Demography, for example, has provided us with group-specific expectations by gender, race-ethnicity, and socioeconomic status. The population and some if not all of its relevant categories, however, will continue to change over time. Second, we recognize that a range of possible futures are all contingent on a particular present, that the extent to which future realities are a result of present conditions is sensitive to how many others share the relevant categories as competitors, and that these future realities are also a function of future conditions, and these conditions are similarly sensitive to the population size of relevant categories.

Consider an example. A person born during a baby boom will face a large number of competitors for available opportunities of education and employment. By comparison, a person born after that baby boom will enjoy conditions of relative scarcity of same-aged competitors. A thirty-year-old planning to retire at sixty-five should think about others who might be retiring at that same time or the same age. A relatively large number of much wealthier persons of the same age retiring at sixty-five could make our particular thirty-year-old less competitive in certain markets (for example, housing, recreation, health care, groceries, and so on). In other words, in making our plans for retirement, we must not only anticipate *our* needs, resources, and activities, but we must also anticipate what others in our cohort will need, have, and want. Complex systems operate relative to complex sets of relationships.

This is just a glimpse of the complexities involved in trying to make reasonable plans for probable future realities. One of the beginning points for that effort is a set of demographic projections—that is, estimates of various population characteristics at regular dates between now and then. Demographic projections are necessarily based on assumptions about three processes: fertility, mortality, and the balance between immigration and emigration. The simplest projections assume that the past, or the recent past, is the best predictor of present and future; they merely extrapolate from past and current trends. So long as there are no surprises, these projections prove to be reasonably good; but they also provide no new information, precisely because they tell us what we already expect. In a classic illustration of that conundrum, no one foresaw the Baby Boom; and though a number of observers knew that the accelerated fertility rate would not continue forever, they did not predict exactly when the boom would end or that it would turn to a bust. Consider the Great War, as it was known until the late 1930s: many astute observers saw the storm building and feared a great clash, but probably no one foresaw just how devastating it proved to be, the enormous loss of young men born roughly between 1880 and 1900 in Britain, Ireland, France, and Germany, a lasting mark on the age structure of those national populations for decades thereafter. Likewise, no one predicted the influenza pandemic of 1918, with a death toll of millions of people around the world.

"Every week for the next 18 years, some 88,500 baby boomers will turn 59½ and become eligible to pull money out of their retirement accounts without penalty," *Newsweek* declared (September 12, 2005, p. 82). We know they got part of it right. Federal tax regulations stipulate that money could be removed from certain types (not all) of retirement accounts without penalty after age fifty-nine and a half. Not all of the Baby Boomers had (or have) accounts that permit those penalty-free withdrawals. In fact, some had (have) no private retirement accounts at all, only their Social Security accounts. Further, whether the part of the tax code referred to in the *Newsweek* article remains unchanged during the next eighteen years is open to doubt. No one knows. Likewise, we do not yet know whether the projection of 88,500 newly eligible persons each week until 2024 will prove to be correct. Projecting from current trends, the average of 88,500 per week is certainly a good guess, but it is a guess. It assumes, for example, that age-specific mortality rates (up to age fifty-nine and a half) remain the same between the day the projection was made and September 2023. Mortality schedules could improve or worsen; the shift up or down could be a little, or it could be a lot.

In general, the more complex the underlying processes that result in specific events or outcomes, the more likely that any projection of their future outcomes will be wrong, and the longer the projection—that is, the longer we must wait for that future outcome—the more likely the projection will be wrong. Thus, for example, we can be far less confident about projections that involve not only variables of fertility, mortality, and immigration-emigration, but also variables of, say, labor-force participation, wage rates, hours of labor supply, and the education or skill of the supplied labor (much of which will be relative to the labor markets of other, competing countries). An example is the effort to project future revenues for Social Security payments, projections that are sensitive not only to variables we just listed but also to decisions about taxation and the integrity of a trust fund. When considering that, remember that projections even of the fertility rate, which results from relatively simple behaviors aggregated across a population, have often been wrong by a substantial margin.

Projections also depend on assumptions about future changes in life span as well as mortality rates. Life span has not changed much during the last two millenniums, in the sense that some people who were living 2,000 years ago or more survived well into their eighties, perhaps into their nineties, and possibly on rare occasion beyond the century mark. Plato, for example, lived to about eighty, Epictetus to about eighty-eight, and Democritus to about ninety. The proportion of people who have lived to those advanced ages has no doubt increased, but that is a different matter (though not irrelevant; see below). Some accounts of people today cite them living to 120 or 125, but the evidence for it is usually suspect, and in any case such events are exceedingly rare, a handful of cases among the planet's billions of people. What are the prospects of an increase in life span to 120 or 125 or beyond, in the sense that such events become as common as survival past age eighty today? At present, those aged eighty or beyond are the fastest-growing age group in the United States. Improvements in medical-surgical and other health-care technologies, along with greater popular awareness of healthier lifestyles, will probably continue to add to current old-age life expectancy rates, of course. Other techniques, however, including a three-way wedding of biotechnical, cybernetic, and nanotechnical procedures, are already leading to such capabilities as growing person-specific replacement organs and intra- as well as inter-organ tissues, cleaning out the garbage that accumulates inside our bodies, using new materials to augment skeletal structure, and tuning electrochemical functions in the human body to external energy and information supplies. Capabilities that we have not yet imagined could be within a short reach. If we think we have major problems now with the management of demands and supplies associated with the older and oldest segments of the human population, just imagine the challenges ahead, when and if significant proportions of men and women live robustly to 120, 125, or even longer.

Finally, projections, no matter how good, are only tools that must be used with care. Unfortunately, they are all too easily subject to misuse, either out of ignorance or in a deliberate effort to mislead. A simple case in point is that among the patently false statements wielded in the Social Security debate is the claim that, when the program was devised during the mid-1930s, the full-benefit retirement age was set at sixty-five because very few working people lived to that age. Therefore, the argument went, as life expectancy increased, the program faced inevitable insolvency. In 1930, life expectancy at birth was fifty-eight years for men, sixty-two for women. That meant that at birth about half the male babies would probably be dead by age fifty-eight, and half the female babies by age sixty-two. But the single biggest factor in those mortality curves was infant death, followed by childhood death. Neither infants nor children would be contributors to the Social Security accounts. The pertinent question is (and was), what proportion of people who survived infancy and childhood would be alive at age sixty-five? We are here setting aside another significant factor in mortality curves, deaths from war, which primarily affected young men, even during the Civil War. In fact, in 1940 about 54 percent of men and 61 percent of women had survived from age twenty-one to age sixty-five; moreover, the men who had survived to age sixty-five could expect to live another 12.7 years, on average, and the women another 14.7.[1]

Dependency Ratios

Statistics, like mathematics more generally, is a tool we can use to make systematic comparisons and detailed descriptions. As with any piece of information, however, we must be careful to state clearly exactly what the statistic measures. When statistics are used in everyday discussions, the tendency to use nonspecific language can create a lot of confusion. For example, we have a variety of statistics that calculate average values. The statistical literature is quite specific about which measures are appropriate for various sorts of questions and distributions. Even so, by choosing measures—only one of which can be the best—each side of a debate can make claims about what is typical, and these claims can be quite different. Explaining what that difference means and why it occurred is not an easy task, however. People need to know enough about basic statistics that they understand why the selection of one measure over another is preferred and what sense they can make out of the difference in the values of the two statistics.

Persons who want to prove a claim or a message can be very ingenious, even duplicitous, in using statistics to get the answer they want. One statistic that has often figured prominently in debates about Social Security is known as a dependency ratio. There are various ways to calculate such a ratio, and it shouldn't surprise us that each side of the debate tends to cite only the ratio that best supports their position. All these ratios are descriptive of something and all show changes over time. They differ in their approaches to economic dependency. The difference in the values and trends therefore relates to that substantive point: how do we assess economic dependency in our society? When economic dependency is defined more broadly, the future appears less problematic. When it is tightly focused on those aged sixty-five and older, eyebrows are raised.

Well before Social Security entered its latest controversy, the age dependency ratio was the one most commonly used in basic demographic descriptions of a country's population. It categorized a population into one of three age groups, those too young or too old to be in the paid labor force and everybody else (the economically active). Those too young or old made up the numerator, the economically active made up the denominator.[2] In 2000, the age dependency ratio, using ages twenty and sixty-five as the cut points, was .69 (see table 2.1). That is, there were sixty-nine age-dependent persons for every 100 aged twenty through sixty-four. This ratio is projected to be about .81 in 2040 and about .83 in 2060. The increase from .69 to .81 or .83 might seem large. Consider, though, that in 1960 the same ratio using the same age boundaries was .91. This ratio was higher when the Baby Boomers (those born between 1946 and 1964) were children, and it will increase again as they age beyond sixty-five. What might be a little surprising to the reader, however, is that in 2030, when the last of the Baby Boomers will have passed age sixty-five, and the oldest is eighty-four, the ratio will be quite a bit smaller than it was in 1960—that is, about .79 versus .91. Not until 2070 will the ratio again reach .91, and that is according to the high-end projections.

Table 2.1   Dependency Ratios

	Total			Old-Age		
Historical data						
1950		.73			.14	
1960		.91			.17	
1970		.90			.19	
1980		.75			.20	
1990		.70			.21	
2000		.69			.21	
Projected data	Low	Med	High	Low	Med	High
2010	.66	.66	.65	.21	.21	.21
2020	.72	.71	.70	.26	.27	.28
2030	.81	.79	.78	.33	.35	.37
2040	.82	.81	.80	.33	.37	.42
2050	.81	.81	.82	.33	.38	.45
2060	.83	.83	.86	.33	.40	.49
2070	.82	.85	.91	.33	.42	.54
2080	.82	.86	.95	.33	.43	.58

Source: Office of the Actuary 2005, table V.A.1.
Note: The three assumption sets pertain to projected rates of fertility, mortality, and net immigration; total age dependency ratio has both young age (under twenty) and old age (sixty-five and older) in numerator; old-age dependency has only the old age category in numerator.

Table 2.1 reports a parallel set of projections, focused only on old-age dependency, thus excluding persons under twenty from both numerator and denominator. As inspection of these numbers will no doubt suggest, it is this ratio that critics who define the crisis of Social Security prefer to cite. By 2030, this ratio will have doubled relative to its size in 1960 (that is, about .35 versus .17).

The merit in this old-age dependency ratio is that most children are supported by household budgets, whereas older citizens generally do not rely directly on their adult children for financial aid but on public programs. Furthermore, when public funds are used in support of children, these funds are mainly from state and local budgets, not the federal budget. (Politicians' critique of public transfer programs has been primarily focused on federal programs.) Note the importance of the term "directly" in the earlier sentence. In fact, older citizens as a group do rely on financial assistance provided by their adult children as a group, but the connection is indirect, occurring through governmental agency. The fact that the transfer is managed by a government agency is, for some critics, adequate reason to retain the narrower focus.

Table 2.2   Beneficiary per Worker Ratios

	OASI			DI		
Historical data						
1950		.061			na	
1960		.189			.007	
1970		.243			.028	
1980		.267			.042	
1990		.264			.031	
2000		.249			.043	
Projected data	Low	Med	High	Low	Med	High
2010	.256	.259	.264	.053	.056	.065
2020	.312	.324	.336	.052	.062	.074
2030	.368	.393	.418	.054	.068	.083
2040	.376	.419	.463	.053	.070	.087
2050	.366	.424	.491	.054	.073	.093
2060	.364	.437	.529	.054	.074	.096
2070	.361	.453	.575	.054	.074	.096
2080	.358	.465	.614	.055	.075	.097

Source: Office of the Actuary 2006, table IV.B.2.

Both ratios described so far are rather crude approximations in that they assume that age groups are homogeneous in their economic activity. Obviously, they are not. If the central issue is the fiscal integrity of Social Security, why not focus on beneficiaries[3] of the several programs and on those in the paid labor force paying FICA taxes, given that it is specifically these people who are supporting the beneficiaries as well as themselves (see table 2.2). Proportionately fewer people aged twenty through sixty-four are not in the paid labor force today than in 1950 or 1960, primarily because women are much more likely to be in paid employment today than in 1960. The proportion of men aged twenty through sixty-four in paid employment has declined. Even so, the proportion of those aged sixteen and older in paid civilian employment increased from 55.4 percent in 1960 to 63.7 percent in 2000.

But those who are not engaged in paid labor cannot be left entirely out of the picture. They, too, must be supported, even if they are not in one of the Social Security eligibility categories. So, as Reno and her associates have described (for example, Reno and Olson 1998), let's examine the ratio of support-dependent people to paid workers. In 1950, it was 2.48 (248 support-dependent to every 100 workers). In 1960, it was 2.62. By 1970, it was 2.47. By 1980, it was 2.28. By the end of the century, it was approximately 2.0 (the worker and one other), mainly because of the increase in the number of women in the paid labor force. Projections of this sort of ratio are even more tenuous than the relatively simple age dependency ratio, because more variables are involved (for example, the relative size and composition of the labor force). With that large caveat in mind, by 2030, each worker will have to support about 2.21 persons (herself or himself and about 1.2 others). By 2050, the ratio will be only very slightly higher, about 2.23, which is still smaller than the 2.62 in 1960. Here is the broader economic context: whether through direct or indirect means of support, those not directly involved in economic production must rely on those who are.

Projections are useful, even indispensable, if we are to attempt rational planning for future contingencies. In rational planning, however, we have the advantage of revised knowledge; the projections are continually updated as new information comes into the picture. Plainly, any number of events could upset the projected estimates detailed with double-digit precision in table 2.1, but if any changes could be anticipated with enough information about the when, where, and how much, their effects would have already been factored into the projections. Of course, one should also give due weight to the importance of resolve. Projections concerning the Baby Boomers, relative to the Baby Bust cohorts that followed, were available as early as 1970, and implications for future policy, including Social Security, were not obscure.

Markets and Hierarchies

The debates about Social Security also engage several fundamental issues of human experience. One major focus is the notion of market, which is extensive in substance and ramifications. People perceive and evaluate the strengths and weaknesses of market processes differently. Some see markets as the problem behind almost everything, and others see them as the solution to almost every problem. But what is a market and what is its counterpart?

Processes of distribution and exchange can be organized several ways. A basic distinction, perhaps the most basic, and a very old one, is between a market model and a hierarchical model (see, for example, Williamson 1975). Although it might seem that the older of the two is the hierarchical (think of paternalism and patriarchy or matriarchy, for instance), archaeological and ethological evidence suggests that the market model could be almost as old (for example, reciprocity in gift exchanges, in the exchange of women in cross-group bonding and conflict management, and so on). In general, however, any market is situated in a broader network of exchanges and distributions that tend to be hierarchical at least in relations of power (see, for example, White 2002).

The two models of organization also apply widely. Darwinian and neo-Darwinian evolutionary processes follow a market model, for instance, whereas some religious views of the development of life processes (for example, creationism, intelligent design) follow a hierarchical model. Markets are often regarded as if they are strictly economic institutions but are in fact intensely political in at least two senses. First, they are structured as relations of power, and those relations are the material of politics. Second, they depend on certain basic conditions of the organization of power, especially the provision and enforcement of individual liberties and property rights. Included is the right to sell or transfer property, with one's person, skills, knowledge, even image, being alienable.[4] The capacity of a market to function (that is, for transactions to clear) is founded in trust, the trust of players in those underlying political institutions and in observance of the basic principles (the ideals) of the market model.

The ideal of the market model has strong democratic components. The market process is supposed to be transparent, with no privileges of information. Any person with alienable property (whether it be a good or a service, present or future) is invited to be a player, without regard to any personal traits (such as nativity, gender, ethnicity, physical ability, education, profession, confession, honesty, prudence, greediness, integrity, or vanity). The market is a sorting mechanism of buying and selling, of trade among free individuals. A market transaction immediately results in setting a price—that is, an agreement, however temporary, on estimated value—and a redistribution of risk, the risk of gain, and the risk of loss. Markets thereby sort winners from losers. But, insofar as the market fits the ideal of the model, each sorting is temporary; it does not accumulate across trades, unless a given trader has very poor trading skills (for example, is more fearful than average, more gullible than average, and so on). Notice that the traits governing this exception are not traits of social ascription or inheritance, about which the individual can do little or nothing (for example, parentage, gender, ethnicity), but instead malleable traits of personal sentiment, mental attitude, skillfulness, and the like. They are not group traits (such as gender or ethnicity or religious confession) but highly individualized ones. They are regarded as traits about which a free individual can be held entirely accountable and responsible. Each player in the market is assumed to have equal status (indeed, equal legal status) in all respects except those judged (by the market model) to be private to the person, to the free individual—namely, personal sentiment and ability. The ideal of the market model is much like that of the bureaucratic model of organization, in that the operative principle is not who one is but what one can do and how well.

Again, in the ideal of the market model, the only information carried forward each day is how the market functioned—the closing prices of the prior session, which transactions cleared and which did not, and so forth. The structure of the market preserves that minimal information, but is not privileged to any trader; all prices and price changes are public—in principle, instantaneously so.[5] The result is an efficient pricing of goods and services, an efficient distribution of rewards (gains) and punishments (losses).

Clearly, markets generally do not fit exactly the ideal of the model, and sometimes do not fit well at all (though there is a point at which market collapse occurs).[6] Some of the disparity is due to the fact that specific markets exist within larger hierarchical structures (for example, the internal labor market of a corporation, internal markets of loyalty, favoritism, and celebrity, as well as the aggregated labor market, and so on, of a society as a whole). The hierarchical dimensions of market contexts necessarily impinge on markets in ways that distort the ideal of a free market. Even aside from those forces, however, markets fail to match the ideal (and sometimes literally fail to function) for reasons internal to the market. Much of the tendency to fail is due to the information function. The likelihood that one or more players has privileged information (for example, insider trading) is a problem that market players try to regulate through self-enforcement, which will generally reveal evidence of the most damaging errors only after they have occurred. External detection and enforcement agents (for example, the Security and Exchange Commission) can at least supply ex post penalties that market self-regulation cannot.

Another kind of failure related to the internal information function follows from the sentiments that markets feed on—greed and fear. Either can become self-reinforcing to such an extent that the market ceases to clear, that is, breaks down, after such a heavy surge of buying (driving up prices) that few buyers remain, or such a heavy surge of selling (driving down prices) that either few sellers remain or little of value remains. The greed cycle of self-reinforcing decisions tends to be more quickly self-limiting than the fear cycle. This is why (after severe crashes of market valuation, as in 1987) external regulators of markets have imposed automatic circuit breakers to stop heavy surges of selling but not heavy surges of buying. Fear dominates greed in the external regulation of markets, due to relative concerns about broader consequences. Fear of loss weighs more heavily than greed for gain.

One of the peculiar strengths of the market model is that it takes advantage of the power of the law of large numbers, which is very useful for making decisions under conditions of uncertainty. The basic notion is that as the number of repetitions of a random process becomes very large the proportionate difference between expected and observed values approaches zero.[7] Application to market process is straightforward. Imagine a new gizmo has been invented. What is its value? How might one determine an answer to that question? We could ask the king, who would be happy to issue a decree. Or ask the gizmo's inventor. Or the village priest. Or pick the first person you meet on the street tomorrow morning and let her or his answer be the correct answer. Obviously all of these sources are interested sources (probably some more than others), and there is little reason to privilege one answer over another. If we can accept the trading price as our best measure of value, then let the market decide.[8] Over time (that is, some number of trades), the market will settle on fair exchange, not because any one player was asked to determine what was fair, but because in effect that is what the large number of traders created on average through their individual buying and selling decisions. (The process is dynamic, of course; prices change momentarily, as a function of relative demands by buyers and sellers.) The overall decision was achieved by indirection, not by any particular person's assertion of what the answer should be. The indirection is manifested as the average of many repetitions of a process (in principle, a random-variable process, which actual markets only approximate) of exchanges between free agents.

A pertinent illustration comes from the study by Victor Fuchs, Alan Krueger, and James Poterba (1998), cited in chapter 1, of how economists' value preferences affect their choices on certain policy questions. Each economist in the study was also asked to give best-guess estimates of certain technical data, such as the fraction of total net worth in the United States held by the richest 1 percent of households. The authors noted that, while the best guesses for the technical data were remarkably divergent, the means of the distributions were very close to measurements independently obtained (for example, through national accounts, the Survey of Consumer Finances, and so on).

The power of indirection was highlighted by Adam Smith when he wrote of an invisible hand that seemingly directs the functioning of a market.[9] The insight is integral to what was once regarded as central to the discipline of sociology: the quintessentially sociological act is an action in which the actors do not entirely understand the meanings and implications of what they do. Sometimes they do not understand that their actions are contrary to, or contradictory of, their conscious intentions and expectations. This is not because they are subject to Freudian delusions or anything of the sort but simply because their actions are social. Paul Seabright (2005) made use of the insight in his study of the many and varied ways in which modern society is a tapestry of leaderless chains of interaction in which actors place blind trust that their interests will be satisfied. Likewise, James Surowiecki (2004) drew on the insight when making his claim that crowds often display more accuracy of estimation than single individuals do, even those accredited as experts on the topic at hand. Of course, crowds can also be self-destructive, and blind trust is not always the best course of action, in markets or elsewhere. One must remember that market transactions involve losers as well as winners, and though the ideal of the model says that markets are without memory (beyond the requirements of their functioning), long strings of loss are possible. Even in a perfectly random distribution of tosses of a fair coin, the probability that any sequence of 100 outcomes will contain a string of at least five heads or five tails in a row is about .8, and even a perfectly functioning market does not protect against gullibility.[10]

Efficiency and Fairness

A term one often encounters in the Social Security debate is *efficiency*, usually intended as a technical term within an economics framework. In ordinary usage, to be efficient means to achieve the desired effects without waste. In a utilitarian sense, it can further mean to select the most effective and least wasteful way to achieve a desired end. The discipline of economics has further narrowed the meaning of efficiency, producing a still more specific technical term, which applies in a variety of contexts, for example, the efficient-market hypothesis.[11] The core principle of that technical usage has been identified with the work of Vilfredo Pareto and therefore is sometimes called Pareto efficiency. In judging how goods have been allocated across people, this principle states that an allocation is Pareto efficient if no possible reallocation would improve the situation of any person or persons without worsening the situation of at least one other person. Thus, if you have ten apples distributed across three people so that the first has one apple, the second has four apples, and the third has five apples, the only way you can make the first better off is by making either the second or third worse off. It should be obvious why this principle is also called a welfare principle or theorem. The idea is that efficiency yields optimal welfare for all persons, hence also the phrase Pareto optimality (see, for example, Hausman and McPherson 1996, 84–99).[12] However, an allocation that is Pareto efficient need be neither equitable nor just. At the extreme, a dictator may hold all the resources, leaving the rest of the population with nothing, yet such an allocation would nonetheless be Pareto efficient, because no one could be made better off without taking away some of the dictator's wealth. As Amartya Sen (1970) observed, an economy can be Pareto-optimal and still be perfectly disgusting by conventional moral or ethical standards.

The notion of fairness in this context typically refers to a distribution—for instance, whether a distribution of risk is fair, or a distribution of reward, and so forth. A word often used in place of fairness in this context is equity, which basically means equal or fair.[13] Equity or fairness has a number of dimensions. It can refer to distributions in the cross-section (that is, across persons or groups at a specific date) or to distributions over time (that is, whether persons or groups are treated fairly in how resources or risks are distributed across time) or to both the cross-sectional and the temporal dimensions at once. As just noted, fairness or equity can refer to persons as individuals or to persons as members of groups or other social collectives; and each of these has both cross-sectional and temporal dimensions. In the context of the Social Security debate, emphasis on individual equity tends to focus on the question of return on investment. Is the person as an individual getting fair compensation for the funds provided? An emphasis on social equity tends to focus on both the cross-sectional and the temporal dimensions of fairness in distributions of both investment risks and investment returns for persons as both individuals and as members of groups, especially status-defined groups (for example, women vis-à-vis men, low-wage vis-à-vis higher-wage workers). Some of the relevant literature distinguishes social equity as social adequacy, in contrast to individual equity. This distinction in terminology could be an effort at clarity, but in fact it misleads. It assumes that the only relevant aspect of social dimensions of distributions (of risks or rewards) is adequacy (that is, a minimalist fit to needs). Clearly, we as individuals are advantaged and disadvantaged by factors over which we have little or no control. Obvious examples include being born into a wealthy family or a poor family, being born female or male, African American or Asian American or European American, and so on, being incapacitated or limited because of war injury or accidental injury or exposure to toxins or other health-debilitating agents. These advantages and disadvantages affect a person's location in subsequent distributions of risk, resource, and reward.

The actual connections between efficiency and a fairness sense of welfare or justice are usually much more complicated than the simple definitions initially suggest. This is in fact true even of the notion of efficiency taken on its own. The basic insights are hardly new; formulations can be read in works by Immanuel Kant, Adam Smith, and other eighteenth-century scholars. But refinements of the basic insights lead us to a better understanding of the issues. In his treatise on the matter, James Meade defined efficiency in terms of the efficient use of resources—"resources are so used that it would be impossible to make one citizen better off without making any other worse off" (1964, 19)—and then pointed out that the inherent relation must be dynamic: the "any other" must be any other at any point in time, any future date. He also made it clear that pricing only for efficiency in the strict sense can "result in a very undesirable distribution of income and wealth" (13). For example, where the marginal product of labor tells of the efficiency of labor, it is the average (or total) product that tells of distribution. As the marginal product increases (that is, through increases in "worker productivity"), the increase in total product (total output value) goes mostly to those owners of property who are already wealthy (25).[14] The enormous surge in recent decades in the ratio of CEOs' compensation to the wages and salaries of typical workers in the corporations they head strongly illustrates the point.

The Paretian notions of efficiency and optimality "have some real ethical appeal, for, other things being equal, it is better to make people better off, and the satisfaction of [individual] preferences surely has something to do with well-being" (Hausman and McPherson, 1996, 88–89). However, they have no automatic or necessary connections to the fairness of exchanges and distributions—that is, between preference satisfactions and perceptions of what is a fair distribution of rewards and punishments or benefits and costs—even though empirically it is clear that perceptions of fairness do have implications for efficiency. To the extent that a market functions with perfect competition, it increases economic efficiency by reallocating resources from those who value them less to those who value them more.[15] Although this is generally a positive effect of the market, public opinion and politicians sometimes rebel against it.[16]

To the extent that a market is functioning efficiently, it not only does not know, it cannot know, anything about the players except their buy and sell offers. This high degree of anonymity is both a condition and a consequence of market efficiency. Whether any given player more often wins than loses, or wins (loses) more than her fair share, is not simply information the efficient market does not have; it is also a normative judgment wholly alien to the vital principle of market transaction. The bet is that in the long run—that is, under conditions of the law of large numbers—market outcomes will tend to be optimal for the total number of transactions. These transaction need not be distributed across the total number of players according to any normative principle (that is, beyond the principle of efficiency). Thus, in any long patch of transactions, some proportion of players will, with high probability, win significantly more often than the average, and some proportion will lose significantly more often than the average.

Moreover, the efficiencies gained from market transactions narrowly defined[17] can be gained as a result of externalizing certain costs, charging them to a resource outside the agents (individual or firm) of the transaction. Pollution is a commonly cited example of a cost externalized onto the broader society, but there are also more specific externalizations by specific firms within the market. For instance, successful hedge fund strategies, such as those that long-term capital management applies, leverage tiny differences in asset pricing to reap large gains, at least for a while (see Dunbar 2000), at the externalized cost of creating a lot of volatility in affected markets.

The conventional understanding is to think of externalized costs as material "bads" that no one wants (polluted air, for instance). It can, in fact, instead be the entire contents of a concept that market players seek to externalize. This can occur when an analysis uses simplifying assumptions to get around a problem of ignorance. For example, if we do not know how a specific process works, we can assume the effect and then address our concerns. It also occurs when we want to get around an inconvenient fact or concept. Some narrow treatments of efficiency externalize the concept of fairness. Defining efficiency too narrowly makes it difficult to notice that issues of fairness (and the consequences of ignoring those issues) are inherently involved in the processes being described or analyzed in the (narrowed) terms of their efficiency. Indeed, much of the discipline of economics has traditionally regarded issues of fairness, vis-à-vis efficiency, as a matter of politics, not of economics (but see, for example, Rabin 1993). This tendency remains quite visible in strategic aspects of the debate over Social Security, most especially in the fact that technical analyses usually feature issues of efficiency, as reflected in comparative rates of return on investment capital, for instance, and exclude (or minimize) attention to the advantages of collective treatments of risk in regard to postemployment income.

Efforts to manage the terms of a debate come from all sides, of course. To take a common illustration, critics of a standard economic argument about the costs of a production process will say that the argument externalizes certain categories (and concepts) of cost, such as the cost of polluted air or polluted water. When, however, economists answer the criticism by bringing the previously externalized categories back into the analytic framework—which they do, understandably, by conceptualizing markets in air or water pollutants—many of those same critics will then complain that economists are now degrading the value of clean air or water by their well-known penchant for pricing everything (Hausman and McPherson 1996, 197–200).

Investment, Intertemporality, and Insurance

We treat the terms investment, intertemporality, and insurance together because they share the perspective of a person making decisions today on behalf of a sequence of future selves. These decisions take into account one's future well-being but also have implications (whether present self is aware of them or not) for the futures of other people, because an actor's present behaviors usually ramify in ways, some unexpected, that affect others at a future time.

Intertemporality is a term coined by economists to mean between times or periods (see, for example, Loewenstein and Elster 1992). The perspective is not new, but it is increasingly important: present decisions and actions have consequences in future periods, some of them intended, others not intended but nonetheless anticipated, and still others neither intended nor anticipated. Intertemporal periods are defined first of all as involving transactions between oneself in the present and oneself at various points in the future. In these transactions, the present self acts as agent for each future version of self as principal. Present self attempts to determine how much consumption each future version of self will require or want (or is entitled to have from a principle of fairness), relative to the consumption needs of present self, and therefore how much present self must save or invest for his/her future consumption needs, given specific assumptions about total longevity, rates of inflation, returns on saving and investment, and risk aversion, and related factors such as the personal discount rate. This transaction is actually, or should be, repeated over multiple periods, because later periods will have updated information about trajectories and one's future states. Taken systematically, the transactions are repeatedly integrated over remaining intervals of investment time. Whereas the preceding description focuses on the individual actor, actor's present self can consider in these determinations any number of social or collective factors. For example, one can take into account the expected proceeds from an insurance program that pools risk, where one's risks include the likelihood and consequence of being wrong as an individual (for example, in assumptions, or disciplined behavior) or as a member of a specific birth cohort (for example, membership in a cohort that approaches retirement age just as investment markets sharply decline and then remain in a bearish state).

Most economic models for the analysis of postemployment income insurance assume two periods, one of present workers who pay taxes (whether as public tax or as private saving) to fund the insurance, and the other of former workers who at the same time draw benefits from the insurance fund (whether contributions are paid by present-period taxation or past-period investment). In a program such as Social Security, contributions are made by taxes paid on present worker's wages or salary (subject to an earnings ceiling), and benefits are drawn from the same fund by former workers (retired or disabled, and so on). The transaction is analogous to adult children providing financial support to their retired parents, except that the transaction is not individualized (that is, from adult child to his or her father and mother) but is made by pooling risks and capital that has the aggregate of adult children paying the aggregate of postemployment parents.[18] A three-period model is sometimes used, the added period being the children of present adult workers (as described in the discussion of dependency ratios). Of course, regardless of how many periods are defined, the periods are arrayed in sequences, with individuals moving from one state (for example, paid employment) to another (retirement) on a regular basis. Until recently, the common practice was to treat the periods as exclusive of one another. In fact, of course, they overlap, because all members in one period do not move to the next period at once: whether defined as birth cohorts or as generations, period membership is continuously changing, as individuals move from one state to the next, and the present and future (or past, present, and future) periods are therefore partially simultaneous (Samuelson 1958; Hausman and McPherson 1996, 16–20).[19]

Even in a two-period model that simplifies dynamic properties of the period sequencing, the analytic challenge can be quite daunting for someone prepared with an armory of analytic skills. Once overlapping is allowed, the task is much more daunting. Imagine, then, the situation of the typical adult worker, trying to optimize the stream of consumption between present periods and future periods. What portion of possible present consumption should be put aside, as investment, for consumption in future periods? The tasks of planning for retirement income security are essentially efforts to determine the current value of anticipated future needs. "How much money should I save or invest today and during each successive period of paid employment, to have sufficient wealth to convert to income so I can maintain a desired level of consumption during my retirement?" Many uncertainties must be considered. For example, what will be the rate of inflation at each future period? Inflation erodes the value of a dollar, so that the present value of a future dollar is less than a dollar.[20] An account that contains $100,000 ten years from now will have $74,400 today, if the annual rate of inflation is a constant 3 percent. (Putting this another way, the present value of the $100,000 at $t + 10$ years (ten years in the future) is $74,400 at time t (the present), assuming constant annual inflation of 3 percent).

To repeat an important point made in the discussion of the market model, past and present conditions cannot contain full information about any future. Surprise, shock, the unexpected is experienced often enough that a prudent consumer will not discount it to insignificance. This is at the kernel of the problem of time. How should one respond to it?[21] If total product increases between now and then, either because of more producers or (better) because of greater productivity per producer (or both), future self should be better off than present self. Moreover, future self should be more knowledgeable (have better information about future needs as well as actual events between now and then) than present self. Perhaps, then, one's present self should discount the future at a substantial rate? What exactly does that mean? What about all the uncertainties between now and then?

By pushing consumption into the future (that is, deferring consumption or gratification), we settle on a way to value or price that consumption in an equivalent way across time. In that respect, we establish something like a personal interest rate, which is generally called the discount rate, or the rate at which we discount value-in-the-future relative to value-in-the-present. If I am impatient to consume a future good (I want it now rather than later), I would (if I could) shift it from future to present and buy it at a premium relative to its value in the future. The more impatient I am, the larger the premium I am willing to pay, or the higher its value to me now relative to its value to me in the future. When the present discounted value of the future good (its value now) is less than its value in the future, the size of the discount becomes a measure of my impatience or my preference not to wait. It is tantamount to saying that a future dollar is worth some fraction of a dollar today.[22] In that regard, it is similar to inflation; but inflation is systemic, whereas discounting varies from person to person, depending on personal intertemporal preference (that is, consume now or consume in a later period).

A standard assumption in economics has been that a consumer's discount rate should be set relative to the prevailing interest rate (which is the price of money, the cost of borrowing). That is, a consumer's decisions of whether to consume an extra unit of a good now or in some future period (a preference category known as the marginal rate of time preference, measured as the discount rate) should be governed by trade-offs across periods such that their discount rate on average equals the interest rate. The reasoning behind this expectation is simple. A rational actor if presented with an investment option that pays below the market rate of interest (r) will reject the option, but if presented with an investment option that pays at a rate higher than r will accept the option, borrow money at rate r, and have greater consumption in every period. This seems to be a sound theoretical expectation.

The problem with that expectation and reasoning is that empirical evidence abundantly demonstrates that typical actors, typical market players, make decisions that imply very different discount rates, ranging from negative rates to rates as high as several hundred percent per year.[23] Not only do implied discount rates diverge widely from the prevailing interest rate; they diverge from time to time, and from situation to situation, for a given actor, despite the theoretical expectation that a given actor will be consistent in discounting. At a systemic level, for example, the economy as a whole, most of the effect of this inconsistent and highly variable discounting seems to wash out. Market players, to the extent that they succeed by skill and not just luck, tend to be relatively disciplined in their discount behavior. The very fact of saving and investing is a discipline that reveals a relatively low (but positive) discount rate. A person who accepts negative discount rates is giving money away (though he or she might see as an acceptable bargain a service in return for the money) and generally will not perform well in market actions.

All of that description follows quite well from observations of behavior, but it has proven very difficult to evaluate the specific effects of variations in personal discount rate on specific actions and outcomes. The main impediment is the difficulty we face in measuring personal discount rates in a way that is conceptually independent of the actions that theoretically should be affected by differences in discounting. Although certain behaviors imply a lower or higher discount rate on the part of the actor, those behaviors are a function of other factors as well. Some of these other factors cannot be directly measured well if at all; therefore, specifying the discount component is inherently problematic, and we rely instead on the implied discount rate. Several economists have demonstrated that little of the variation in household wealth can be accounted for in terms of the sorts of predictors that economists thought would be important (for example, differences in saving and investing portfolio choices) drawing on theoretical as well as empirical work (for example, Bernheim, Skinner, and Weinberg 2001; Venti and Wise 2000). In searching for better predictors of wealth inequality, they have made good efforts to measure such factors as discounting. On the one hand, their results confirm how difficult that measurement problem is but, on the other, also suggest that perhaps variation in discounting is too irregular to account for differences in saving and investing behavior (see Ameriks, Caplin, and Leahy 2002). Some theorists consider such results more evidence that behavioral departures from a rational-action model do not matter because intentions of behavior make little systematic difference in the actual distributions of outcomes at a population level. Although it might seem odd for scholars to make such a claim, there is considerable sense to it, however discouraging that might be of one's own sense of rational ability. However, separating the effect of measurement from the measured effect can be far more difficult than is often acknowledged.[24]

Judging from observations of behavior, it seems clear that some persons are aware of the temptations of either negative discounting or a very high discount rate (or both, in different situations); being aware of their poor discipline in regard to those temptations, they purchase insurance to protect their future interests. As already noted, the negative discounting itself can be, under certain circumstances, a kind of insurance (as when a person makes an interest-free loan to the federal treasury rather than readjust the rate of tax withholding). It is always possible in principle to purchase self-insurance, in the sense of saving or investing for future self, but that does not solve the discipline problem.[25]

Facing a discipline problem, one tends to look for an enforcement mechanism, something that will establish inertial advantage. Committing to the habit of making premium payments to a for-profit insurance company can establish that inertial advantage, but using this mechanism is sensitive to one's level of wealth or income. It is not unusual to see people pay the profit premium to another when they could in fact better afford to self-insure. The imposition of a tax, whether indirectly by self, as in an agreement to participate in an employer-sponsored saving or investment plan, or by some external agency such as a government or a church, is an enforcement mechanism that has the additional advantage of overcoming that sensitivity to level of wealth or income by including poor persons in the risk pool.

As the foregoing statements illustrated, insurance mechanisms vary in the structure of risk pooling. Here, too, risk is symmetrical: in the case of a for-profit firm, for example, the firm's actuaries attempt to calculate an acceptable balance between risk of gain to the firm (profit) relative to risk of loss (the insured person's loss becomes the firm's loss, although usually within some limits), at a loss premium that is attractive to market buyers. How is the pool of risk of loss determined? One approach is to make it as large as possible (rather, as large as is profitable), so as to take advantage (again) of the law of large numbers. A contrary approach is to tailor it as finely as possible (as finely as is profitable), so as to calibrate the premium level to the probability of loss of each specified amount.

The choice between these approaches depends on a number of factors. Some of the factors are explicitly moral. What, for example, is the obligation of any one member of a group (family, firm, society) to other members? Structuring the risk pool in a way that is relatively insensitive to wealth or income (ability to pay premium) is one example of a statement about moral obligation. Pooling in the opposite direction reflects a different morality. Another factor affecting the choice of approaches is information, both its known existence and the cost of search and acquisition. Holding morality aside (or not, if one assumes that one's only moral obligation is to maximize profit to one's firm, its officers and shareholders), an actuary who knew with high probability the death date of potential clients, and had acquired that information at acceptable cost, could tailor life insurance policies accordingly, with the inevitable consequence that some persons would be priced out of the market (but they would be dying relatively soon).

This second and admittedly extreme hypothetical case illustrates what can be called an actuarially individualized insurance function. The approach has become increasingly popular in segments of the insurance industry, especially health and life insurance. Are you a smoker? If so, you necessarily have an unacceptably high discount rate, and any insurer willing to sell you a policy will charge a very high premium. Consider also the prospects of genetic testing. Concerns about future health by employers as well as insurance companies could lead to use of genetic information either to select employees and insurance-eligible individuals or to graduate the schedule of premiums according to actuarial likelihood of developing future health problems. The implications can be highly complex. Late in 2005, for example, IBM announced that it had begun to promise its employees not to use genetic information in decisions on hiring or on eligibility for its health care or other benefits plans (Steve Lohr, "IBM to Put Genetic Data of Workers Off Limits,"*The New York Times,* October 10, 2005). It was not clear whether the company intended the prohibition to include variation in employee matching rates or payout rates. Nor was or is there any guarantee that the company's privacy policy could be enforced in future years. Unless the company is willing to pool insurance risks across all IBM employees, it might encounter increasing resistance from its insurance underwriters.

From the standpoint of an insurance company and its shareholders, an imbalance of information in their favor allows them to eliminate high-risk patients. If the information is known by the employee and not disclosed to the employer, the imbalance can work against the insurance company. That is, any person could undergo secret testing for known markers of impending health problems (for example, a genetic marker for early onset Alzheimer's) and, if the test result should be unfavorable, hide that fact while purchasing insurance for long-term health care. Conversely, persons who undertake an available battery of tests for all known genetic markers and find themselves to be free of threat could then band together and lobby their congressional delegations to pass legislation mandating such tests and the use of resulting information as a means of lowering their health insurance premiums; they might argue that such an action would lower the average level of health-care costs (or at least the average rate of increase in those costs), on the assumption that insurance companies would charge fully funded (and thus, for most, probably unaffordable) premium rates of applicants whose test results showed an unacceptably high probability of developing a specified health condition. If employers have the genetic information, however, they could use that knowledge much like the actuary just described, and lower its present and future health-care costs.

The implications for postemployment income insurance are clear insofar as the insurance program includes provisions for disability, as does Social Security. But the implications go well beyond that, depending on the availability of information about individual preferences and the ability to realize them. One illustration is company pensions. For years, firms such as General Motors have attempted to structure the benefit provisions to encourage employees to retire at specified ages, sometimes at relatively young ages (so-called early retirement incentives). In practice, these efforts have achieved the firm's desired outcome to a limited extent, usually far less than the firm's management had hoped when they designed the incentive structure. One key element of that structure is known as the cliff effect. Assets grow very slowly until an employee approaches eligibility age, then accumulate rapidly. After eligibility, the rate of return on the asset valuation declines precipitously and soon becomes negative (for further illustration, see Hardy, Hazelrigg, and Quadagno 1996, 70–74). Whether this cliff effect achieves the result intended by the company is a function of the worker's preference. If the preference is to maximize total income over all periods, the cliff effect cannot dominate the income benefit of continued employment with the firm, even though future-period income (from the firm's pension program) is thereby diminished.

A final example of the involvement of investment, intertemporality, and insurance in this debate relates to the notion of intergenerational transfers, a featured component in predictions of generational warfare. In fact, of course, transfers across generations do occur. Parents invest wealth in their children, who then do the same for their children, and so on. More generally, wealth that is not destroyed (by design or by ignorance) will be transferred to future collections of persons. By the same token, negative wealth, or what is otherwise called public debt, is also transferred to future collections of persons. Again, there is nothing novel in either event. The variance is in quantity, composition, and mechanism of transmission. In an earlier era, older adults who were unable to be independent relied on their adult children. Today the same is true. But now it is also older adults as a collectivity relying on their adult children as a collectivity; this indirect reliance is accomplished through a government agency acting as conduit or intermediary. This indirection is not popular with some of the same people who sing the praises of indirection in the operation of markets as transfer devices (market-based solutions). One is supposedly natural, the other a contrivance.

Use of the word *generation* in the *intergenerational transfer* phrase is a bit misleading. There is indeed an intertemporal dimension to the transfer, but whether the donor and recipient groups are separated as generations or only as birth cohorts depends on context. Intertemporal transfers are common. Consider investments in infrastructure such as roadways, bridges, airports, seaports, and public schools. These are present decisions funded in part by present payers and in part by future payers (via bonds, tax revenues, and so on), with future cohorts reaping most of the benefit. Consider, on the other hand, parents investing in children through education, diet, health care, and so on. These are present decisions funded by one generation for the benefit of the next generation, with some of that benefit perhaps being realized only after the parent generation is dead. Likewise, adult children investing in their elder parents' well-being (for example, Social Security, Medicare, and the like) are present decisions funded in the present for the benefit of the older generation, but all of that benefit will be realized during the older generation's remaining lifetime. Relations of familial structure are generational, and can link multiple generations over hundreds of years. The temporal sequences of donor-to-recipient linkages in some transfer processes (for example, Social Security) are more accurately described in terms of shorter categories such as birth cohorts than in terms of generations.[26]

As already noted, those temporal sequences, though always arrayed in present-to-future chains, can be differentiated between those in which the donor-to-recipient perspective looks forward (for example, public investments in infrastructure) and those in which the perspective looks backward (for example, younger cohorts investing in older cohorts' well-being, as in Social Security). It can be argued from game theory that these differentiated transfers are linked together as an intertemporal exchange or trade, and though the backward-looking component of the trade can be self-sustaining even among actors who are strictly and only self-interested, the forward-looking cannot (Rangel 2003). The reason is that in the backward-looking component, the donor pays first, providing a good for an older recipient and gaining a benefit for self later, from the next cohort in the chain. In the case of the forward-looking component, the present donor has already received the benefit from investment by prior cohorts, only later (if at all) donating a benefit to a future cohort. The interesting upshot of this reasoning for purposes here is that the self-sustaining chain of the backward-looking component of intertemporal trade is sensitive to social norms of trust governing the links. If that norm of trust is damaged enough to break the chain, the break is not reparable within current terms of trade, and the backward-looking component also becomes unsustainable. In that conclusion, from an application of game theory, there is also an implied political strategy. Enough damage to public trust in the chain among young cohorts can kill Social Security. A person who does not believe that Social Security will be there when his or her turn comes is less likely to be supportive of the trading relationship now.

Risk, Uncertainty, Probability

Some words are expected to do too much work, and *risk* is one of them. The word is used as a synonym for danger, jeopardy, and uncertainty, the thing or condition that poses danger or hazard, as a name for a particular kind of volatility, and more. For present purposes at least, two meanings suffice: risk names a particular kind of volatility, and it names a condition that could be termed jeopardy, hazard, or danger. This latter meaning is the one intended in the notion of value at risk, a phrase that has become the name of an appropriate model in the economics of finance: a VAR, value at risk, model. Putting a valued good, such as money, at risk is to put it in jeopardy of being lost. Why would anyone put a valued good at risk of being lost? Because, among possible other reasons, such as ignorance, by putting it at risk one is creating the opportunity of reward, a gain, as well as opportunity of punishment, a loss. That symmetry of opportunity is crucial to a useful understanding of risk. The rational task is to evaluate the likelihood of gain, relative to the likelihood of loss, for any value put at risk.

Uncertainty is not the same as risk, but is a condition of risk. That is, if an impending event is certain to occur to someone or something, it makes no sense to say that person or thing is thereby at risk of the event happening. More specifically, a rational person who is certain to lose something of value (such as invested money), if put at risk, is unlikely to take that risk (assuming knowledge of the certain outcome). A rational person who is certain to gain from putting something of value at risk would of course like to do just that, but will be unlikely to find anyone willing to accept the other side, the loss side, of the risk (again, assuming all parties have equivalent knowledge of that certain outcome). On the other hand, if a possible event is uncertain, a person might be at risk of the event but might also alter circumstances to avoid being at risk of that event, yet the uncertainty of the event is not necessarily altered. It is this condition of uncertainty that makes the concept of risk, value at risk, meaningful.

As just exemplified, knowledge (factual information) is a vital component of the condition of risk and its evaluation. This component is itself subject to uncertainty. A rational person who knows that she or he knows some particular fact or facts is not necessarily correct in that confidence. One of the peculiar features of a market, to the extent that it is an efficient market (as described), is its ability to lessen the burden of inevitable ignorance, but even a perfectly efficient market cannot abolish all of that burden, or the burden of all sorts of ignorance. A market player who does not or cannot invoke a rational calculus for evaluating the relative likelihoods of gain and loss for any given value put at risk undoubtedly will sustain losses, in the long run, if not immediately.

Uncertainty comes in two varieties: possible events for which one can estimate a probability of realization and those for which one cannot make such estimates. Physics tells us that some vacuums are inherently unstable; an unstable vacuum can unpredictably and suddenly unzip, inside out, utterly changing everything in its path, as it reaches a new (but temporary) state. We do not know how to estimate the probability of such an event in earth's vicinity. For a great many events pertinent to our near-term futures, however, means for estimating relevant probabilities have been devised and frequently used. This is not to say that all interested parties always agree in the estimations.[27] In general, events that are regulated in hierarchical relations are more predictable than those regulated in market relations. Events that are not regulated at all, of course, are not predictable. Market events vary in predictability, according to a number of factors, many of which are summarized in the notion of efficiency (see chapter 4).

The law of large numbers tends to work across risks at any given time, as well as overtime, though the effect of increasing numbers is reduced by a positive correlation among the discrete risks. Structuring one's risk in a way that lowers this positive association can be a good strategy. Diversifying assets in one's portfolio, for example, is a recommended strategy of market investment. Exactly the same principle is at work whether the risk pooling in question is across the discrete risks of different types of assets or across the discrete risks of different groups of risk-takers. The nugget of that principle is the other meaning of the concept risk—namely, volatility.

Again, the law of large numbers tells us that as the number of trials in a random process increases our estimate of the true value of some process parameter converges to that true value. Think of it this way: if you are asked to guess the number of white marbles in a jar that contains 10,000 marbles, with some proportion (unknown to you) being white, how should you proceed? Ask to randomly sample them—that is, blindly select one marble, record its color, put it back, shuffle the whole collection, then take out a second, record its color, replace it, and so on, some large number of times. Based on this information, you can make a pretty good guess as to the proportion (and therefore total number) of white marbles in the jar. Two, three, or four trials will not get you much leverage, not much better than a simple eyeball inspection. But as the number of trials grows, the distribution of outcomes will begin to favor an ever smaller range of answers, eventually clustering around one most likely answer. That central tendency of the distribution is your best-guess answer to the expected value of the distribution of possible answers (outcomes). It is not the only information you have witnessed about the process, however. You will also have witnessed the degree to which observed outcomes were dispersed around, or diverged from, that central tendency: the wider the dispersion, the greater the variance in the underlying process, or, to put it another way, the more volatile the underlying process.

In general, as volatility increases the risk of relying on the expected value as a predictor of future states of the process also increases. Or as volatility increases, the opportunity of doing better than average (the expected value) increases, but so does the opportunity of doing worse than average. Insurance is a way of reducing the cost of doing worse, but the premium is also charged against the opportunity of doing better. Diversifying types of assets to reduce the positive correlation across discrete risks is a relatively inexpensive mode of insurance. Likewise, diversifying across risk-takers is another relatively inexpensive mode of insurance. Not every person will be as shrewd or as lucky in risk-taking; not every birth cohort will be as large or small, or face the same chance of reaching expected retirement age when investments have on average turned sour. Because most people are more sensitive to loss than to gain of the same magnitude, risk hedging tends to focus on loss, hence the classic insurance function, but it is the upside of risk, the opportunity of gain or the insurance company's profit that balances the transaction against the risk of loss. This transaction takes place across persons (market players, some winning as others lose) as well as across types of asset. How that distribution of risk is divided among players depends, however, on how explicitly they are willing to negotiate—or indeed even to acknowledge—the collective dimension (see, for example, Thaler 2000, 137; Hirshleifer and Riley 1992, 25, 26–27, 129–31, 159). Here is a case in which the power of word choice is apparent. Risk pooling is one thing, collectivization of risk is quite another.

Chapter 3

Trust and Trust Funds

T HE TERM *trust* figures prominently in the discussions about Social Security as a central element of both its short-term and its long-term sustainability. On the one hand, trust is a principle that provides legitimacy to the operations of the federal government. It is the confidence we place in the social contract that requires us to pay taxes today so that we can collect benefits when we retire. It also buttresses our acceptance of the complex interdependencies inherent in the division of labor (and division of responsibilities) that characterize our society. The Social Security program was built on trust, and as our society shifted to new modes of production and to a new industrial system, it was trust that helped sustain people shaken by their vulnerability to economic trends they didn't understand and could not control, people made acutely aware that their individual actions could not guarantee their futures. On the other hand, claims that the Social Security Trust Fund[1] is worthless have undermined public confidence in the program. By trying to convince the public that it doesn't hold any real assets, these claimants undermine public trust in other aspects of the federal government as well. After all, if the federal government can suddenly declare that the designated use of trillions of dollars of already paid taxes for benefit payments was some kind of hoax—a hoax perpetrated by none other than the federal government—how can we trust the same government to keep its word on any of its promises?

Efforts to manipulate public opinion by repainting the Social Security Trust Fund as illusion have been quite common. For example, as Warren Vieth and Richard Simon reported in the *Los Angeles Times*, in April of 2005, President Bush visited a facility of the Bureau of Public Debt in Parkersburg, West Virginia, looked into the news cameras, and, referring to a four-drawer filing cabinet that contains about $1.5 trillion in government bonds, declared, "There is no Trust Fund. Just IOUs . . . that future generations will pay . . . either in higher taxes or reduced benefits or cuts to other critical government programs" ("Social Security 'IOUs' Piling Up, Bush Warns," April 6, 2005). The intended take-away message of his remarks was plain: the Trust Fund contains nothing of value. Imagine, he continued, the retirement security for future generations is sitting

43

in a filing cabinet. Imagine the reaction of foreign governments in Beijing, Seoul, and elsewhere, if the value of their substantial holdings of U.S. Treasury bills were so resolutely dismissed. For that matter, imagine telling the American public, bankers, commercial agents, and so forth, as well as international creditors, that the U.S. dollar is merely a piece of paper, no longer worthy of trust. The three statements would be fundamentally the same. The U.S. dollar, a Treasury bill, and a Treasury bond are each a promise to pay (an IOU) issued by an agency of the U.S. government, supposedly in good faith and credit. Each promise to pay is fundamentally an act of trust. If your banker declared that your checking account is now worthless or your employer declared that your claim for wages or salary at the end of the current pay cycle is worthless, you would assume one of two things: the bank or the employer was being dishonest (stealing your assets) or they were bankrupt (in which case you would then stand in the line of claimants against federal bank insurance or on the liquidation of remaining assets).

What in fact is the Social Security Trust Fund? Answering that question will take us on a brief detour into the history books. Before making that turn, let's deal initially with three questions. First, is there a Trust Fund? Yes, a Trust Fund was created by the original Social Security legislation of 1935. Is the Trust Fund in fact empty? No. It presently holds those government bonds, U.S. Treasury securities, which are legally mandated as the only investment that can be made with the Social Security surplus. Last, is it in danger of becoming empty? Yes, it is. How quickly it will empty depends on what assumptions one makes about factors affecting the flow of funds into and the flow of funds out of the Trust Fund, as noted in chapter 1. The technical problems of Social Security are about the conditions of those assumptions—that is, predictions about future events— that impinge on the continuing financial solvency of the Social Security retirement and disability insurance programs. We will return to these questions later. For the moment, let's review the history.

The question of a Trust Fund was a major point of contention in the debates over the initial Social Security Act. Disagreement focused on whether benefits should be paid only after enough contributions had been collected to fund the benefits and on whether a person's benefit should be tied tightly to the contributions made through payroll taxes. These two issues intersect. Assume that an account is tied to a specific person, that receipt of benefits must be in proportion to what that individual has put into the account, and that benefits can be collected only after the account is fully funded. What does fully funded mean in that context? How do you know when that goal has been reached?

An actuary can make a best-guess estimate about how long the person will live and, if still alive after eligibility age, what a bare minimum existence would cost. If the person does not live to eligibility age, or does not live as much beyond eligibility age as the actuary predicted, what happens to the assets in that person's account? They could be assigned to surviving family members (if any), or to a general pool of assets held by the agency. What if the individual lives longer than the actuary predicted?[2] He or she could appeal to friends or relatives, but these avenues already had been seen as problematic, which is why some notion of social security was on the table. Perhaps that person could be assigned benefits from the general pool. But that would contradict the idea that an account must be attached to a specific individual.

During the 1930s, many adults were unemployed, many others were employed only intermittently, and many of those who had managed to keep their regular employment were paid very low wages. If accounts were to be individualized in both revenue and disbursement, many people would probably receive little if any relief from the system of accounts. The alternative was to pool revenues, pool risks (the risk of unemployment, the risk of disability, the risk of living longer than expected, and so forth), and disburse benefits from the pool according to a formula that recognized both the level of contribution and some minimum level of support per person. How do we determine the meaning of a fully funded account in that context? Exactly how much revenue should be accumulated before disbursements begin? All of the uncertainties associated with the possible differences of life trajectory for each specific person now had to be accumulated to the whole of all persons. Also, given the dynamic nature of the estimation problem, differences from period to period in size of birth cohorts, rate of unemployment, and other systemic traits, had to be factored into the mix as well. Once again, the law of large numbers came to the rescue: more reliable predictions could be made for the aggregate of cases than for any individual case. Recall, however, that the accuracy of a predicted value (average) for a large population declines as the volatility (variance) around that value increases. Said differently, errors associated with using the average as the best guess for all members of a population increase as inequality[3] increases.

Of course, even the very best actuarial predictions can be stymied by political failures, and the programs of Social Security have been continually subject to political failures of one sort or another. The designers of the program understood that as the system matured—as more workers became eligible and as benefits were based on higher contributions made over larger segments of their working lives—the number of beneficiaries and the amount of benefits would both increase. To accommodate the growing cost of benefits, a schedule of increases in the contribution rate (the FICA tax) was proposed. Without those scheduled increases, the combination of Trust Fund resources and incoming contributions would not be enough to support a mature program. But Congress repeatedly failed

Figure 3.1   Provisions of the Social Security Trust Fund

(a) There is hereby created an account in the Treasury of the United States to be known as the Old-Age Reserve Account, hereinafter in this title called the Account. There is hereby authorized to be appropriated to the Account for each fiscal year, beginning with the fiscal year ending June 30, 1937, an amount sufficient as an annual premium to provide for the payments required under this title, such amount to be determined on a reserve basis in accordance with accepted actuarial principles, and based upon such tables of mortality as the Secretary of the Treasury shall from time to time adopt, and upon an interest rate of 3 per centum per annum compounded annually....

(b) It shall be the duty of the Secretary of the Treasury to invest such portion of the amounts credited to the Account as is not, in his judgment, required to meet current withdrawals. Such investment may be made only in interest-bearing obligations of the United States or in obligations guaranteed as to both principal and interest by the United States....

(d) The interest on, and the proceeds from the sale or redemption of, any obligations held in the Account shall be credited to and form a part of the Account.

(e) All amounts credited to the Account shall be available for making payments required under this title.

Source: The Social Security Act of 1935, Sec. 201, Title II.

---

to enact the recommended increases in the FICA tax rate required to build the Trust Fund.

The initial Social Security Act of 1935 stipulated that revenue collection would begin in 1937, but benefit payments would be delayed until 1942, with the surplus contributions held in government bonds. (Monthly benefit payments actually began in 1940.) Here was the first appearance of the old-age reserve account, which evolved into the Social Security Trust Fund (see figure 3.1). After 1935 and until the amendments of 1939, the Trust Fund was the basis for maintaining the Social Security program as a funded program.

The 1935 act stipulated that Congress would transfer funds from general revenue into a Trust Fund so that reasonable funding levels could be maintained across generations. Assets in this Trust Fund were to be invested in government bonds. Provisions governing benefits and taxes were described in different titles of the legislation (benefits in Title II, taxes in Title VIII), because the authors of the bill feared that the Supreme Court would otherwise find the legislation unconstitutional. Given the political context of the time, a constitutional challenge was thought inevitable. In 1932, Franklin D. Roosevelt had been the first Democrat since Woodrow Wilson (1913 to 1921) in the White House, and only the third elected since the Civil War (the other was Grover Cleveland). Roosevelt's first administration was proposing programs that, though hardly novel by international standards, encountered immediate opposition as being radical ideas and threats to the moral fiber of the country.[4] Indeed, the court challenge came quickly. However, the Supreme Court sustained the act, citing the general welfare provision of the Constitution as basis. Because separation of the tax and benefit provisions was now unnecessary, Title VIII was repealed in February 1939 and replaced by a new provision, the Federal Insurance Contributions Act (FICA), which designated a tax separate from other payroll taxes as the main financing mechanism for Social Security. This change eliminated the need for congressional appropriations each year because the distinction between revenues intended for Social Security and other payroll taxes (for example, federal withholding for personal income taxes) was now made at the point of collection.

The failure of the constitutional challenge meant that critics of the program had to find other ways to undo what they believed to be bad policy. Lingering concerns over the program led to an almost immediate reconsideration of central program features. Critics of the original program's financing structure wanted another chance to reshape it. By the same token, the program's proponents were disappointed by the program limitations. In response, the Social Security Board and the Senate Finance Committee jointly chartered the 1938 Advisory Council so that certain features of the original legislation could be revisited. The resulting revisions, known as the 1939 amendments, changed Social Security from a fully funded to a partially funded program, making funding contingent on a schedule of tax increases to be passed by Congress. Without the scheduled increases, benefit payments relied almost exclusively on current contributions, plus an occasional supplement from general revenues to ensure the payment of full benefits until tax rates could be adjusted, thereby making the program an entirely pay as you go (PAYG) program.

In 1983, Congress passed amendments that called for increases in FICA taxes beyond the level necessary to pay current benefits;[5] the Trust Fund would accumulate the surplus contributions in anticipation of the retirement of the Baby Boomers. Whether a government trust fund could be used as a savings account for another government program continues as a major point of contention. To better understand the basis of this disagreement, we must enter the sometimes arcane world of federal budgets.

Different Taxes and Different Budgets

The principal source of government revenue is taxation. Other sources include credit from lenders, which is what happens when U.S. citizens purchase U.S. Treasury bonds or bills and when agents outside the U.S. economy, such as the central bank of another country, purchase U.S. Treasury securities. Taxes have generally not been popular, even though, as several scholars have pointed out (for example, Macdonald 2003), taxation as a means of financing long-term government debt has been instrumental in the development of political institutions of representative democracy. Politicians are often quick to avoid responsibility for taxation, either denying the need or, when need can no longer be evaded, using some wordplay. Thus, as noted above, even in the authorizing legislation, proponents of Social Security prefer to call FICA taxes payroll contributions, or just contributions. In contrast, opponents take every opportunity to stress the word *tax*. Proponents of taxes for maintenance of infrastructure such as bridges and ports prefer to call these taxes user fees. And so forth. The convention has been to regard any revenue that is raised for the public good as a tax. The line, however, is hardly that clear. For instance, contributions made by an employee (and, if matched, by employer) to a 401(k), 403(b), or similar pension plan amount to a self-tax on employment earnings, arranged by the worker through an agreement with the employer. Some critics would say we do not call it a tax because the government is not involved, but indeed it is: those shorthand designations, 401(k) and 403(b), refer to the U.S. Tax Code.

Recall from earlier discussion that during the initial design of Social Security there was some uncertainty about revenue source, and in particular whether program assets should be subsidized from general revenues (that is, the taxes collected to administer the federal government in general). With the 1939 enactment of the FICA payroll tax, that uncertainty was settled in favor of a self-sustaining program. From that time until the 1960s, Social Security was treated as separate from the routine operations of the federal government and from general revenues. Benefits were paid from the incoming flow of FICA revenues (contributed by employers and employees), with minor occasional help from the Trust Fund. During this period the Trust Fund gradually accumulated assets, as FICA revenues frequently exceeded benefits, and the Trust Fund served as an instrument of financial fine tuning, used as a contingency fund for years when FICA revenues could not meet all benefit obligations. Because the Social Security accounts of FICA taxes, Trust Fund, and benefit payments were legally separate from the federal government's general revenues and disbursements accounts, the Social Security programs were defined as off budget. That changed during the late 1960s.

Waging a war in southeastern Asia that was becoming increasingly expensive and increasingly unpopular, the administration of Lyndon Johnson sought to reduce perceived costs by a variety of manipulations. One consisted of slogans such as "guns and butter," and behind that was a search for new revenues without obviously raising taxes. Johnson appointed a Commission on Budget Concepts, which, in its 1967 report, recommended that the federal government adopt a unified budget, one that combined all revenues, all expenditures, and all government programs into a single set of accounts. Implemented in fiscal year 1969, the new unified budget meant that Social Security accounting was now on budget, and the Social Security surplus could be used to camouflage costs of financing the war. Social Security remained on budget until 1985.

In the meantime, a number of changes were introduced to improve the benefit structure of Social Security. Benefits were indexed for inflation, the benefit formula was changed to provide significant real increases in benefit level, and individual earnings histories were adjusted to reflect changes in average wages.[6] FICA taxes were set at a rate designed to pay for the improvements. Unfortunately, the design was faulty, and by 1977 the financial solvency of Social Security had severely deteriorated. Part of the problem lay with the general economy, which also had severely deteriorated to a persistent condition of both very high inflation rates and economic stagnation. This state, together with problems in the new benefits formula, meant that Social Security revenues were not keeping pace with disbursements. Changing the rules for people already in or near retirement was viewed as unfair as well as highly unpopular, given that people had been planning in certain terms of eligibility and benefit levels. The corrective measures therefore consisted primarily of an increase in the FICA tax rate and base—that is, the level of wages and salaries subject to the FICA tax (Snee and Ross 1978).

Although Ronald Reagan as presidential candidate promised to exempt Social Security from budget cuts, he later proposed some significant program changes, including lowering the earnings replacement rate for future retirees and even larger cuts for persons electing early retirement (Light 1995). Political reaction was strongly negative, however, and few changes were made. Social Security benefit payments continued to outstrip FICA revenues. From 1975 through 1983, the Trust Fund declined in value, as millions of dollars in Treasury securities were redeemed to cover the cost of benefits: $790 million in 1975, increasing to almost $5 billion in 1978, dropping back to $2.9 billion in 1979 and $1.3 billion in 1981. A bipartisan commission was appointed to solve Social Security's problems. This led to an agreement that was later enacted, with some additions by Congress, as the 1983 amendments that restructured key aspects of the program. The full benefit eligibility age (that is, normal retirement age) was increased from sixty-five to sixty-seven, with gradual phase-in from 2000 to 2022. Reduced benefit eligibility age (that is, early retirement), still possible at age sixty-two, carried a greater penalty in benefit level. Cost of living adjustments were delayed. Last, scheduled FICA tax increases were accelerated. It is this last change, moving up the scheduled increases in the tax rate, that greatly raised the profile of the Trust Fund. Although it was not new, and using assets from it to augment FICA revenues when necessary was also not new, few people had given it much attention until the mid-1980s.

From the 1939 amendments to the 1983 amendments, the PAYG structure of Social Security maintained a largely budget neutral program, with tax rates set to generate revenue sufficient to make benefit payments. Legislated benefit increases and programmatic expansions to cover spouses and survivors were supported by the favorable demography of the times and by an unprecedented period of wage growth. The changes to the program in the late 1960s and early 1970s were more than cost-of-living adjustments, however. They were real increases in benefits, coupled with program stabilization measures designed to maintain a given level of earnings replacement. This latter provision—the notion that the Social Security benefit should be assessed as a replacement of employment earnings—was a significant change. The benefit formula moved from being governed primarily by a criterion of minimal sustenance to a criterion of earnings replacement. One other change was at least equally as significant. The series of amendments passed during the 1970s sought to remove Social Security benefit provisions from the arena of congressional floor politics, where it could always be made into a convenient hot potato for horse trading and various ideological postures. Whereas previous Congresses had considered each benefit change, even those linked to inflation, now the program would be put on automatic pilot. Benefits would be increased automatically as the cost of living rose (because of inflation), and earnings histories would be adjusted automatically for changes in the average wage rate (because of economic growth and increased productivity).[7]

We come nearly to the end of our detour through the history books. One last scene occurs during the mid-1980s, when concerns about rising government deficits and poor economic growth brought the distinction between on-budget and off-budget programs back to center stage again. Social Security was not the only program to have been given off-budget status. Politicians had learned that by putting favorite programs off-budget they could sometimes succeed in insulating them from the threat of budget cuts. An off-budget program was supposed to be evaluated solely in terms of its own revenues and expenditures. Surplus revenues in an off-budget program were put in that program's own trust fund as investments in (that is, purchases of) U.S. Treasury securities. As of 1985, the U.S. Postal Service, the Federal Financing Bank, the Synthetic Fuels Corporation, and the lending activities of the Rural Electrification Administration were all off-budget programs.

The Balanced Budget and Emergency Deficit Control Act of 1985 repealed the off-budget status of each of those programs. At the same time, it returned Social Security to off-budget status, where it had been until removal during the Johnson administration.[8] Social Security was now legally excluded from coverage under the congressional budget resolutions. Giving Social Security off-budget status should have enforced consideration of the program's financial status on its own terms—that is, financing through FICA and the dedicated Trust Fund, which continued to accumulate resources. But a curious thing happened—or rather, did not happen: in spite of its off-budget status, Social Security accounts continued to be quietly included in reports about the government's unified budget.

In the late 1990s, former Senators Sam Nunn (Democrat, Georgia) and Warren Rudman (Republican, New Hampshire), co-chairs of the Concord Coalition, argued that Social Security surpluses should not be used to mask the budget deficit. Clearly, Social Security was by then officially and legally off-budget, but as Nunn and Rudman noted, convincing politicians to address pressing issues of the federal budget deficit without evasions and deceptions was proving virtually impossible. They urged in a letter to Representative Bob Livingston (Republican, Louisiana), who was to become speaker of the House, that change was needed: "Politicians from both parties, White House and Congress alike, still talk, act, and legislate as if laws removing Social Security from the federal budget had never been enacted. . . . *Changing the rhetoric will change the way we think about fiscal policy, and that in turn will help to change policy decisions*" (emphasis added).[9] Their request did not change the general practice, but the distinction did for one brief moment become moot. At the end of the millennium, the budget deficit had been eliminated—not just the deficit-camouflaged-by-FICA-surplus, but the on-budget deficit, a much more substantial feat.

The Social Security Trust Fund has thus evolved from a long-term funding mechanism to an instrument of deception. Used to conceal deficits resulting from an unpopular war, it has most recently masked deficit spending of a magnitude larger than most people realize, because one budget trick is to count as new debt only that part of each year's deficit that the Social Security surplus cannot cover.

There are two issues in this latest instrumental ruse. One is the technical-financial issue. The Trust Fund is maintained by the Department of Treasury, not the Social Security Administration. The Trust Fund contains real money. As of December 31, 2005, these assets were worth $1.663 trillion, $1.57 trillion in Treasury bonds and the remainder in certificates of indebtedness. Those who want the public to believe otherwise say that the Trust Fund contains only IOUs, the implication being that those IOUs (that is, government bonds) are not real money. Surely any adult in the United States who has a bank account understands that the account is not a fruit jar or wall safe containing stacks of dollar bills that sum to the account's balance. That money is being used elsewhere (for example, in loans to other clients) by the bank as a basis for generating its own profits. That said, the account holder can appear at the teller's window (physically or electronically) and demand hard cash up to the amount of the account balance, and succeed in doing so. The same principle applies to the Social Security Trust Fund. The bonds are special issue, meaning that the bonds are not marketable, but sheltered from market forces (excepting the level of the interest rate, as explained below). They guarantee interest as well as principal and can be redeemed at any time.

When revenues (FICA taxes) exceed disbursements, the surplus is placed in the Trust Fund as a U.S. Treasury security that bears interest. The interest rate is determined at the end of each month for the following month's assets. It is defined as the average market yield on all of the outstanding marketable U.S. securities that are due or callable more than four years into the future. The bonds held at the end of 2005 had fourteen interest rates and maturities, in keeping with date of purchase. The rates ranged from 3.5 percent, with maturities from 2007 to 2018, to 8.125 percent, with maturity in 2006. These latter bonds, having current asset value of almost $17.5 billion, were obviously purchased at a time when market interest rates were relatively high. The longest maturity for any of the bonds was 2020.[10]

The surplus for 2005 added about $154 billion, which brought total assets in the Trust Fund to $1.9 trillion. Estimates of future surplus amounts are about $178 billion in 2006, about $195 billion for 2007, and so on until 2014, when the year's surplus will be about $259 billion. Within a few years of 2015, the size of the annual surplus will cease to grow each year, assuming no change in the current tax rate and base. By the beginning of 2015, the Trust Fund will have grown to about $3.932 trillion.[11]

Thus, the surplus is not only saved, it is also invested in what has been one of the most secure investment assets available—U.S. Treasury bonds—and the relatively low rate of return on that investment reflects that high degree of security of principal and interest. The saving-investment is made on behalf of future claimants on Social Security. That is, if during any future period revenues (FICA taxes) cannot meet obligations to claimants (persons retiring, persons on disability, and so on), the gap can be met by cashing assets held in the Trust Fund. It currently contains about $1.663 trillion in assets. Primarily because of the large number of Baby Boomers coming to retirement, combined with the fact that for too long actuarial recommendations to change the rate or the base of FICA taxes have been ignored, revenues will cease to equal disbursement obligations in several years. Estimates of the exact year vary, another of the political footballs kicked back and forth in the Social Security debates. The fact is, no one knows. When that year arrives, saving and investment assets in the Trust Fund will once again need to be converted into liquid assets (dollars) that can be used to fill the gap between FICA revenues and disbursement obligations. Fund assets have been converted before, at least ten times since 1940. The difference this time is that, again because of the size of the Baby Boom cohort and the failures to make appropriate actuarial adjustments of revenues in previous years, the assets held by the Trust Fund will eventually be depleted. When that time comes, only the FICA revenues being received will be available for disbursement to eligible recipients.

Some critics of Social Security contend that converting the assets into monthly benefit checks will amount to double taxation in that the assets were first generated by FICA taxes, and the interest accrued on surpluses from FICA, and the cash from the redeemed bonds will also come from taxes, unless we find another buyer for them. Nothing in this is novel, however, nor is it unique to Social Security. The proceeds from FICA taxes could have been invested in the stock market or corporate bonds, instead of government bonds, from the beginning. During the 1930s and 1940s, however, many people were frightened of being exposed to the stock market, and others disliked the idea that an agency of the federal government would be investing in private enterprise.[12] The more secure option of government-guaranteed bonds was possible politically, where the option of stock and corporate-bond markets was not. By definition, a government bond is a category of public debt. The FICA proceeds that did not immediately return as benefit payments (that is, the surplus) bought government bonds, which means that the money was used for other purposes (that is, treated as if it were part of the Treasury's general revenue), in return for the government's promise to pay the principal and accrued interest of a bond on demand by the Social Security Administration (that is, because the bond proceeds would be needed to pay benefits). When the Treasury Department pays the redemption value of a bond, it does so with money acquired from other sources; and nearly all sources of Treasury revenue are taxes or user fees (excluding the possibility that the Treasury will deliberately inflate the currency by printing new money). Exactly the same is true when any holder of a U.S. Treasury bill or bond (for example, the central bank of another country, a U.S. citizen, and so on) redeems that bill or bond.

The second issue in the instrumental ruse of attempts to convince us that the Trust Fund is worthless is not technical-financial. It is political. More fundamental than all the cynicism that has dominated the politics of electorate persuasion and governance, there is the issue of property rights. All too often, recent discussions of the Trust Fund in its technical-financial aspects have neglected or belittled the fact that government debt obligations to its own citizens are in fact property rights. A citizen has the right to expect that the contract implicit in the purchase of a government bond, a contract reached in good faith, will be honored by all relevant parties. But it remains the case that the citizenry of a representative democracy gets the politicians it elects, and therefore the government it deserves, and sometimes these politicians and resulting officials breach that good faith, either as a deception concocted in aid of election or because they genuinely seek to alter the bases of government.

National Debt

Some critics of Social Security deride it because, they charge, it is unfunded and contributes to the public debt. It does indeed. As we have just indicated, and as many others (mostly economists) have pointed out, a PAYG system such as Social Security is equivalent to public debt (Bohn 1997; Borgmann 2005, 8–11). What some of those same critics fail to acknowledge is that even a private pension plan, insofar as it invests in public debt (for example, government bonds), is to that extent also unfunded. The simple reason is that it does not build capital. The same would be true of any program designed as a transition from the PAYG system of Social Security to a fully funded system and that pays the transition costs by issuing new government bonds (Feldstein, Ranguelova, and Samwick 2001). Although the Social Security surplus must necessarily purchase public debt, it would not have to purchase new public debt. In other words, rather than using the surplus to disguise deficit spending, the surplus (some of it) could have been used to retire public debt, that is, to reduce the national debt rather than to cover an annual deficit. Since the 1980s, however, when this run of surpluses began, the most common strategy has been to incur more and more new debt by running sizable annual deficits, thereby driving up the size of total national debt as well as the amount of interest paid on that debt. Only in the 1990s, during the Clinton administration, did we shift to a strategy of reducing annual deficit spending to zero. Beginning in 2001, however, increased spending coupled with tax reduction returned us to large deficits, routine legislation raising the amount of national debt we could carry, and increasing the amount of interest we pay to service that debt. Not surprisingly, the critics who ignore the property-right aspect of government debt obligations to citizens are often also the critics who ignore certain other aspects of public debt when it is convenient to their political cause. Issues of public debt are another store of weapons that can be used for purposes of deception, confusion, and manipulation.

Moral Hazard

Sometimes when people feel protected against loss, or of loss replacement should it occur, they tend to behave in ways that make a loss more likely. How much it costs to get that protection or replacement is one major factor determining whether that tendency is realized. If the cost is small relative to the value of the potential loss, this tendency is generally greater than if the relative cost comes close to the value of the potential loss. This tendency is known as moral hazard or hidden action, an asymmetry of information flow (see Hirshleifer and Riley 1992, 296–304). It is a problem associated with the use of insurance. The cost factor can be well illustrated by considering the difference between two people. One person self-insures against loss by hiring another party, an insurance company, to provide loss protection. A second person self-insures by accepting any loss as a reduction in personal wealth. A person who drives a ten-year-old car, for instance, rationally accepts that collision insurance (for own vehicle) is not worth the insurance premium. In contrast, one who has just purchased an expensive new car is less likely to accept that chance of loss (and if the car is purchased with borrowed money, the lender will require it).

Moral hazard is a controversial notion—not whether it exists (it is indeed a real phenomenon), but in what specific situations it applies. One major site of this controversy has been health care. For instance, the Economic Report of the President for 2004 invoked moral hazard in an effort to buttress its argument that many people have too much health insurance, or use it unwisely, and that many without it voluntarily choose not to have it (though the other side of that choice might be food on the table) and therefore do not contribute to moral hazard (see Office of Management and Budget 2004a, chapter 10). Because of the attention that this controversy has raised, we will illustrate the concept of moral hazard first in terms of health-care insurance, and then turn to its possible applications in the area of postemployment income insurance. The two areas are hardly unrelated, given that a large demand on retirement incomes is and will continue to be the cost of health care.

Critiques of the high costs and the failures of delivery of health care in the United States are plentiful. This dissatisfaction often invokes country differences in health expenditures—fully 15 percent of GDP versus about 8 percent in the EU and Japan. Except for the rich, the quality of health care purchased does not compare well with the quality of health care available to the average citizen of other countries (for example, Sweden, Norway, Switzerland, Japan). Some commentators argue that health-care costs have risen so much and so rapidly in the United States mainly because of moral hazard; they contend that people use too much health care because of insurance and that introducing private medical accounts will stem the surging costs.[13] As other observers have noted, however, this is a misapplication of the concept of moral hazard (see, for example, Nyman 2002). Insurers prefer to cover the healthy, not the ill; they have been increasingly successful in making this segregation, using health-actuarial accounting techniques, to the benefit of their profit margins and to the detriment of—whom else?—the poor and the ill. Susan Sered and Rushika Fernandopulle have detailed some of the consequences (2005).

To the extent that something like moral hazard operates in this area, it is due more to the behavior of health-care providers than to patients. Physicians have a serious interest in maximizing successes of diagnostic and treatment regimes, simply because of the belief that more information is better than less. Patients, too, share in that interest but generally do not declare what tests should be made and what treatments should be prescribed. Some critics have argued that physicians are excessive in their diagnostic and treatment procedures because of fear of litigation. No doubt medical liability costs have increased, hugely, as insurance companies have capitalized on fears fed by a small number of dramatized litigations. But the fact remains that physicians do have an inherent interest in getting as much diagnostic information as might be useful and, similarly, in erring on the side of too much rather than too little treatment. They are also sensitive to a patient's ability to pay, which generally means insurance coverage, when making decisions.

The culprit here is not the moral hazard of too much health insurance, however. Remember, insurers prefer to sell coverage to the healthy, not the ill, and they generally succeed in doing so. Rather, we need to look to a number of other factors. One of these is the understandable preference of health-care consumers as well as providers to want the best, which is often assumed to be the latest—the latest pharmaceutical advance, the latest diagnostic machinery, and so forth. Whether it is a new drug, a new scanning machine, a new telecommunications device, or an entertainment gadget, the latest is usually the most expensive. Innovators rightfully expect to amortize the costs of innovation and development as rapidly as possible, before the next innovator comes along and takes all the market; unit costs generally go down only as volume goes up, and so forth. Not that there are no problems with aspects of this process; however, John Abramson (2004), a recently practicing physician, describes some of the detrimental effects of pharmaceutical marketing procedures, including the fact that the most expensive drugs are the most likely to be overprescribed (Harder 2005).[14] But the problem that we focus on here is different: in wanting the best and thus the latest, both consumer and provider are sometimes incorrect in equating the two.

A case in point is the use of the CT scanning technology for lung cancer. CT scans are very sensitive to lung tissues with lesions that are cancerous or pre-cancerous. As a result, CT scans have a high false positive rate, in the sense that many people (the exact proportion for the general population is unknown) who test positive have at worst a form of cancer that progresses very slowly if at all (indolent cancer). As researchers Steven Woloshin, Lisa Schwartz, and Gilbert Welch from Dartmouth Medical School reported in *The New York Times*,

> Imagine a city in which 1,000 people are found to have progressive lung cancer following evaluation for cough and weight loss [the traditional

diagnostic approach]. At five years after diagnosis, 150 are alive and 850 have died: a five-year survival rate of 15 percent. However, if everyone in the city were screened with CT scans, perhaps 5,000 would be given a cancer diagnosis, although 4,000 would actually have indolent forms. These 4,000 would not die from lung cancer in five years, and the five-year survival rate would increase dramatically—to 83 percent—because these healthy people would appear in both parts of the fraction; 4150/5000. But what has really changed? Some people have been unnecessarily told that they have cancer (and may have experienced the harms of therapy), and the same number of people (850) still died. ("Warned, but Worse Off," August 22, 2005)

To drive the point home, let's shift to a situation that is more realistic in the sense that, unlike the scenario described just above, we don't already know all the relevant facts. Assume that a new diagnostic test for a disease with a high mortality rate has just been approved for use. Like all tests, this one is not perfectly accurate. It has a known risk of false positives and false negatives. Because the test is very sensitive, the risk of false positives is not small, but the risk of false negatives is quite small. The cost of a false positive is that any positive test should lead immediately to seriously invasive procedures first to confirm the diagnosis and then to commence treatment. Seriously invasive procedures always involve risk of trauma and mortality. Now assume that the trial data show that the five-year survival rate of people who were correctly diagnosed by the new test as having the disease and who then began appropriate therapy is 80 percent. The corresponding five-year survival rate of people who were correctly diagnosed with the older, less sensitive test and who then began appropriate therapy is 15 percent. Further assume no difference in appropriate therapy across groups. Shouldn't the new test be used in all future cases, despite the fact that the new diagnostic machinery is much more expensive and the new test has a higher false positive rate than the older test (which also increases costs)?

The answer is not necessarily, and for the same reason as described in the previous scenario, though it is less obvious here. From what we know at this point, we have no basis for ruling out the possibility that no one diagnosed with the disease through the new test gets even one extra day of life. We want to jump to the welcome conclusion that an 80 percent survival rate is so much better than a 15 percent survival rate, but are in no position to draw that conclusion until we know where the observations are made in the process of the disease. The greater sensitivity of the new test means that people with the disease are diagnosed earlier than they would have been with the old test. It is possible that because of that fact alone those diagnosed positive by the new test have a much higher rate of surviving five years from date of diagnosis than do those with the disease who are diagnosed later (that is, with the old test).[15]

Thus, insisting on newer (and more expensive) diagnostic technology would not be rational.[16] Does the presence of insurance encourage irrational use of the newer technology? It might, to the extent that physicians are less likely to order the newer, more expensive, but no more effective technology unless insurance coverage includes it. The patient's motivations to use the newer technology, however, derive from interests more fundamental than moral hazard. A person who believes that chances of survival are more than five times better using the newer technology will strive mightily for that choice even without insurance coverage.

We present this illustration of how the moral hazard argument is sometimes (mis)applied in the health-care area at some length, in order to unfold some of the complexities that can be hidden beneath the (mis)applications. Does moral hazard reasonably apply to the dynamics involved in postemployment income insurance? The short answer is that, though several commentators have tried to argue conclusively in one direction or the other, as if all or most of the facts were on their side, there is as yet no conclusive answer, because the dynamics of the underlying processes are very complex.

The most common argument that favors a role for moral hazard focuses on substitution effects. If workers are automatically compelled to save or invest for their retirement years, whether via the present programs of Social Security or by a mandated program of IRAs, are they therefore less inclined to supplement that saving-investment by voluntarily committing to additional saving-investment? Or, focusing just on Social Security, is worker saving-investment behavior depressed because they are overinsured by the mandated provisions of Social Security? Judged within a macroeconomic framework—that is, in terms of the national accounts of the economy as a whole—there is general agreement that the aggregate of saving and investment with Social Security is less than the aggregate would be if the FICA taxes had been put in the stock market. This conclusion was established four decades ago by Henry Aaron (1966). He demonstrated that the yield of a system such as Social Security equals the total growth rate of the economy (or, net of productivity growth, the growth rate of the population), whereas the yield of a fully funded system equals the interest rate—if one assumes, as Christoph Borgmann notes, the principles of neoclassical growth theory. In particular, we must assume "the neoclassical production function and competitive factor markets where the interest rate is equal to the marginal product of capital." (2005, 15). The difference in yields is often described as Social Security's implicit tax, which then raises two questions. What is purchased by this tax? Is the purchase efficient, fair, and productive? In fact, the tax pays for the between and within generation redistributive components of the postemployment insurance function. The redistribution is dictated by need rather than by contribution, and the need is defined by the benefit amount required to maintain someone who worked thirty-five years at little more than minimum wage above the poverty line. Whether the purchase is efficient, fair, and suitably productive is another disputed point, largely because of inherent trade-offs between efficiency and fairness, as well as disagreement about which goods are defined as economic and allowed inside the framework of evaluation.

The difficulty with that general conclusion from within a macroeconomic framework is that it rests on some major theoretical assumptions about how economic actors behave (for example, their decisions about saving, investment, consumption, and the like, their potential susceptibilities to moral hazard, and so on) and how those behaviors sum to form the national accounts of an economy as a whole. As an empirical argument, it proceeds through some counterfactuals. For example, what if we had chosen to retain a fully funded system? In retrospect, it is clear that the aggregate yield (investment return) of a fully funded system would have exceeded the aggregate yield of Social Security, but such hindsight appraisal is artificially narrow. First, it considers yield as a measure of monetary value, something from an accountant's spreadsheet. Other types of returns, such as improvements in well-being, reductions in social discord or political conflict, and all that might flow from those improvements are not so easily calculated. Second, if we engage in this imaginary time travel and change this one decision, we can only speculate as to the social, political, and economic ramifications of that other choice. Had the system of postemployment income insurance been fully funded from the beginning, in place of the pay-as-you-go public debt system of Social Security, other dynamics of the economy might well have been changed as well.[17]

One last point is significant. Whereas one often hears about the danger of moral hazard in regard to the insurance functions for health care and retirement income, less is generally said about its operation in other domains. For instance, one could make a case for the undesirable presence of moral hazard in behaviors of the Federal Reserve Bank (FRB). If people learn to factor FRB efforts to keep a tight lid on the rate of inflation into their saving, investment, and consumption decisions, will those decisions increasingly underestimate the risk premium that should be paid against the probability of future inflation? In fact, no one knows. The FRB policy on inflation is always a work in progress, a rather large experiment, in the midst of changing conditions, but it is certainly possible that FRB actions promote moral hazard. When the stock market bubble burst in 2001, the FRB responded by pumping in liquidity—sharply lowering interest rates, especially against the threat of price deflation. Has that response encouraged investors to take greater risks of future loss? Has it encouraged housing investors to adopt the view that, should the

Figure 3.2   Personal Saving Rate, 1950 to 2004

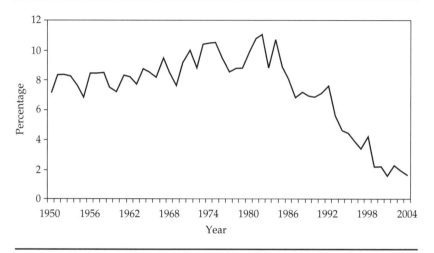

Source: Author's compilation from Reinsdorf 2004, chart 1.

housing market become a bubble that then bursts, the FRB will respond with comparable behavior? These are questions that a few economists take seriously. These categories of moral hazard, however, have not become the sort of issue of public morality that has typified the politics of health-care insurance or retirement-income insurance.

Saving and Saving Rates

Another issue bound up in the controversy over Social Security is the saving rate of individuals and households—that is, to what extent do people defer consumption in the present to some future period. As figure 3.2 shows, the rate of personal saving has declined very sharply since the early 1980s, perhaps to zero (Summers 2004). If citizens are to be expected to fund their retirements solely or primarily through their saving and investment accounts, it is clear that the rate at which they save must be substantially increased (Thaler and Benartzi 2004).

The fact is, no one knows exactly what the rate of private personal saving is or has been. The data portrayed in figure 3.2 are approximate, as are all data on private personal saving. This ignorance does not reflect a lack of effort. Once again, measurement has been a problem.

Two general ways to measure saving are from the bottom up and from the top down. The bottom up method is to use household surveys and similar means to determine how individuals who have disposable income in fact dispose of it—in particular what portion of their disposable income they save or invest. The next step is to aggregate this information across all such individuals to find the average rate of saving and investment (as well as component rates, such as the average rate of investing in mutual funds, in direct stock purchases, in certificates of deposit, and so on). In contrast, the top down approach begins with the total amount of disposable personal income(for all individuals combined, as measured from the National Income and Products Account (NIPA)). It then subtracts total personal spending, interest paid, and transfer payments to the rest of the world. Each approach has a number of variants, but the basics are dominant. One of the problems is that the two methods yield significantly different answers, always rather than occasionally, and by variable rather than a constant amount. Which approach is better?

Both have known flaws. Those of the bottom-up method are generally more serious, the most significant being that people too often do not know the answers to the questions asked of them, fatigue at the interview process, and prefer not to give accurate answers (if they do know or think they know) or even any answers.[18] The flaws of the top-down (or NIPA) approach tend to be systematic in known ways, and reliable estimates of measurement errors are thus possible.[19]

Disagreement about why the personal saving rate has declined so much since the 1980s is considerable. We will not go into the various proposed explanations but note only that part of the decline probably manifests a wealth effect (Poterba 2000). Judging from estimates by the Federal Reserve Board, almost all of the decline in the aggregate of personal saving since 1989 (the first year for which there are data on saving rates by quintile of income) was due to change in saving behavior among households in the top fifth (the 20 percent of households with the highest incomes) of the income distribution (who account for nearly two-thirds of aggregate net worth of U.S. households). This correlates with the fact that total household financial wealth, expressed as a proportion of disposable personal income, increased after the early 1980s at about the same rate of change that the personal saving rate declined. Of course, that households in the bottom 80 percent of the income distribution contribute virtually nothing to total personal saving is of prime relevance to the Social Security debate. If this debate has indeed stimulated more uncertainty about whether "Social Security will be there for you," as Jeff Dominitz, Charles Manski, and Jordan Heinz (2003, 1) have suggested, one might expect to see an increase in personal saving by households in that bottom 80 percent.

Alice Munnell, Francesca Golub-Sass, and Andrew Varani (2005) have shown that the NIPA measure of the saving rate is biased downward in that it does not distinguish between those with earnings income and those without, such as retirees. Employment earnings account for two-thirds or more of total personal income. It is well known that the personal saving rate as calculated in the NIPA framework is almost certain to be negative in any given year among retirees. Thus, if the NIPA measure of saving excludes persons aged sixty-five or older, the saving rate is somewhat higher than otherwise reported, though still in decline since a high point of about 11 percent in 1992. It is also apparent from these age-category estimates that virtually all of the personal saving by members of the working-age population has been through employer-sponsored pension plans. If pension plan saving is excluded, the personal rate of saving even among members of the working-age population has been negative since the mid-1990s. Again, this would fit the wealth effect explanation mentioned. Current saving behavior tends to be sensitive to expectations about future income and wealth. As asset prices in corporate stocks and then housing real estate greatly increased during the 1990s, households that contribute the vast bulk of personal saving and investment experienced large increases in net worth, which perhaps led them to expect greater postemployment income security even if they decreased current saving and investment (excepting commitments in employer-sponsored pension plans). After all, current saving is only the acquisition cost of new assets. If one has locked in major growth in the value of assets already acquired or is optimistic of more growth in future years, or both, the driving force of current saving might diminish in future years. The argument is plausible. Whether it accounts for the decline in the NIPA personal saving rate is an open question.

The relationship between a person's private saving rate and her or his benefit from Social Security can be illustrated by a typical idealized two-period model of income and consumption. We borrow an account from Dominitz, Manski, and Heinz because it is brief, lucid, and a good illustration of the (simplified version) of calculations that a private saver would be expected to make (or have made), if the saving function should become privatized and actuarially individualized.[20]

> Suppose that we divide our lives into two periods. In the first period, we work, receive wage/salary income as well as income from other sources (INC_1). We must allocate our income between [immediate] consumption and retirement savings [delayed consumption]. Savings may be invested in two ways: in a mutual fund, with an uncertain real rate of return, and in a risk-free asset. We retire to begin the second period and now must rely on two different sources of income: Social Security retirement benefits (SS) and realized savings (the amount that has been saved during the first period plus the return on that savings). Now let us shift from income to consumption. In the first period, we can consume our income minus what we save. In the second period, we can consume our Social Security benefits plus our realized savings. To frame it in what economists call budget constraints, consumption in the two periods must satisfy the following:

$$\text{Consumption}_1 = \text{INC}_1 - \text{Savings}^{\text{mutual fund}} - \text{Savings}^{\text{risk-free}}$$

$$\text{Consumption}_2 = \text{SS}_2 + \left(1 + r^{\text{mutual fund}}\right)\text{Savings}^{\text{mutual fund}}$$

$$+ \left(1 + r^{\text{risk free}}\right)\text{Savings}^{\text{risk-free}}.$$

[In both parenthetical expressions, the r stands for rate of return; adding the '1' simply adds in the principal, for example, if $100 earns 5 percent interest, we have (1.05)100 or $105 at the end of the period, assuming one end-of-period payment.]

What we gain from our consumption choices across the two periods, $U(\text{Consumption}_1, \text{Consumption}_2)$, is the sum of the utility gained from consuming during the first period and some portion of the total utility gained from consuming during the second period. That portion is determined by the discount rate, the rate we use when we assess value-in-the-future.

Suppose that when trying to decide how much to consume and how much to save in the first period, we know the amount of income we currently receive, INC_1 and the rate of return on our risk free investment, but we do not know either our future Social Security benefits or our return on the mutual fund. Suppose we try to imagine all the possible income values we could realize in the second period from these two sources (the possible combinations of Social Security benefits and realized savings) and make decisions to maximize our expected utility (our anticipated happiness) across both periods. To do that, we must solve a problem: how much should we save in the first period? What amount of savings will produce the most contentment across both present and future periods? The answer to that question depends on our first-period income INC_1, our preferences [captured by our individual utility functions and discount rates], and our expectations of Social Security benefits and mutual fund returns. (2003, 3–4)

If that seems too complicated, realize that placing the decision of how much to save for retirement in this framework is a simplification in a number of ways. Assuming a two-period division of a lifetime is one. People move in and out of employment, with many changes that are not expected, yet when such events occur, they likely have implications for present and future decisions. We borrow (incur debt) as well as save. That the model ignores dynamic properties of a person's preferences (for example, of discount rate), expected remaining years of life, ability to find and then use relevant information rationally, and so forth, adds many specific simplifications. Preferences can change. People can get better at gathering new information and putting it to good use, and more if we assume that learning and development continue throughout one's lifetime. But as Frank Hahn and Robert Solow point out in their critique, as the simplifications are removed, the model quickly becomes so complex that analytical solutions cannot be found using any available mathematical procedures (1995, 140).[21]

Even so, these are the types of decisions we all must make. We can make them explicitly, deciding to have a certain amount taken out of every paycheck and opting for some distribution between risk-free and riskier investments. We can also make them by default, believing that we cannot afford to allocate any of our current income to future consumption; we barely have enough income to meet our current needs. We might decide to fund our current consumption by taking out loans and accumulating debt on credit cards and assume that we'll manage to turn things around sooner or later. The circumstances under which we make these decisions—what we believe we can count on and what we view as less certain—bring us back to the concept of trust, an important part of the glue that holds these complex relationships together.

= Chapter 4 =

Preservation or Privatization

B OTH SIDES agree that changes need to be made. Exactly what must be changed and how quickly the change needs to be implemented are immediate points of disagreement. But these choices have taken a backseat to the question of when we should decide. Timing the changes in the program, per se, has become secondary to skirmishes around timing the decisions about the changes. The changes are sensitive to the demographic and economic concerns we discussed in previous chapters, and making decisions about exactly what to change is only part of the answer. We also need to figure out when and how to stage in the changes, which cohorts are affected and how they are affected, and how the behavior of affected cohort members needs to adjust to the new program rules. Once all this is determined, we need to emphasize public education, so that people understand the new rules, grasp the implications of those rules, and adjust their strategies in light of the rule changes. Nevertheless, how to time the decision about exactly what changes should be made has been treated largely as a political question, given that it involves attempts to push for a decision when external conditions appear favorable and to delay the decision when conditions appear less favorable to one side or the other. It also means that reports on any number of subjects—employment, pensions, economic growth, interest rates, among others—are invoked as further cause for alarm (or calm).

Given the importance of the issue and the lag time required for any changes that are agreed on to be factored into household budgeting behavior, why do we still linger at the fork in the road? Perhaps more important, why do we continue to view our situation as a choice between preservation and privatization? One would think that the debate would involve a great deal of discussion about a great many options. Instead, it seems to be limited to choosing either straightforward modifications of existing program features or a radical transformation of program design. Given that our options actually include everything between those extremes as well, why are we stuck on this much more limited question?

Proponents of preserving the current program structure often emphasize interdependence, social insurance, and redistribution as important principles to reinforce in designing Social Security for the future. They argue that such a program neither absolves individuals of responsibility for their own well-being nor suggests that markets are bad, that all beneficiaries are equally deserving of what they receive, or that all of those who are disadvantaged are victims of bad luck, social apathy, or structural barriers to success. Instead, program proponents see markets as effective and efficient for many types of exchanges, but not the best distributional mechanism for all purposes. Bad luck and poor decisions, they point out, can put people in dire circumstances, even when they are trying to behave responsibly, and that although structural barriers do not preclude the possibility of success, they do lower the odds. For these reasons, among others, those who have worked for U.S. industry from early to late adulthood deserve a sound foundation of basic security on which to build their resources to sustain them in old age.

Opponents of the current program structure—those who favor moving to a funded system—emphasize independence, personal choice, efficiency, and fairness as important considerations in revising the program. Concerned about both the macroeconomic consequences of an unfunded or even partially funded system and the moral implications of the current program structure for individual decisions about work and saving, opponents emphasize how programs based in nonmarket principles can distort both labor and capital market operations. These distortions translate into losses, which mean that whatever is gained from the public program is less than what could be gained from a system of private accounts. Moving to a privatized system, they argue, does not mean that the federal government is absolved of its responsibility for the income of the aged, or that we as a society should ignore those who enter old age without adequate resources. Rather, the federal government will continue to supervise rather than administer the program by making contributions mandatory, limiting the types of investments, limiting or penalizing premature withdrawals, and providing assistance for the most disadvantaged through an old-age social welfare program. The key difference is that the principal will be in the hands of individual citizens (as private capital and private savings) rather than under the control of the federal government (to be spent on other programs, given that the federal government cannot save current revenues for future use). Operating on the premise that government investment in private companies is bad policy, the Social Security surplus can only be used to fund public debt. By individualizing the investment accounts, national savings (as the cumulative savings across all units) will increase, even if people save no more than they are currently contributing through FICA taxes, because each dollar of savings they control will, by definition, increase the level of national savings by one dollar.

Because both sides of the debate make claims that assume knowledge of some of the basic attributes of Social Security, and the Old-Age and

Survivors Insurance (OASI) portion in particular, we will present some factual information before turning to each of the two main camps.

Social Security Basics

Social Security receives its primary revenue from FICA taxes. Its secondary revenue is the interest on the government bonds held in the trust fund. The FICA tax rate cannot change except by congressional legislation initiated in the House of Representatives. In 2006, the FICA rate for the OASI portion of Social Security was 10.6 percent of taxable earnings. The FICA rate for the disability insurance portion of Social Security was 1.8 percent of taxable earnings. Thus the total FICA rate for OASDI in 2006 was 12.4 percent of taxable earnings.[1] This 12.4 percent is divided into two equal parts, one coming off the top of an employee's payroll income and the other coming from the employer's payroll disbursements. Some critics have argued that both halves must be charged against the employee, that an employing firm passes its portion of any tax on to the employee or the customer unless specifically prohibited from doing so. Any tax that an employer pays on the wage bill could, of course, in principle be paid directly to the employees rather than to the government. Similarly, from the employee's point of view, the FICA portion paid by the employer could also be understood as a deferred compensation to the employee, in the form of insurance against risk of loss in postemployment income. Both perspectives are correct, as far as they go. They are correct in describing what has happened in completed transactions. But does anyone really believe that, if the half of the FICA tax charged to the employer were suddenly abolished, the employer would then add that money to the wages paid directly to the employees?

In the case of FICA taxation, taxable earnings are defined as earnings by covered workers up to a ceiling amount, which in 2006 was $94,200. This ceiling now increases each year, having been tied to an automatic inflation indexing, just as the benefit level has been indexed through a cost of living adjustment (COLA). The portion of all paid-employment workers who have earnings at or above that ceiling is variable over time; it can decline as well as increase, depending on the average wage rate and hours of paid employment (and the variance of each). Although Social Security covers about 96 percent of all American workers, the vast majority of uncovered workers are state, local, and federal government employees.[2]

Social Security disbursements to beneficiaries vary over time because of changes in the numbers of beneficiaries who are newly eligible, who die, who elect early retirement and thus accept some reduction of benefit level (which varies depending on age at early retirement), and who elected to delay receipt of benefits until age seventy. Disbursements also

Table 4.1   OASI Retired-Worker Beneficiaries

	Total	Men	Women
All beneficiaries			
Average monthly benefit	959.90	1082.00	830.80
Number of cases (millions)	30.36	15.61	14.75
Beneficiaries with reduction for early retirement			
Average monthly benefit	898.10	1004.00	793.60
Number of cases (millions)	22.06	10.96	11.11
Beneficiaries without reduction for early retirement			
Average monthly benefit	1124.30	1265.50	943.90
Number of cases (millions)	8.30	4.66	3.64
Number of cases as percent of all beneficiaries	27.3	29.8	24.7

Source: Office of Policy 2004, table 3.

vary in relation to changes due to the COLA provisions and changes in the composition of earnings histories (for example, by gender), which affect the formula by which a specific person's benefit level is calculated. Thus, comparing average benefit levels over time (in constant dollars) can be more complex than one might initially suppose, though short-term comparisons are relatively straightforward.

As can be seen in table 4.1, there were approximately 30.4 million retired-worker beneficiaries of OASI on September 30, 2005. Just over half (51.4 percent) were men. Most had elected to retire early—70.2 percent of the men and 75.3 percent of the women. The mean monthly benefit level was $959.90; if they retired early, it was $898.10; if they did not, it was $1,124.30. The mean benefit for all (the $959.90) was slightly more than 3.5 percent higher than it had been exactly a year earlier. Most of the difference was due to the COLA provision.

The Case for Preserving Social Security

Social Security advocates often complain about the rhetoric of crisis that has become so prominent in the current debate, claiming it is nothing more than a political tool designed to undermine public confidence in this program. Likening it to the Bush administration's use of the threat of Iraqi weapons of mass destruction as the basis for initiating the Iraq war, they argue that the talk of a crisis in Social Security is not based in reality, but is instead a tool of manipulation.[3] Rather than propose program adjustments that would place Social Security on a more stable long-term trajectory, the crisis talk has preempted serious discussion of ways to fix the program in favor of strategies to dismantle it. Because those who wish to destroy the program routinely paint a picture of catastrophic intergenerational warfare to promote the belief that substantial and fundamental restructuring is required, those who favor social insurance have been maneuvered into minimizing the seriousness of the financial issue, defending all aspects of the current structure of redistributions, and trying to avoid any talk of tax increases or benefit reductions as likely components of preservation.

The annual Social Security Administration Trustees report is an authoritative source on the current status of Social Security—the program, the trust fund, current receipts and payments, and expected receipts and payments under differing assumptions. According to it, the time frame of program stability extends until 2042. In 2018 or thereabouts, payment of all promised benefits to entitled recipients will require more than the revenue generated through collection of the FICA payroll taxes. At that point, the Social Security Administration will begin to redeem some of the Treasury bills held by the trust fund. The current revenues from FICA coupled with the funds from the redeemed Treasury bills will allow coverage of current and anticipated benefits until about 2042. At that point, the trust fund reserve will be exhausted. Even then, the current collections from FICA will allow coverage of two-thirds or more of anticipated benefits. All of this assumes that we do nothing to prepare for the shortfall we will face in 2042. We have a variety of options at our disposal, including different combinations of benefit adjustments, small increases in the payroll tax, increasing eligibility ages, restructuring spousal benefits, and rethinking the number of years or the form of indexing used in calculating average earnings or the income threshold on which the payroll tax applies.

As a review of the last ten or so years of reports on Social Security makes clear, the length of time during which the Social Security program is solvent has been adjusted. Often, though not always, the year in which revenues are predicted to fall short of promised benefits has been pushed further into the future. Suppose, for the sake of argument, when the trust fund was depleted, we decided to enforce a 25 percent benefit cut. Because people tend to think in terms of current benefit levels, they imagine the impact of such a reduction on what retirees currently receive. But 2042 is thirty-five years in the future.

During the second half of the twentieth century, average Social Security benefits increased for a variety of reasons. Workers accumulated more years of covered employment as the program matured, thereby increasing their average monthly earnings on which benefits were based. Congress frequently increased benefits, including ad hoc cost of living adjustments until these adjustments were made automatic in 1974. Congress also changed the benefit formula and the way earnings were indexed. Last, improvements in worker productivity and healthy rates of economic growth were reflected in real increases in average wage levels and the average standard of living. In 2005, the average monthly benefit was $960. If we assume 1 percent growth in annual real wages (that is, net of inflation) over the next twenty-five years, the average real benefit levels will have increased substantially by the time this cut would be enacted.

For example, in 1975, the average monthly Social Security benefit for retired workers was $207.18. By 2000, it was $844.60. We need though to adjust for inflation over this period, so we calculate the average monthly Social Security benefit for retired workers in 1975 using 2000 dollars. If we want to know what the $207.18 benefit is worth in 2000 dollars, the answer is $675.29. In other words, for the average retired worker to have the same standard of living in 2000 as he had in 1975, he would require a monthly benefit of $675.29. By 2000, however, the average benefit for a retired worker was almost $170 more than that, or in percentage terms, average benefits in 2000 were 25 percent higher in real dollars. This so-called growth in average real benefits reflects the growth in average real wages.

No one is suggesting that we solve the problem this way, but it is important to consider the question of benefit cuts in the appropriate context. First, the program will continue to enjoy a steady stream of revenues unless current law is changed. Second, assumptions about growth in real average wages is part of any set of projections, as are assumptions about economic growth and inflation. The rates may differ, but we should use the same assumptions—the same rates—to evaluate different options. Third, because real Social Security benefits are expected to continue to grow (in concordance with real wages), any talk of a 25 to 30 percent cut in future benefits must be assessed relative to an expected level of real future benefits 25 to 30 percent higher than they are today. Once again, the claim that the benefit formula will have to be adjusted to cut back on future benefits and the counter claim that real benefits can be the same as they are now both contain some truth.

Why Social Insurance?

The centerpiece of Social Security that proponents want to maintain is the social insurance model (Dionne 1999). As members of a complex, modern, and democratic society, we necessarily rely on each other. The efficiencies introduced by organizing the production and distribution of goods and services around a division of labor necessarily mean that our society is characterized by a high degree of interdependency. Although this web of mutually reinforcing connections does not eliminate our individuality—our personal skills, talents, preferences, and dispositions—it does place limits on what individuals can routinely accomplish on their own. That we rely on farmers and ranchers to provide us with food, local utilities to supply us with water and power, educators to teach our children, physicians to treat our illnesses, and mechanics to fix our cars means that our current standard of living is possible because we can del-egate responsibility for all these important tasks to other people even as we rely on our government for protection against unfair or unsafe exchanges.

This interdependence also places us at some risk. First, we must have enough financial resources to purchase what we need, which means that we must have a steady source of income to maintain access to the goods and services we require. For most people, a steady source of income is received as compensation for work. In modern societies, therefore, an important risk shared by most people is the risk of being without a job. This risk is experienced as the risk of unemployment, disability, or retirement without access to sufficient earnings replacement for workers and their dependents.

The notion of social insurance is based on this presumption of inter-dependency as well as belief in advantages of addressing shared risks with collective programs. If we jointly share these risks and desire some protection from the adverse consequences of these risks, then designing a federal program that will replace some proportion of our earnings is seen as advisable. They argue that the program has worked well for more than sixty years and can be continued with some straightforward adjustments as long as trust in the social contract remains strong. Unfor-tunately, the rhetoric of crisis in the financial status of the plan has undermined public confidence in the program and raised doubts among cohorts of younger workers.

The Benefit of Spreading Risk

An important difference between collective approaches and individual accounts involves the allocation of various types of risks. Although arguments that favor individual accounts focus on the potential benefits of managing one's own investments, recent experience has driven home the real cost of misjudging the market. In thinking about investment options, we should consider separately the questions of diversifying investments beyond Treasury bills and dismantling a large component of the collective enterprise of social insurance by establishing individual accounts as the core of the new Social Security program.

Two central concerns are investment risk and longevity risk. Invest-ment risk addresses the probability that our investment choices will not perform well enough to fund retirement. In other words, managing investment risk involves the prediction of rates of return. Longevity risk is related to the length of time during which we will need to rely on our investments for support. Here, we run the risk of outlasting our funds or incorrectly choosing the number of years over which we spend what we have saved. If we are too conservative in our estimate, then we spend less money per year than we could have spent; the remainder of our retirement funds becomes part of our estate. If we underestimate, we will exhaust our funds before we die because we will have spent the money too quickly and will, for the remainder of our years, have to rely on family, charity, or government welfare programs for support.

The contrast between large defined benefit pension plans and defined contribution accounts provides us with evidence of the advantages of investing retirement funds through large pooled accounts (the DB approach) rather than on an individualized basis. Regardless of whether the fund is pooled or individualized, the risk of an inadequate rate of return must be addressed. Managing investments through a large single fund creates economies of scale unavailable to individuals. Not only can transaction costs be more widely spread, but the temporal aspect of investment risk is much more difficult for individuals to handle. When funds are pooled, those directing investments can diversify with respect to time horizons, because those pooling their funds will need to cash out at different times. In addition, pooled fund managers can often use a longer time horizon than individuals, thus allowing for riskier investments, which are more profitable. Depending on the individual investor's age, opportunities for higher long-run returns may not be feasible because of the time frame in which retirement savings will need to be converted to retirement income. As retirement nears, individual investors must either choose to invest less aggressively and accept lower rates of return, or run the risk of having to delay retirement until their financial picture changes. Another option for individuals is to buy a lifetime annuity, though diseconomies of scale are introduced in the process.

If lifetime annuities were mandatory, then those who die later would be counterbalanced by those who die earlier. The risk addressed by the annuity is longevity, but the insurer can assume it at a better price because of the heterogeneity of the group. Those buying lifetime annuities will vary widely in the number of years they receive the benefits. However, when the purchase is not mandatory, insurers must address the impact of adverse selection. Those people most concerned about longevity risk are those who expect to live many years beyond their retirement. Those who have more modest or even pessimistic life expectancies will be more inclined to manage the longevity risk themselves. From the insurers' standpoint, demand for the product is highest among those for whom the payout will be most expensive.

Certainly, many of today's elderly are surprised by their own longevity, a sentiment captured by the joke: "If I'd known I was going to live this long, I would have taken better care of myself!" Social Security protects against longevity risk by paying benefits until the retiree dies, and then continuing survivor benefits until the spouse dies. Because of the lifetime annuity provision, retirees need not worry about outliving their pensions. The cost of furnishing the annuity is minimized because it is, essentially, a mandatory provision. Although individual investors can also buy a lifetime annuity, insurance companies charge a premium for these policies, given that the retirees most concerned are those who expect to live a long time. Because Social Security requires participation and does not allow lump sum payments, it eliminates the problem of adverse selection. Managing both investment risk and longevity risk collectively is therefore the most efficient solution.

The Advantage of Predictability

A major advantage of the Social Security program is its transparency. Although some of the calculations may be more suited to accountants than the average worker, potential beneficiaries receive an annual statement that both reports their earnings histories and projects the level of benefits they can expect if they follow certain patterns of employment and choose either sixty-two or full entitlement age as their time to retire. Clearly, these reports cannot guarantee specific benefit amounts, but the assumptions on which the projections are based are easy for the typical worker to understand. Given that level of expected retirement income, any worker can begin to formulate a fuller picture of what to expect in retirement by factoring in any potential benefits from employer-sponsored pensions or potential income from savings and investments. Because many workers have little accumulation in the category of savings and investments, especially when we factor out home equity, the key additional source of retirement income is employer-sponsored pensions.

If the pension plan from work is a defined benefit plan (DB), expected retirement income is often a function of seniority and earnings. Because DB formulas are part of contract negotiations, the information necessary to make these estimates is available to workers. Those represented by unions can often find help in projecting retirement income from their union office. Even if workers are disinclined to be that systematic, however, they can get a good approximation of their future benefits by learning the benefits received by those like them who have already retired or who have done the calculations. Of course, expectations for DB income in retirement assume continued employment with the firm and the firm's continued investment in the plan. Neither of these requirements can be guaranteed.

Estimating retirement income from defined contribution plans is not nearly so straightforward, and because it can fluctuate as the market improves or declines, the amount a person needs to contribute to meet any given goal also fluctuates. Making projections about retirement income generated from a DC plan is somewhat less complicated if DC funds are invested in very conservative (and therefore very low risk and relatively low return) securities. Workers with a sizable portion of their accounts in stock are accustomed to the fluctuations in the value of their accounts as reported in their quarterly statements. Fluctuations in the value of accounts translate into fluctuations in the level of retirement benefits one can expect at any given retirement age. On occasion, the level of expected benefits or the age at which retirement can occur change in more favorable ways than anticipated, as those who invested in technology stocks experienced in the 1990s. Of course, many of these experienced the sudden jolt of significant losses as the trading value of the same stocks dropped when the bubble burst and their account values took a nosedive.

For the half of the workforce not covered by employer-sponsored pension plans, the retirement income promised by Social Security is what can be counted on. What we can see is that a central element of the security provided by employer-sponsored defined benefit plans and Social Security is its predictability (Thompson 1998), with Social Security being the more reliable of the two. First, the public can be confident that the benefits promised during the years of contribution will materialize when they satisfy the eligibility requirements and file the necessary paperwork. The full weight of the federal government is behind this agreement—that those who pay into Social Security will receive benefits that will support them until they die. Second, those on the verge of retirement understand that the standard of living they've enjoyed during their working years will not disappear when they retire. In other words, they know not only they will receive benefits, but also that they will be able to live on the benefits they receive.

The Social Benefits of Progressivity

Whereas an individualized framework evaluates a benefit program in terms of average rates of return on investments, proponents of collective programs argue for a more expansive framework for program evaluation. With Social Security, one's individualized return is found by calculating how much was paid in taxes over one's career and comparing it to how much one receives in benefits during retirement; this calculation is possible only in retrospect, after retiree, spousal, and survivor benefits have been received. Although an individualized investment framework sees any deliberate redistribution as a negative, those who favor social insurance see the guaranteed benefit floor as an important component of the security offered by social insurance. Early debates over how to structure Social Security benefits weighed the relative merits of adequacy and equity as the principles behind benefit calculation. The equity principle held that people should receive in benefits at least what they made in contributions. The adequacy principle held that benefit levels should maintain retirees above the poverty line. Reducing the poverty rate among the elderly was linked to two features of the program. First, a minimum benefit (or benefit floor) was established. In

1940, the minimum benefit payable at age sixty-five was $10 per month. This minimum benefit remained in effect until 1981. Supplementary Security Income, the original old-age assistance program from 1940 to 1973, now provides average benefits of $330.04 per month per recipient.

The second feature involves the formula used to compute benefits. Based on the adjusted earnings history, each individual is credited with an average indexed monthly earnings amount (AIME), which is the average of what they earned per month during the best thirty-five years of employment, adjusted for how long ago the earnings took place and how average wages have changed since that time. If someone retiring at age sixty-five in 2003 had an AIME of $2,000, his or her monthly Social Security benefit would have been calculated as $991.48—that is, .90 (606) + .32 (1394) = 545.40 + 446.08 = 991.48.

If a more highly paid sixty-five-year-old retired in 2003, someone whose AIME had been $4,000, the benefit would have been $1,572.49— or .90 (606) + .32 (3,047) + .15 (347) = 545.40 + 975.04 + 52.05 = 1,572.49.

In other words, the retirement benefit replaces 90 percent of the first $606 of average indexed monthly earnings, 32 percent of the next $3,047, and 15 percent of the next $3,653. Keep in mind that your earnings history is based not on your total annual earnings, but on your earnings up to the tax threshold. In 2003 that was $87,000. Thus, if you earned $90,000 in 2003, you did not pay FICA on the last $3,000 you earned.

To explore another context, we can compare the AIME and monthly benefit amount for five profiles: someone who never earned more than minimum wage, someone who earned 75 percent of the average wage, someone who earned the average wage, someone who earned 150 percent of the average wage, and someone who earned the maximum taxable earnings in all thirty-five years.

What is clear from the chart is that a person who earns minimum wage throughout his or her career has a higher replacement rate for average earnings. Relative to the benefit formula, this rate reflects the 90 percent of the first $606 of averaged indexed monthly earnings. The maximum family benefit includes a spousal benefit calculated as 50 percent of the worker's benefit, also referred to as the primary insurance amount. The combination of the two benefits replaces 90 percent of AIME. The proportion of AIME replaced gets smaller as AIME increases. The maximum family benefit replaces about 83 percent of AIME for the average wage earner, about 70 percent for someone who routinely earned 150 percent of average wage, and about 57 percent for someone who earned the maximum taxable amount in all thirty-five years. For those who earn more than the maximum taxable amount, the percent of total earnings replaced is smaller, but because they paid no payroll taxes on those extra earnings, the relevant replacement rate is the proportion of earnings that were taxed. What is also clear is that the family benefit is

Figure 4.1   Monthly Benefit Amount for Selected Wage Levels

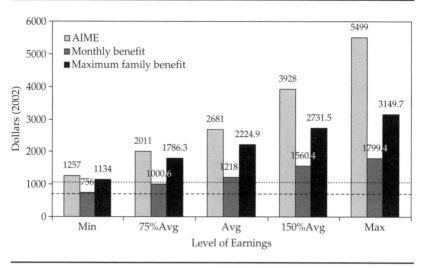

Source: Office of Policy 2004, table 2.A26.

an important component of higher replacement rates. The difference between the middle (and always smallest) bar and the bar on the right of each triad (always between the smallest and largest in height) represents the size of the family (generally spousal) benefit. The middle bar represents the worker's benefit only. We will return to this point later in our discussion, but this chart illustrates one of the fairness issues being debated.

This progressivity of replacement rates has been instrumental in reducing poverty rates among the elderly. To demonstrate the relationship between Social Security retirement benefits and poverty, we superimposed two lines on this chart. The dashed line is the poverty level for individuals in 2003, which is set at $8,980 per year, or about $748 dollars per month. A thirty-five-year minimum wage worker who retires at age sixty-five receives an individual benefit amount (or, if married, a family benefit amount) slightly higher than the poverty level. The dotted line represents the poverty level for couples, which is $12,120 per year, or about $1,010 per month. By minimum wage worker, we mean someone who worked 2,080 hours each year (fifty-two weeks at forty hours a week) for at least thirty-five years. Not all retirees who collect Social Security benefits can expect to live their retirement years above the poverty line, but, in the judgment of policy makers, someone with this level of work commitment should be able to anticipate enough retirement benefits to do so, even if only by a few dollars.

Figure 4.2   Percent Poor, 1959 to 2001

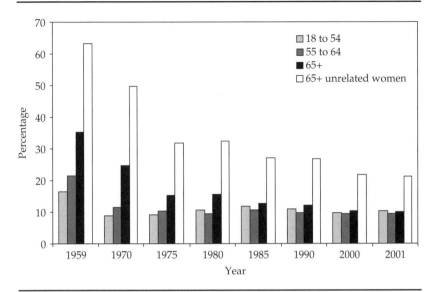

Source: Office of Policy 2004, table 3.E2.

In figure 4.2 we see how the poverty rates for different aged groups have changed in recent decades. Three age groups are represented in this chart: eighteen to fifty-four, fifty-five to sixty-four, and sixty-five and older. This last group is reported as a whole, and then also for un-related older women. Although more than 30 percent of the elderly lived in poverty in 1959, that proportion steadily declined. By 2001, the poverty rates for all three age groups hovered around 10 percent. For older women, we also see a reduction—most notably between 1959 and 1975, when it declined by half. During the last quarter-century, the rate declined by about one-third (from three out of ten to one out of five older unattached women), twice as high as for the other three groups represented.

History from the Proponents' Viewpoint

Proponents of preservation view Social Security as a success story, a demonstration of how government programs can work well, can be managed at very low administrative cost, and provide something important—financial security in old age—to a wide range of constituents. Their view of the history emphasizes the development of the trust fund, the 1939 and subsequent amendments that broadened the impact of the program on old-age poverty. Since its enactment, Social Security has faced a

number of challenges—so-called crises by those who would dismantle
the program—but public support and the program's accomplishments
continued to provide the political will not only to maintain the program,
but also to improve it in a number of respects. As initially passed, the
program provided too little too late. The real crises—of unemployment,
of poverty, of hopelessness—needed a real solution, not the promise of
a solution in the making. That the 1939 amendments allowed benefits to
be paid sooner than the original (1935) legislation had scheduled and
expanded benefit entitlement to spouses and dependents helped make
Social Security an antidote to some of the country's ills.

The history of the trust fund, which has been a major point of contention from the beginning, can be described as a series of skirmishes—
flares of conflict when conservatives tried to prevent the accumulation
of assets in the fund or eliminate it altogether. From the start, claims and
counterclaims about whether a trust fund would be real or illusion were
apparent. Those who opposed using the trust fund argued that it would
hold only IOUs, that paying interest on or redeeming Treasury securities held by the trust fund would amount to double taxation, that the
trust fund was a sham. These same arguments resurface again and
again, and are regularly addressed by Advisory Council reports. In one
instance, the report of the Advisory Council noted that much of the current controversy centered on the long-term financing and how benefits
decades in the future would be paid:

> Dependent old age has become a national problem. A steadily rising
> proportion of aged, technological change, mobility, and urban life have
> combined to create a condition which cannot be met effectively by state
> governments alone. The council has indicated its conviction of the impor-
> tance of an adequate contributory insurance program in the prevention of
> the growth of dependency in a democratic society. Since the nation as a
> whole will materially and socially benefit by such a program, it is highly
> appropriate that the Federal government should participate in the financ-
> ing of the system. With the broadening of the scope of the protection
> afforded, governmental participation in meeting the costs of the program
> is all the more justified since the existing costs of relief and old-age assis-
> tance will be materially affected . . . The prevention of dependency is a
> community gain in more than social terms . . .
>
> Under social insurance programs it is not necessary to maintain a full
> invested reserve such as is required in private insurance, provided defi-
> nite provision is made for governmental support of the system. The only
> invested fund then necessary would be a reasonable contingency fund as
> outlined above . . . If the method of accumulating a relatively large reserve
> is eliminated, there must be, instead, the definite assurance that the pro-
> gram will be financed not by payroll taxes alone but, in addition, by gov-
> ernmental contributions from other sources. Without interest returns on
> a relatively large fund, payroll taxes alone would prove insufficient to

meet the current disbursements necessary as the system matures. For this reason, the council insists that the principle of adequate governmental contributions should be definitely established in the law when tax provisions are revised, if the reserve policy under the old-age insurance program is changed . . .

The receipts of the taxes levied in Title VIII of the law, less the costs of collection, should through permanent appropriation be credited automatically to an old-age insurance fund and not to the general fund for later appropriation into the account, in whole or in part, as Congress may see fit. It [is] believed that such an arrangement will be constitutional.

The old-age insurance fund should specifically be made a trust fund, with designated trustees acting on the behalf of the prospective beneficiaries of the program. The Trust Fund should be dedicated exclusively to the payment of the benefits provided under the program and, in limited part, to the costs necessary to the administration of the program.

At the time the Social Security Act was drafted it was deemed necessary for the constitutional reasons to separate legally the taxation and benefit features of the program. It is believed that in the light of subsequent court decisions such legal separation is no longer necessary. Since the taxes levied are essentially contributions intended to finance the benefit program, it is not only logical but expedient to provide for automatic crediting of tax proceeds to the old age insurance fund. It is believed by the Council that such a procedure would enhance public understanding of the contributory insurance system. Since the tax proceeds thus credited are intended for payment of benefits, it is recommended that they be deposited in a trust fund under the control of designated trustees in accordance with appropriate legal provisions. The Trust Fund should be dedicated to the payment of benefits and, to a restricted amount, to the costs necessary to the administration of the program. It is recommended that these funds should continue to be invested in securities of the Federal government as at present. (Advisory Council on Social Security 1938, 18–20)

Not only did the council emphatically reject the proposal to abandon reserve funding. Its recommendations strengthened this form of financing by creating a formal Trust Fund to hold Social Security reserves. Further, in the appendix to the report, the council rejected arguments against the decision to partially fund the program through reserves:

The special securities issued to the old-age reserve account are general obligations of the United States Government, which differ from other securities of the Government only in the higher rate of interest they bear and in the fact that they are not sold in the open market. The issuance of such special securities is not only expressly authorized by law, but is required by the provision of the Social Security Act that the old-age reserve funds are to be invested so as to yield an interest return of 3 per cent.

The U.S. Treasury uses the moneys realized from the issuance of these special securities by the old-age reserve account in the same manner as it does moneys realized from the sale of other Government securities. As long as the budget is not balanced, the net result is to reduce the amounts which the government has to borrow from banks, insurance, companies and other private parties. When the budget is balanced, these moneys will be available for the reduction of the national debt held by the public. The members of the Advisory Council are in agreement that the fulfillment of the promises made to the wage earners included in the old age insurance system depends upon, more than anything else, the financial integrity of the government. The members of the Council, regardless of differing views on other aspects of the financing of old-age insurance, are of the opinion that the present provisions regarding the investment of the moneys in the old-age reserve account do not involve any misuse of these moneys or endanger the safety of these funds. (Advisory Council on Social Security 1938, 22)

The Trust Fund was retained, and the plan continued to designate some portion of current contributions to build a reserve, allowing the program to be partially financed through the accumulation of excess contributions. However, the implementation of this plan required that Congress keep to the schedule of recommended tax increases. They did not. Building the proscribed level of reserve funding in the account required that these tax increases occur, even though the additional revenue was not immediately required to pay benefits. Accumulation was necessary so that when the demography of workers to beneficiaries turned less favorable, payroll tax increases could nevertheless be slow and incremental. Actuarial projections predicted that the reserve would build until 1980 when, for the first time, benefits would exceed receipts. By then the Trust Fund was to have accumulated $46 billion, and the interest alone would provide the needed funds to pay benefits.

Between 1942 and 1947, Social Security payroll tax rate increases were postponed seven times. Senator Vandenberg, the vocal opponent to establishing the Trust Fund in the first place, was now focused on a tax freeze (Kollmann and Solomon-Fears 2001). Proponents of the payroll tax freeze argued that because additional funds were not immediately required to pay current benefits, no such increases should be implemented. Unsuccessful in his attempts to eliminate the Trust Fund, Senator Vandenberg was now successful in blocking the flow of funds designed to accumulate in it, despite protests by President Roosevelt that

a failure to allow the scheduled increase in rates to take place under the present favorable circumstances would cause a real and justifiable fear that adequate funds will not be accumulated to meet the heavy obligations of the future and that the claims for benefits accruing under the present law may be jeopardized. (Kollmann and Solomon-Fears 2001).

Although supporters of the recommended tax rate schedule warned that the freeze would require either sharper tax increases in the future or general funds to be used to meet obligations (or both), the freeze prevailed with bipartisan support. In this case, as in others, a coalition could be established among those who were anxious to keep taxes at a minimum as a desirable end in itself, those who were focused only on the short-term health of the program, and those who saw the tax freeze as a way to prevent the federal government from having access to this surplus revenue (and perhaps limiting the size and long-term viability of the new social welfare program).

Regardless of the reasons for opposing the tax increases, the Trust Fund was not accumulating the necessary reserve the council thought would be required to pay benefits after 1980. The unfunded, PAYG nature of the program was accomplished by the 1939 amendments in conjunction with congressional refusal to allow the scheduled increases in FICA taxes to become effective. The de facto level of the Trust Fund was thereby significantly reduced, and the idea of Social Security as a PAYG program was absorbed in collective memory as though such a design had been the initial intent.

Even with these changes, the actual level of retirement benefits paid by Social Security during the 1940s were so low and the entitlement group so limited that the old-age assistance programs of the states (OAA) continued to shoulder much of the responsibility for wage replacement among the country's elderly, given that benefits under the federal old-age insurance (OAI) program were significantly lower (approximately 60 percent) than under the states old-age assistance programs (Berkowitz 1991). The gap between OAA and OAI was especially wide in the farm states.

Another advisory council was appointed to address these issues. The council's 1948 recommendations became the basis for the 1950 amendments to Social Security, which expanded coverage and increased benefits (Cohen and Myers 1950). As Edward Berkowitz noted,

> In a more fundamental sense, the 1950 amendments marked the start of Social Security's golden age, in which rising wage levels and expanding employment levels made possible the continued rise of Social Security benefits without substantial tax increases. The 1952 amendments set the postwar pattern. Both Democrats and Republicans backed a substantial rise in benefits, and the Social Security actuaries ruled that no new taxes would be necessary to fund the increase. (1991, 27)

In the absence of a tax increase, the benefit expansions were to be financed by further reductions to the Trust Fund accumulations. In other words, the changes made in the 1950s furthered the transition of the Social Security program to a fully unfunded (PAYG) system in that it increased the proportion of program revenues that were paid out immediately in benefits and significantly reduced the proportion of surplus revenues invested in Treasury securities.

That fact did not escape notice, when in the mid-1950s concerns about the failure of the Trust Fund to keep pace with expanding long-term liabilities began to attract media attention. In response, the staff of the 1957 to 1959 Advisory Council prepared a report addressing these "Misunderstandings of Social Security Financing" (1958). Citing newspaper articles and editorials arguing that the Trust Fund had a shortage of $300 billion, the report responded to each charge. The claim that the Trust Fund had a $300 billion deficit was fundamentally a critique of the PAYG financing of the current program rather than the fully funded design initially envisioned. The Advisory Council response was that full funding was necessary for private life insurance companies, for example, because one could conceive of a given company's failing to sell another policy but still having to pay off on policies already sold. A compulsory government program such as Social Security was not similarly constrained, given the federal government's power to tax and the reasonable assumption that contributions would continue to be collected in the future.

Second, the Advisory Council report noted that the program was "designed to provide receipts exceeding disbursements in most years during the next several decades," and that the program was therefore not in trouble because estimates suggested that paying benefits in calendar years 1958 and 1959 would require dipping into the Trust Fund reserves (1958, 4). Third, the report asserted that paying interest on and redeeming some Treasury securities in which the Trust Fund was invested did not represent double taxation, because the Treasury securities are issued to fund public debt, and the government must pay interest on all public debt, regardless of who holds that debt. Fourth, the Trust Fund does not consist of IOUs, a claim that rests on the assumption that Treasury securities in the Trust Fund are issued by the government to itself. The report argues that the federal securities purchased with Trust Fund dollars are not materially different from the securities issued to private investors. All Treasury securities are debt obligations. Finally, the report noted that investing the Trust Fund in Treasury securities to partially finance the national debt did not, in and of itself, increase the national debt. The debt is increased only when the federal government spends more than it collects in taxes. We will return to this point later.

Once again, the concerns were laid to rest—at least temporarily, and attention returned to groups and contingencies that were still unaddressed by the program. During the next fifteen years, a number of changes were made. The program became nearly universal in coverage. A disability program was added. Medicare was added. Early retirement benefits were authorized. The level of benefits was significantly increased. Benefits were indexed to the cost of living. Annual earnings were indexed to average wages so benefit levels across cohorts could be stabilized at an average proportion of previous earnings—what is often referred to as the replacement rate. Many of these adjustments provided a framework that allowed benefit determinations to switch to an accountant's version of automatic pilot. Rather than making periodic adjustments to the level of benefits, increases would be built into the process of benefit calculation. By adjusting earnings histories relative to current average wages, average earnings of new beneficiaries were calculated in today's living standards without privileging earnings that came late in a career over earnings that came early. By adjusting benefits annually according to the consumer price index, benefits would always stay in current dollars—being stabilized in terms of purchasing power rather than fixed in nominal amounts.

Concern about the financial trajectory of Social Security surfaced in the 1970s and culminated in the 1983 amendments that recommended a combination of benefit reductions and tax increases. By enacting tax increases earlier than had been scheduled, program revenues exceeded what was necessary to pay for current benefits, thereby yielding a surplus, which was routinely invested in U.S. government bonds. The strategy to put the program on a better footing thus followed the blueprint from 1939 by restoring the program to a partially funded status. This positive balance in Social Security accounts—the positive difference between contributions collected and benefits paid out—is expected to continue until about 2017.[4] Given the return to the 1939 partially funded design, perhaps we should not have been surprised that the same kinds of claims intended to undermine the Trust Fund were launched anew. It would appear that the Social Security Trust Fund—and particularly the decision to accumulate a significant level of securities to fund future benefits rather than a minimal accumulation to round the edges of minor shortfalls—is the real focus of the political struggle. Recall that in the 1940s, critics of the design were able to derail the strategy to move the program to a partially funded status by blocking the tax increases that would have created the flow of surplus funds. Since 1983, however, the Trust Fund has financed more and more of the federal debt, as one administration after another has authorized expenditures in excess of general revenues. Instead of using surplus FICA takes to reduce national debt in anticipation of redeeming Treasury bonds, we have created substantial new debt, shifted tax burden toward flat taxes and reduced progressive income taxes.

Providing enough benefits to prevent people from slipping into poverty, though a stated goal of some, was not part of the original program. During the 1940s, benefit levels were maintained but not increased. As a result, by 1949, twice as many people were receiving old-age assistance (the state-run welfare program that ultimately became the Supplemental Security Income program) as Social Security retirement benefits. The average benefit under old-age assistance was $42 per month and under Social Security $25 per month (Schieber and Shoven 1999). Although the average retirement benefit had increased by about 10 percent in nominal dollars, the increase was due to the longer coverage period. In other words, each successive cohort of retirees had participated in the Social Security program for a somewhat longer period of time than previous cohorts. The increase in coverage period translated into somewhat higher benefits, but even this meant that the real value of the benefits had declined over the decade. The extremely low benefits were not routinely adjusted for inflation. A series of amendments in 1950 extended coverage to new categories of workers and increased benefits so that average retirement benefits were at least as high as welfare benefits. To fund the increased benefits, the payroll tax was increased to 1.5 percent—a tax increase that today's opponents would describe as a 50 percent increase in payroll taxes, because the additional half-percent represented 50 percent of the original tax rate of 1.0.

As illustrated in figure 4.3, the ratio of average benefits to average wages fluctuated, declining during the 1940s and then bounced back as a result of the amendments in 1950. Throughout the 1950s and the 1960s, it remained somewhere between .2 and .3. We can think of it as an average replacement rate. The ratio of average retirement benefit to average wage tells us what proportion of earnings the average worker had replaced by Social Security benefits. It was still the case, however, that changes in the benefit formula (for those not yet retired) as well as in the benefits received by those already retired were done on a largely ad hoc basis, often to coincide with election cycles (Derthick 1979). During the first Nixon administration, an effort to systematize replacement rates and stabilize the purchasing power of retirees led to substantial increases in benefits and to passage of the COLA indexing of benefits. These changes improved replacement rates for the time being, but guaranteed that the real value of benefits would be maintained rather than gradually eroded by inflation.

Replacement rates were stabilized toward the end of the 1970s, after the notorious notch mistake. The result, however, was an automated accounting system that adjusted earnings history for the growth in average wage to accompany the automatic cost-of-living escalator of benefits. At long last, Social Security had fulfilled its promise of providing predictable, adequate, and sustained income security in old age. From the 1980s through 2006, the program maintained an average replacement rate of about one-third. The wage indexing of earnings histories helped steady replacement rates and ensured that as average real wages improved, real social security benefits would as well. Once the benefit (primary insurance amount) was established, the annual cost-of-living adjustments ensured that the real value of the benefit amount (its

Figure 4.3   Ratio of Average Retirement Benefit to Average Wages, 1951 to 2001

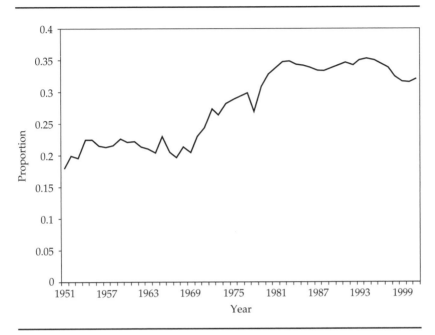

Source: Authors' calculations from Office of Policy 2005, tables 2.A8 and 5.C2.

purchasing power) also would be maintained. Before these changes were enacted, any benefit adjustment required new legislation; failure to act resulted in benefit erosion, given that the nominal benefits of retirees would fall further and further behind as inflation drove up prices. This concern became known as the problem of living on a fixed income—fixed in nominal dollars whose value eroded with inflation. In the absence of other retirement income sources, real retirement incomes steadily declined.

Even at maximum benefits, however, Social Security offered considerably less than a plush lifestyle. By 2003, the maximum monthly benefit payable to retirees was $1,404.30, or $16,851.60 per year. Given that the poverty threshold for a single person in 2003 was $8,980, the maximum benefit for an individual is not even 200 percent of the poverty line. Those depending on Social Security as their only source of retirement income will therefore have to be satisfied with a rather sparse existence. Those who have employer-sponsored pension benefits to add to the mix will be in much better shape, assuming that the company providing the benefits—either the employer paying the DB benefits or the financial institution paying the DC annuity—stays afloat.

Figure 4.4   Dependency Ratios (Intermediate and High Cost Assumptions)

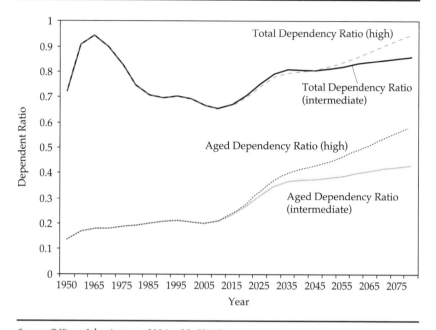

Source: Office of the Actuary 2006, table V.A.2.

Demographic Considerations

In describing the demography behind the Social Security crisis, critics often use some version of the old-age dependency ratio to underscore the burden that workers will have to assume in the near future. Figure 4.4 illustrates, the old-age dependency ratio and the total age dependency ratio, which does not limit the status of economic dependency to the elderly. Raising children, for example, claims some proportion of household income as well as some proportion of GDP. Therefore, any age-based estimate of dependency should have both age groups in the numerator, as reflected in the top lines in figure 4.2. The figure reveals that the total age dependency ratio peaked during the years when the Baby Boom cohorts were born, declined as they aged into the workforce, and will gradually rise as they age into retirement. Under the intermediate assumptions, the total age dependency ratios experienced in the twenty-first century remain below the peak of the mid-twentieth century.

Rather than rely on age groups as a crude way of classifying the population into those who work for pay and those who do not, a refine-

Figure 4.5   Consumer-to-Worker Support Ratios

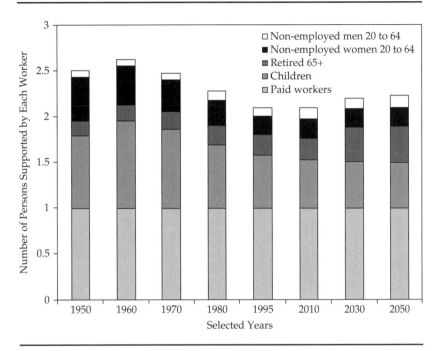

Source: Author's compilation from Reno and Olson 1998, table 1.

ment of age-based dependency ratios compares paid workers with everyone who depends on their productive output. In this way, the consumer-to-worker ratio looks more generally at the issue of dependency (Reno and Cardwell 2005). The numerator counts all those who consume goods and services—a category that includes workers and nonworkers, old and young, men and women. The denominator is the count of all those in the paid labor force. Once again, the support responsibility for workers peaked when the Baby Boom cohorts were children; on average, each worker supported 2.62 people. After declining in the mid-1990s to 2.09 people per worker, this ratio will again increase to 2.21 by 2030. As we saw in figure 4.5, the composition of consumers has changed over time as the proportion of children has declined and the proportion of nonworking older adults has increased. Between now and 2030, the major change occurs in compositional characteristics—the fact that the proportion of consumers who are elderly will increase as the proportion of consumers who are children will decline. However, the total number of consumers to workers will increase only marginally.

Social Benefits and Personal Growth

Proponents of Social Security argue not only that the program provides superior protection for financial security in old age, effectively reduces poverty among the elderly, creates a secure space that encourages risk taking in other sorts of arenas, and counteracts some of the inequities of life that are based in disadvantages of origins, bad luck and poor decision. They also claim that positive side effects stem from a commitment to the principle of social insurance. Given the complex interdependencies of modern society, members of a society face some very real threats. They confront them in the absence of reliable information that indicates, for any given event, who will receive the worst of it and who will escape personal harm. Under these conditions, the principle of collective action allows us to protect not only ourselves but each other in an affirmative strategy that benefits society as a whole. That we choose to support a program that helps all of us, individually, but does so through a cohesive, society-wide endeavor strengthens us by making this accomplishment our shared accomplishment. In strengthening our connectivity, Social Security strengthens our society, strengthens our nation, and helps to create an environment in which our citizens can thrive, and innovate, and create, and build futures. It is that strength in solidarity that we lose through excessive individualization. Our concerted action, our mutual goals, our shared futures receive reinforcement from such enterprises, and in that way, our society is made more secure.

The Case for Privatization

The argument against allowing the Social Security program to retain its present structure generally begins with finances—the program will soon be bankrupt—and then moves to demographics—and even if we could find a short-term financial solution, the program is unsustainable in the long run because we have too few workers paying for too many retirees. The underlying disagreement that fuels the controversy, however, is over individual property rights and private ownership. This ideological issue is raised as an issue of macroeconomics and a concern for fairness.

Martin Feldstein, for example, argues that major reforms of the program are necessary—sooner or later—but that these reforms must address the "basic economic problems" of the system rather than simply "protecting the solvency" of the current arrangements (1998b, 1–27). The fundamental problems he sees are the "large deadweight loss" and the loss of "intertemporal welfare" that a pay-as-you-go (unfunded) system creates. Deadweight losses result from distortions in the supply of labor and forms of compensation; the loss of intertemporal welfare is the consequence of "depressed capital accumulation" and low national savings rates. To the average reader, the exact nature of these problems may remain vague; even so, that they are problems—with terms such as deadweight, distortion, depressed, and loss—has been effectively communicated. That gap in understanding is to be expected, which is why Feldstein argues for the critical role that economists must play in advising politicians on what is feasible and correct.

Consider first the "deadweight loss of labor market distortions." Economic theory holds that any tax on payroll creates deadweight losses because it effectively lowers the wage rate. Because workers offer their labor to employers in exchange for what they consider an acceptable wage, any tax that reduces net wages will result in some number of potential workers evaluating that net wage as unacceptably low. Within the macroeconomic context, this loss means that less labor will be offered than would otherwise be the case, and the loss of labor translates into a loss of product. In the case of Social Security FICA taxes, the fact that these taxes are framed as contributions that result in benefits at some later date is counteracted by the low rate of return that workers can expect on their contributions. In fact, he argues, the deadweight loss from Social Security taxes is particularly bad given that FICA taxes are in addition to federal and state income taxes. They distort not only how many hours individuals will work, the occupations people choose, job locations, and individual work effort, but also the forms of compensation (from taxable cash to fringe benefits, comfortable working conditions, job perks), which ultimately reshape individual patterns of consumption. Finally, additional deadweight losses are incurred because of the unequal links between the taxes workers pay and the benefits they receive. We will return to this point later, but the basic point is one of equity. If person A contributes X dollars more than person B, then person A should expect some function of X dollars more in benefits. This equity concern conflicts with adequacy elements that build in redistribution along the lines of earnings level and family structure. How can we assess these costs? Feldstein's answer is that an estimate of the cost of these losses is the difference between the average return that workers realize on their contributions (the extent to which benefits exceed contributions, on average and in real terms) and the real marginal product of capital (the real return on private investments).

The second basic economic problem with the current system involves Social Security's effect on national saving. In general terms, reductions in national capital income (because of lower levels of accumulated wealth) and economic welfare depend on the relationship between individual savings and social security taxes and benefits. An additional consideration is whether the government acts to offset whatever reductions in private savings might occur. Because the payment of FICA taxes can be viewed as forced savings for retirement, opponents argue that households are less likely to build private reserves. In part, this involves a comparison of public saving through the Trust Fund and private saving through individual accounts.

Feldstein argues that the Trust Fund does raise the level of real investment to the extent that it buys government bonds that would otherwise have been sold to another buyer. In other words, if the government's level of deficit spending is unaffected by the fact that the Trust Fund offers a ready buyer for the overages, then all of the Trust Fund's bond purchases count as real investment. Although deficit spending might have been reduced in the absence of surplus social security contributions, Feldstein argues, it would probably not have been zero; therefore, the surplus does increase projected national saving to some extent, but not by the full amount of the projected surplus. The core issue is how much household saving and investment would increase in the absence of an entitlement program such as Social Security. Feldstein's assessment is that this loss is substantial.

Privatization proponents' concern for fairness is based in the various dimension of redistribution, or income transfer—from generation to generation, from high-wage to low-wage, from short-lived to long-lived, from workers to dependents, from single to married—that are built into the benefit structure of Social Security. They argue that, unlike earlier cohorts of retirees, those who retire in the future will receive less in benefits than they have a right to expect given the amount they have contributed. The most unfair cases are the individuals who die before they receive retirement benefits. Next are those who collect benefits for only a short time. Last are those who may receive benefits for many years but nevertheless will be worse off than if they had been able to invest the money themselves.

Some critics argue that this approach shifts the emphasis from adversity to perversity in accounting for poor economic outcomes. What is often viewed as the moral superiority of market approaches is linked to the claim that programs that incorporate income redistribution—which includes all forms of social welfare—may be well intentioned, but by helping those less fortunate, we undermine their natural inclination toward self reliance. By allowing people to make their own choices— and their own mistakes—we strengthen them, strengthen their moral fiber, and help move them toward self-sufficiency.

This theme underscores the rights of individuals to exercise control over their circumstances, which includes the implicit assumption that circumstances are controllable. Coupled with this emphasis on individuation is the principle of liberty. Individuals should have the freedom to choose how they prepare for retirement rather than having the federal government take their contributions and dictate their benefits. This principle, however, requires the federal government not only to allow individuals to choose among available savings and investment options, but to decide whether to save or invest at all.[5] The subtext to both the assertion and the mandate is a behaviorist approach to moral behavior. People make better choices if they fear the consequences of worse choices; the desire to secure reward and avoid punishment are powerful motivations for those seeking to maximize pleasure and minimize pain.

Privatization advocates note further that preserving Social Security in anything close to its present form not only perpetuates an obsolete program, but also reinforces an entitlement mentality by rewarding dependency and punishing self-reliance. Clearly, the Social Security program served a purpose during the twentieth century by allowing us to make the transition to a wage-based economy. It is no longer a good investment for many Americans, who deserve a reasonable return on the contributions they make. Further, the insurance terminology is a political ploy to generate public support for the program. According to its critics, Social Security is not a true insurance program. They claim that the terminology used to describe it—contributions in support of an insurance program that will ultimately provide benefits—underpins the mythology that built and sustained public enthusiasm for Social Security. Rather than a contribution, FICA is a payroll tax. Benefits are, in actuality, income transfers from workers and their families to retirees. Social Security is a welfare program, not an insurance program.

Instead of increasing the size of the welfare state, we should be deciding how to create a funded retirement pension system that would provide earned benefits. The key to structuring a fair system is to build around the basic principle of equity. Benefits must reflect the level of contributions and a reasonable rate of return, with the yield being a function of the amount of risk the individual prefers coupled with performance of the investment vehicle. Although equity is one factor in determining the level of benefits for which workers qualify, as the program was amended (beginning in 1939), the provision of adequacy was given increasing prominence. Trying to combine both equity and adequacy in the same program created an internal contradiction, because adequacy requires redistribution to lower earners and equity demands a direct mathematical relationship between contributions and benefits. It also sent out an inconsistent moral message by mislabeling as earned benefits what were essentially cash transfers from workers. The emphasis on adequacy expanded the social welfare components of the program, obliterated the insurance features of the original program, and reinforced an entitlement mentality.

Why Switch to Private Accounts?

Clearly, market dynamics have occasionally created immediate crises that required some type of government intervention. Although relying on the federal government to help citizens temporarily weather difficult economic circumstances is sometimes necessary, those who favor privatization generally view institutionalizing these national interventions as a mistake, Social Security being for them a good example of such a mistake. The Social Security program grew out of transitional circumstances that created temporary difficulties for workers in general and older workers in particular. As the U.S. economy transformed from an agricultural to a manufacturing base, worker dependence on wage income increased.

This dependence made workers vulnerable to interruptions in employment, because their ability to be consumers (pay rents, buy groceries) depended on their weekly paychecks. For that reason, labor unions and some employers offered small pensions to their retired workers. The economic environment created by the Great Depression, however, compromised the patch-quilt of protections that were available. The high rates of unemployment meant an unusually high demand for benefits. The unevenness of available jobs or wage replacement programs meant that poverty rates soared. The frequency of bank and business failures meant that whatever savings or investments people had managed to accumulate were wiped out. But all of that happened three-quarters of a century ago.

Workers and their families accustomed to a farm-based economy, generational transmission of farm ownership, and shared reliance on home production were ill-prepared for the new role of labor in an industrial economy that promoted an urban lifestyle. Although Civil War veterans received small military pensions, the workers who became the first generation of wage laborers were unprepared for old age on the new economic terms. Too little savings, an inadequately regulated banking industry, and an economic roller coaster created ever more casualties until business and labor turned to the federal government for a solution (Swenson 1997). In response, discussions about how to structure a wage replacement program centered around two competing models: the Ohio model, which was supported by Isaac Rubinow and Abraham Epstein, and the Wisconsin model, which was backed by John Commons and John Andrews. The Wisconsin model provided a long-term solution to wage-replacement income, but would take decades to make a substantial difference in the lives of workers turned retirees. The Ohio model offered an immediate-relief solution, but gave the federal government a larger role in providing financing.

In contrast to what we now call social insurance, the model under initial consideration was, in fact, a pure insurance model. The Wisconsin alternative allowed people to insure against the risk of a loss of income by contributing to a larger contingency fund. The Ohio alternative proposed that reserves be pooled and subsidized by government funds so that benefit levels would be enough to support workers during unemployment. The pooled funds and benefit structure of the Ohio plan therefore included a redistributive component. The Wisconsin model included no redistribution, no government subsidy. These structural differences also meant lower benefits under the Wisconsin model, and higher under the Ohio model because its government subsidy allowed for an adequacy provision.

Relevant History from the Proponents' Viewpoint

Providing income assurance for early twentieth century workers would take some time to put in place. Those out of a job, for either short or long periods, needed access to funds that would help them maintain some level of consumption while they searched for the next job. Older workers who wanted to retire needed some financial assistance to supplement whatever saving they had accumulated and whatever family assistance was available to them. In the short term, the situation called for a transitional program. The private sector needed some time to develop appropriate vehicles for retirement savings, and workers needed to develop financial plans for their old age. Reliance on a funded system would necessarily delay initial receipt of benefits. One proposal set initial contributions to begin in 1937, with initial benefits to begin in 1942. Excess contributions would accumulate in government bonds. This design of old-age insurance would be self-supporting and require no government contributions. An important argument favoring the Wisconsin school rested on a particular interpretation of the Fifth Amendment of the Constitution. According to some legal experts, taking property from one (collecting taxes) and giving it to another (distributing benefits) without due process would lead the Supreme Court to rule the program unconstitutional.

The original Social Security Act of 1935 favored the Wisconsin model. This choice placed certain restrictions on initial benefits, ensuring that retirement benefits for the earliest cohorts would be very small—lower than the level of state assistance—particularly for low-wage workers, because the relatively small contributions over a short period (five years, for workers who would want to begin benefits at the earliest possible date) would yield a low level of earned benefits. But over time, as the program matured and the number of years during which workers made contributions increased, benefit levels would gradually rise.

Those who favored a fully funded approach from the start viewed the growing division between labor and management as instrumental in creating a political opportunity to inject a welfare component into federal social policy while expanding the role of the federal government.

Instead of taking a minimalist approach that attended to the immediate crisis, those who believed that the federal government needed to play a larger role argued for a social welfare apparatus that would increase in size and cost over time. Advocates of the basic insurance model wanted to maintain a uniform structure so that benefits returned lifetime contributions under the rubric of individual equity. Those who favored the social welfare model continued to argue for income redistribution through a progressive benefit schedule and benefit adequacy that would involve revenue subsidies. No sooner had the 1935 legislation been passed and reviewed by the Supreme Court than efforts were under way to fundamentally reshape the program, moving away from the insurance model and toward the social welfare model.

Delaying the receipt of initial benefits until 1942 meant that the problems of poverty and unemployment saw no immediate improvement. However, the original legislation created two old-age programs—old-age assistance, which was to be the welfare program (run by the states), and old-age insurance, which was to be the contributory program (administered by the federal government). Discontent with state-by-state variability and the low levels of support provided by old-age assistance programs, social welfare advocates pushed to add welfare components to the old-age insurance program as well. What happened next can be cited as an example of either the corrupting effects of ready cash in the hands of the federal government, or the power of the federal government to act as problem solver, depending on one's political philosophy.

As contributions poured into the Treasury, some politicians thought it made sense to use these funds to meet the need for wage-replacement income. This continuing tug of war over the appropriate foundations for the program led to the 1939 amendments, which transformed Social Security by invoking the principles of social insurance, emphasizing adequacy over equity, basing benefits on average monthly covered earnings (rather than lifetime cumulative covered earnings), adding spousal and survivors benefits, eliminating the lump sum provision, and moving up the date of first benefits by two years. Shifting from a funded program to a pay-as-you-go program—spending rather than accumulating—meant that benefit distribution could begin the next year, in 1940. It also meant that benefits could be paid to nonworkers—those who had never contributed a penny to the program—in the form of dependent and survivor benefits.

The program restructuring that occurred through the 1939 amendments made the intergenerational structure of the program much more complicated than originally designed. First, the connection between contributions and benefits was much looser after the 1939 amendments. Second, by emphasizing adequacy (the welfare function) over equity (the market function), rates of return received on contributions became an inverse function of both income and cohort. Speeding up the time frame for initial benefit payout meant that early beneficiaries received benefits far in excess of their contributions, establishing the basis for gross inequities across generations of participants.

The 1939 amendments introduced the intergenerational or worker-to-retiree transfer approach to the program. Whereas the initial approach based benefits on total lifetime earnings (an approach that encouraged sustained employment, rewarding those with long and continuous work histories through the summation of annual earnings), the revised program opted instead for average monthly earnings. The number of years on which this average is based has changed frequently beginning with a minimum of three years—the span between 1937, when contributions were first made, and 1940, when benefits were first paid—and gradually increasing to twenty-five and then thirty-five years. The initial cohort of beneficiaries received windfall benefits rather than the low level justified by their limited contribution time. As the program matured, successive cohorts would progressively contribute more than previous cohorts, but receive ever lower rates of return on their lifetime contributions.

Even though contributions exceeded benefits, a series of payroll tax increases were scheduled to build reserves for future demographic changes. These increases, however, were blocked by those who saw a trust fund as a mechanism for expanding federal expenditures. Joining those trying to limit the role of the federal government were those unwilling to vote for tax increases when the funds were not required to pay current benefits. During the 1940s, neither taxes nor benefits were increased. Even so, benefits grew because of the longer contribution period, as did the Trust Fund. As conservatives were trying to avoid a large fund, others were trying to move toward institutionalizing the adequacy of benefits by developing a benefits formula that would improve the replacement rate of benefits to wages. The rate had declined during the 1940s and the amendments of 1950 returned it to its original level. At a rate of roughly twenty-five cents to the dollar, though, retirees required additional sources of income to be able to approach their preretirement standard of living.

By 1950, two very different sorts of concerns were surfacing. On the one hand, those who supported the adequacy provision were working to increase benefits. Not only were average social security retirement benefits considerably less than old-age assistance benefits, but the benefit growth due to longer-term coverage was also less than the real benefit reduction due to inflation. On the other hand, the increasing size of the Trust Fund made conservatives nervous. These two perspectives found common ground in proposals to extend coverage to additional groups and substantially increase benefits. Even though these changes required an increase in the payroll tax (from 1 percent to 1.5 percent) and further scheduled increases to 3 percent by 1965, this approach would quickly spend down the Trust Fund as it relieved the relatively high poverty rates that older adults endure. Keep in mind that the 1950s were an era of strong economic growth and rising wages. The increased benefits could thus be viewed as a kind of retroactive sharing of the post-war boom with the pre-war labor force.

Because of the substantial increases in retirement benefits adopted during the 1970s, the Social Security program's long-term financial viability was severely compromised. The problems were made all the more evident by the macro-economic conditions that prevailed in the late 1970s—double-digit inflation and slower than expected wage growth. One consequence was that though retirees saw their Social Security benefits increase because of the automatic cost-of-living escalator and their returns on savings increase as interest rates soared, workers were falling behind. The conditions that made circumstances difficult for young families—wages that did not keep pace with inflation and the high cost of borrowed money—meant relative gains in retirement income for seniors.

The series of changes adopted in the 1970s—including the increases in real benefits, the automatic cost-of-living adjustment to benefits, the wage indexing of earnings histories, and the indexing problems that led to the notch cohort—were designed not only to place the program on automatic pilot, but to do so at a level of benefits that provided an adequate floor. To avoid having to rely on congressional action to increase benefits, those who favored emphasizing the adequacy provision proposed automatically indexing benefits to the consumer price index, ensuring that the real value of benefits would be maintained. In addition, rather than have the adequacy provision result in a series of ad hoc benefit formula adjustments, adequacy proponents sought to introduce indexing to the benefit formula, as well. Where an equity approach matched benefits to contributions, an adequacy approach aimed at replacing some proportion of earnings with retirement benefits, with the proportion of earnings replaced declining as earnings increased.

These program features strengthened political support for the program, especially among lower and middle-income households. Cohorts of retirees, who routinely received much more in benefits than they contributed, were understandably enthusiastic about the new program. But people in general were finding that they could afford to retire in their sixties, even if they had no occupational pension and only a modest amount in savings.

However, this revised benefit structure also set the stage for substantial inequality in rates of return across generations, a fact now becoming apparent to younger workers. Rather than grow stronger as it matured, the program promised too much. With declines in the average age of retirement, increases in longevity, and the changing age structure of the population, those who favor privatization view the current Social Security framework as precarious and eventually unsustainable, given the huge intergenerational transfer with which the program began.

Emphasizing Replacement Rates

Where an equity principle (implemented through rates of return) matches benefits to contributions, the adequacy principle (implemented through replacement rates) establishes a sliding scale of wage replacement in which the rate declines as wage levels increase. Low wage workers thus have the highest replacement rates and high wage workers have the lowest. Within this progressive approach, high wage workers subsidize low wage workers through redistribution. The benefit formula implements this approach through the percentage multipliers associated with different dollar brackets of average monthly earnings.[6] Each worker's annual covered earnings (the earnings on which FICA taxes are paid) are multiplied by the wage index (to adjust each year's earning to the average wage level when the worker is sixty years old) to produce the worker's average indexed monthly earnings. The progressive percentages in the formula remain the same, but the AIME bend points in the formula are also indexed to wage growth.

This approach accomplished two things. Replacement rates remain uniform across cohorts, but benefit levels continue to grow as a reflection of the improved standard of living allowed by gradual increases in average wages. In other words, on an annual basis, Social Security retirement benefits pay about 30 to 40 percent (on average) of what retirees earned during their working lives. Also, at age sixty, retirees are able to lock in improvements in living standards achieved through the gradual wage growth of the previous thirty-five years, which means that each new cohort of retirees has enjoyed a better standard of living than previous cohorts. Whether stabilizing replacement rates produces a fair distribution of benefits across generations depends again on how you define fairness and whether a federal program should be involved in the distribution of benefits on the basis of relative versus absolute criteria. In developing social welfare programs, we have generally adhered to an absolute standard. For example, the poverty threshold is not determined proportionately—as some percentage of former income—but is based on an estimate of basic consumption needs. It is variable only with regard to the size of the household under consideration (the number of consumers) and the age of the household head. That it is set at such a minimal level is supposed to encourage people to take care of themselves. As the Social Security program has matured, more generous benefits (it is argued) have undermined a more general emphasis on self-reliance. One consequence is that individual households fail to save for retirement as they should, and this failure has implications for the formation and availability of capital. Rather than rely on themselves—their hard work, intelligence, and savings—retirees were to rely on a federal program; all they had to do was clock the time on their jobs and their financial security would be taken care of.

No sooner had these increases been enacted, however, then the program was once again facing a shortfall. Economic conditions in the second half of the 1970s coupled with the programmatic changes just described wreaked havoc with the program's financial balance sheets. Another conclave and another quick round of changes, which included increases in the FICA tax, delays in the age of full entitlement, the taxation of benefits, and increased penalties for retirement at age sixty-two, and the gradual renegotiation of retirement had begun. Until this time, changes in Social Security meant expansion of coverage and increases in benefits. But 1983 marked a turning point. Calls for a reduced role for the federal government and an increased role for individual workers in providing retirement income grew stronger as the century drew to an end. By making so few changes on the benefits side, the commission reinforced the view that these benefits were sustainable. But the other changes made clear that paying for retirement was not going to get any easier.

The acceleration in FICA tax increases adopted in 1983 was legitimated as a partial funding of the program—a prepayment for benefits that would be disbursed at some later date. By ensuring that the program would run increasingly large surpluses, the claim was that the OASI Trust Fund was saving money to pay for the future benefits of Baby Boom retirees. But does the Trust Fund represent real assets? The actual cost of continuing the program in its current form beyond 2018 depends on whether its assets can be cashed in as easily as bonds held by any small investor. Can we access the accumulated savings in the Trust Fund, or have they already been spent?

The Empty Trust Fund

Whether one believes the money was invested or spent is as much an issue of semantics as economics. Proponents of privatization argue that because the saving occurs in one branch of the government, and the spending occurs in another, what we think of as accumulation in the Trust Fund and the subsequent cashing in of assets to pay benefits are simply accounting tricks. What the federal government collects in taxes—income taxes, corporate taxes, payroll taxes—is either spent on current programs or used to retire some of the federal debt. These are the only two options. In all the years of Social Security surpluses, only once, in 2000, did we use any of it to retire a portion of the national debt. In every other year it was used to incur new debt. In other words, it was spent on other programs.

Beginning in 2017 or 2018, annual FICA revenues will not be enough to pay 100 percent of promised Social Security benefits. Although some argue that when this occurs, that the Social Security program will have to supplement FICA funds with revenue from the Trust Fund, others claim that it is when we will have to supplement FICA taxes with general revenues, which may require raising income taxes. The money collected for Social Security has been spent on an annual basis as federal expenditures have exceeded general revenues. One portion of this negative balance is reflected in the budget deficit, which indicates the amount of new debt we are adding to old debt (represented by the national debt). But the second portion is where the Social Security Trust fund enters the picture, given that these are the dollars used to finance some of the extra expenditures. Has the money, then, been spent? Yes, it has. Does the Trust Fund hold assets that we can cash in to pay future benefits? Only if we have a buyer, which in this case must be the federal government.

In recent decades, billions of dollars collected through FICA taxes have been used to pay for other federal programs. This shift in funds was accomplished through Treasury bills. To finance federal operations when general revenues were inadequate to cover the cost (taxes too low, or expenditures too high), we needed to find the money elsewhere. We did—in the Social Security Trust Fund, where billions of dollars were transferred into the federal budget in exchange for billions of dollars worth of Treasury bills, the same Treasury bills that finance the national debt. Therefore, beginning in 2017 or so, to pay all the promised benefits, we will need to supplement the newly generated revenue from FICA with money from elsewhere. Because Social Security assets are held in Treasury bonds, we have two choices. First, we find another buyer for the bonds (which is the same thing as saying we must find someone else, for example, some combination of other countries, corporations, or individual investors, to take over that portion of national debt). Second, we collect through general revenues enough to pay for both ongoing federal programs and to retire some portion of the national debt currently financed by the surplus in social security collections. If we use general revenues, we have to raise taxes or reallocate funds from other domestic programs, or both.

The Social Security program represents a very large share of federal spending, and the payroll taxes collected through FICA make up a large share of our tax burden. Social Security expenditures approach 5 percent of GDP. As the proportion of elderly grows from 13 percent to 20 percent (by 2030), the proportion of GDP spent on Social Security will grow by about 2.2 percent. If we exclude the annual interest paid on the national debt, 40 percent of the federal budget is spent on Social Security and Medicare. If we look at what is paid in federal taxes—payroll taxes and income taxes—we see that FICA is more than 30 percent of the federal tax burden. The Social Security Trustees project that the employer and employee share of FICA taxes would have to rise from 6.2 percent (current level) to 8.53 percent in 2030 to cover costs, and then keep rising to 9.42 percent by 2075 (Office of the Actuary 2006). Social Security has already crowded out much of domestic spending, so further cuts would be very difficult. If we rely on borrowing, we will have to allocate more money to service the national debt. Any of these actions will likely have adverse effects on the economy, including upward pressure on interest rates, slower growth in employment, and downward pressure on economic growth.

Why Do We Have a Trust Fund?

The Trust Fund has been a major focus of dispute since the earliest days of Social Security. Different positions on this issue were clearly linked to differences in political philosophy. Although the initial 1935 legislation established the Trust Fund, the reason for doing so was simply to avoid having the act struck down as unconstitutional. To guard against that outcome, the provision for taxation was described in one title, and the design of the benefit structure was described in another. Payroll taxes were to be collected from workers and employers, but were to be part of general revenues. Each year, Congress would make an appropriation to the Social Security Trust Fund in an amount equal to the benefit outlay. The connection between taxes and benefits was accomplished by linking both to covered earnings. Once the Supreme Court ruled that the act was constitutional, this separation was unnecessary. Contributions started to flow in 1937, but their accumulation required some type of investment vehicle. Limiting investment to government bonds was a compromise. Conservatives did not want the federal government to invest in the stock market. Treasury bonds gave the federal government a place to put the money.

A major reason for objecting to the Trust Fund was outright rejection of the claim that the federal government could save excess contributions to build reserve funding for future benefits. The 1935 design of the program was consistent with saving principles. By individualizing the program and defining equity and fairness in terms of a direct connection between contributions and benefits, beneficiaries would receive all of what they contributed. To the extent that the program was a collective endeavor, it was a collective enforcement of these saving principles.

The 1939 amendments replaced the framework of individual accounts accumulating within a general trust fund with a benefit formula based on average monthly earnings and intergenerational transfers. The trust fund mechanism remained as a repository for the excess taxes collected. Concerned that such a fund would encourage social investment, promote unwise spending (as government officials succumbed to the temptation to spend what was available rather than what was necessary), or increases in benefits simply because they were affordable, conservatives feared the direct and indirect negative consequences of too much surplus revenue from Social Security.

Even limiting Trust Fund investment to Treasury bills was problematic in the long term. The steady accumulation of excess contributions (because the ratio of covered workers to beneficiaries was so top heavy), would gradually increase the Trust Fund's share of the national debt. Because investment in Treasury bills was a conservative (low risk, low yield) investment, it was a common component of a diversified portfolio. Some feared that making Treasury bills unavailable to the general investor would weaken financial markets. This fear may seem puzzling, given that limiting the amount of debt held by foreign countries appears to be a positive outcome. We will return to this point later because it is one of the key issues we must address. For now, a few background factors should provide some context.

First, the national debt was much lower in 1940 and the economy was much smaller. In 1940 the national debt was about $51 billion, with a GDP of $97 billion. In 2003, the debt was about $6 trillion, with a GDP of almost $11 trillion. At both times, total debt was more than half of total GDP—52.4 percent in 1940, and 59.2 percent in 2003. But in 1940, the Trust Fund was projected to grow to $46 billion by 1980. Within the economic context of 1940, the projected magnitude was almost half the size of the total 1940 economy, almost enough to totally wipe out the national debt. So, although the 1939 amendments kept the door to the Trust Fund open, having funds flow through that doorway depended on enacting routine escalations in the FICA tax. Congress was unwilling to take this step, preferring instead to maintain rough equivalence between inflow (FICA taxes) and outflow (benefits).

Generational Fairness

Issues of fairness are comparative, though the basis of the comparison can vary, depending on the specific fairness issue being addressed. In an achievement-oriented culture such as our own, some people believe that a fair distribution of resources is based on merit, where merit refers to the value of one's contribution. If we can assume an even playing field with the same opportunities available to all the players, then distributions based on merit have much to recommend them. Is this assumption of equal opportunity reasonable? For some, to say that all players have the same opportunities is to say something more than that windows of opportunity are open to all who try to pass through them. It is to suggest that all began the race from the same starting position. Because we know that is not the case, then for some people fairness must also involve some kind of recalibration, some recognition that differences in starting points can cast long shadows.

In addressing questions of fairness, we need to consider several questions. First, how do we understand the differences in starting positions? Within the economics literature, this discussion is often framed in terms of endowments. One is endowed at birth with certain advantages or disadvantages; these endowments are unequal, but all positions are considered modifiable through hard work. Whether we consider differences in starting positions as external to the game or part of the game is also at issue. If we think about endowments as external to the game, then allowances for these differences are unnecessary. They simply reflect the many elements of diversity, some of which may matter in the long run, and others may prove irrelevant. Further, predicting the consequences of these variable endowments for achievement is not easy. What appears to be an initial advantage may become a weakness, and what appears to be a disadvantage may become an asset. Finally, at issue is whether we evaluate fairness issues fully aware or from behind a veil of ignorance.

Second, how do we understand the process that takes people from their initial positions to those they occupy later in their lives? In other words, how does the process of attainment operate? If it operates the same way for all players, then all players can parlay any initial advantage into greater advantage by following a common formula, regardless of the initial position. But what if the process, at least to some degree, depends on one's origin status, with initial advantages leading to a smoother road to achievement? That the rate of accumulation is a positive function of one's beginnings means that initial endowments are a two-pronged advantage.

Third, how do we understand the relative importance of the components of this process—factors such as initiative, effort, and luck? How we understand the role of luck may be particularly important. Some people believe we make our own luck, create our own opportunities, whereas others believe that luck plays a much larger role—a role we cannot shape or control. If we consider initial endowments to be luck, then they recede into the more general category of individual differences. If we consider them to be part of a structured edifice of advantage, passed from one generation to the next, then they are translated into an unfair inheritance that may require some form of compensatory adjustment. Luck factors into the achievement process in another way, as a catch-all term for the seemingly random and unanticipated occurrences that can either help or hinder our progress. Accidents, injuries, illnesses, serendipitous encounters, being in the right (or wrong) place at the right (or wrong) time—and it is this factor that introduces a healthy dose of uncertainty into all our lives.

Sometimes we make fairness judgments by comparing groups to see whether differences on some set of outcomes can be reasonably explained by factors legitimately related to those outcomes, or whether groups whose outcomes are the same really deserve the same treatment. At other times, we think about fairness within a counterfactual framework, comparing how a process did unfold to how we think it should have unfolded. We can also ask whether the outcomes are consistent with an underlying principle that we consider of paramount importance. Assessments of the fairness of Social Security have involved all three frameworks. If we use the first criterion, we look to see whether the benefits received are systematically linked to factors that should determine their distribution and whether differences are explained by these (or other) factors. If we use the second criterion, we can examine how the program changed over time and whether we would be better served by a different programmatic structure. If we use the third criterion, we can evaluate the program relative to what we believe should be the principle governing distribution. For Social Security, those two competing principles are adequacy and equity. They can be assessed by comparing the quantitative measures of these principles—replacement rates and implicit rates of return.

If we work from an equity standpoint, then fairness is assessed at the level of individual choices, actions, responses, and the consequences of those behaviors. Within a retirement benefits framework, the equity principle holds that benefits be paid in proportion to contributions made. Deviations from that model are then by definition examples of unfair treatment. Basing benefits on lifetime contributions (plus a reasonable rate of return) is one way to accomplish a fair distribution of outputs based on inputs, though guaranteeing the rate of return in advance takes the uncertainty out of the program from the standpoint of benefit receipt, but not from that of program management.

As currently configured, Social Security is not based on individual accounts, nor does it pay interest on contributions on an individual basis; benefits are not based solely on contributions and interest rates. Even so, many analysts argue that one basis for evaluating program fairness is to compare implicit rates of return (IRR) on contributions across cohorts and across demographic subgroups. The IRR is calculated as the average interest rate contributors would have had to earn on their contributions to pay for all the benefits received (by primary or secondary beneficiaries). Average IRR on FICA contributions depend on long-term demographic and economic trends.

Generational differences in IRR are apparent when we compare average IRR across birth cohorts. Earlier and current retiree cohorts received

**Figure 4.6   Estimated Real Internal Rates of Return
on Social Security Contributions**

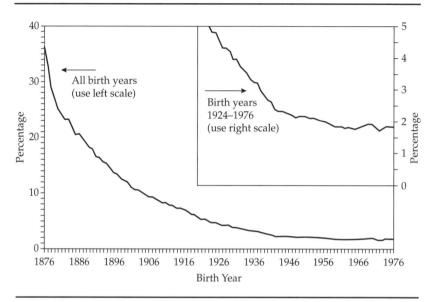

Source: Author's compilation from Leimer 1994.

or will receive relatively high rates of return on their Social Security contributions (Leimer 1994). Until a PAYG program matures, the balance
between taxes and benefits is most favorable for the early cohorts of beneficiaries, because they contribute to the system for a relatively short
period but then are able to collect benefits that exceed their contributions, at least on average. This balance gradually becomes less favorable
as the coverage period lengthens and lifetime contributions increase.
Although benefits also increase, they do so at a slower rate. Published
estimates of inflation-adjusted internal rates of return demonstrate this
pattern; rates decline from 36.5 percent for the 1876 birth cohort to less
than 2 percent for birth cohorts now entering the labor force (Leimer
1994). IRR for future cohorts are projected to be approximately 1.5 to
2 percent.

Now that the program is mature, the rates have stabilized, reflecting
the relationship between long-term average rates of return for a PAYG
system and national trends in total covered wages. If we assume constant demographics, stable economic conditions, and no changes in program provisions, the benefits of one generation of retirees equals the
contributions paid by their children's generation, these contributions are
equal to the retiree contributions plus wage growth, and wage growth
reflects increases in labor productivity and growth in the labor force.

Therefore, as long as wages grow, long-term average returns on contributions will generally remain positive (GAO 1999).

There are two issues here worth discussing. The first involves the conclusion that, on average, rates of return should remain positive, though relatively small. It is this element of Social Security's financial structure that makes the comparison of the program to a Ponzi scheme inaccurate. Ponzi—or pyramid—schemes rely on transfers from subsequent waves of investors to pay the returns to all previous waves of investors, hence the notion of the pyramid. A small group of initial investors each recruits some number of second wave investors, who then each recruit a given number of third-wave investors. In a Ponzi scheme, this number increases exponentially and quickly becomes unsustainable. Social Security is not a Ponzi scheme. The number of beneficiaries does not increase exponentially, early beneficiaries exit the system, and IRRs remain positive.

However, because benefits paid to initial cohorts of beneficiaries significantly exceeded their contributions to the system, the start-up costs of Social Security involved a cash transfer from younger, working-age adults to older retirees. Therefore, generation after generation, worker contributions go first to repay the previous generation's transfers to their parents' generation, leaving subsequent generations to do the same. As figure 4.7 illustrates, cohorts born before 1936, those reaching age sixty-five before 2001, received a net transfer (or subsidy) from other later cohorts through the Social Security benefits they received. This transfer—the excess of their benefits over contributions—was highest for cohorts born around 1906, who reached age sixty-five in 1971, building from the transfers provided for the first cohorts and then declining and turning negative for those born after 1936. One argument for raising the contribution rates as a result of the 1983 amendments was that the Baby Boom cohorts would actually be prefunding some of their own benefits; their excess contributions would accumulate in the Trust Fund, and when the inflow of contributions was not enough to cover their benefits, the Trust Fund would be drawn down gradually to maintain the promised flow of benefits. Whether this interpretation is reasonable given the nature of the Trust Fund is an issue we will return to later.

Although a 1.5 to 2 percent IRR is not unlike interest rates that have been paid on certain types of low risk assets, as a long-term average, it is disappointingly low. Given the range of choices offered by other investments, few fund managers would be satisfied with such a small return. However, if reforms are to be evaluated on this basis, analysts caution that comparisons should be based on concrete reform proposals so that all costs are captured and projections of future economic and demographic trends are consistent across alternatives. Second, compar-

Figure 4.7   Social Security Net Intercohort Transfers

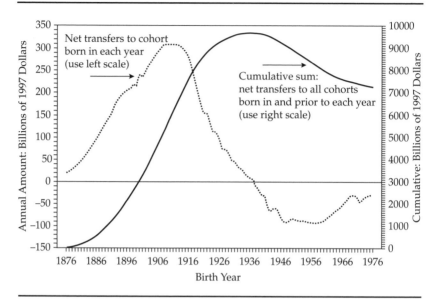

Source: Author's compilation from Leimer 1994, figure 2.

ing rates of return limits the comparison to issues of individual equity. Finally, any comparison with individual accounts would need to reflect the costs of individualization, such as account management, annuitizing accounts at retirement, and the variability around historical averages that would necessarily result from different asset choices, different levels of risk reflected in these choices, and how the timing of investments intersect with general economic trends.

Distributional Fairness: Gender, Race, and Marital Status

Even though projections may indicate a positive rate of return, on average, for cohorts retiring in the future, that is not the same thing as promising that everyone will realize this return on their contributions. These estimated IRRs are averages, averages representing a central value in a larger distribution of values, some of which are larger than 2 percent and some of which are smaller than 2 percent, perhaps even negative. A negative IRR means that you don't receive benefits equal to your contributions, meaning a net loss on your retirement savings through Social Security. Using averages to describe outcomes can be useful, but also deceptive, especially when the outcome is correlated with any number of status or demographic characteristics.

The characteristics of gender, race, and marital status distinguish between better and worse outcomes. These dimensions of advantage and disadvantage revolve around features of benefit structure that determine either benefit eligibility or the magnitude of benefit payout (Steuerle and Bakija 1994). Marital status coupled with the number of earners in the household affects the ratio of contributions to benefits because of the categorical entitlement of nonworking spouses for benefits based on the entitled worker's earnings history (see Figure 4.8). Racial differences in disability rates and overall life expectancy influence the program under which entitlement occurs (DI or OASI) as well as the likelihood that a worker survives to receive benefits and the number of years benefits are paid. Gender differences are apparent in comparisons of average benefits paid to women versus men—a reflection of differences in earnings as well as differences in the structure of careers. Differences between earner wives and nonearner wives are also apparent in the IRR received by one-earner and two-earner couples and in the relative level of survivor benefits to which wives in one-earner and two-earner couples are entitled.

Clearly receipt of benefits requires survival: one must reach retirement age to collect benefits, and the longer one lives as a retiree, the more one collects. Workers who die before retirement receive nothing. Survival differs by race and by gender, and black men have the lowest survival rates among black and white men and women. More than 30 percent of black men die before age sixty-five. Survival rates are highest for white women (see Figure 4.9). Black men are least likely to reach normal retirement age, but their survivors may receive benefits. Even so, because a claim to Social Security benefits cannot be bequeathed as part of an estate, the value of this asset is constrained relative to the value of a privately owned asset.

Because Social Security is described as having a progressive benefit structure, many believe it provides special advantages to African Americans. Given the weighted benefits formula, many assume that the higher relative benefits assigned to low-earning workers more than offset their lower life expectancy. On the other hand, organizations such as the Heritage Foundation have issued reports claiming that Social Security is an especially bad deal for low wage African American men. After calculating rates of return for various income and race-ethnic groups, they claim that, contrary to long-held beliefs, many low wage workers will not only receive a poor rate of return on the taxes they paid, but also even have a negative rate of return, receiving less in benefits than their total contributions warrant. The Heritage Report notes, for example, that "low income, single African American males born after 1959 face a negative rate of return from Social Security" (Beach and Davis 1998, 2), and these conclusions were reported in a number of national news outlets.

Figure 4.8   Social Security's Implicit Rates of Return

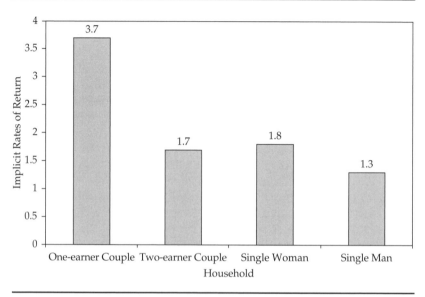

Source: U.S. General Accounting Office 1999, 29.
Note: Inflation-adjusted rates, hypothetical average earners born in 1973; estimates include all Social Security contributions and benefits, including disability, and reflect tax rates that would keep the system in actuarial balance on a pay-as-you-go basis; estimates for hypothetical workers with earnings equal to the national average each year; for one-earner couple, spouse does not work at all.

What received far less visibility than these conclusions was Robert Myers's critique of their methodology. His careful evaluation of their approach led him to conclude that "the foregoing result for young African American males is unrealistic and erroneous" (1998, 5). A former chief actuary (1947 to 1970) and deputy commissioner (1981 to 1982) of the Social Security Administration, Myers noted several flaws in the calculations on which the Heritage conclusions were drawn. Because the projections were based on averages, they were assuming that all members of the group survived until they reached average life expectancy and then dropped dead at once. In Myers's words, "if the computations for young African-Americans had been made correctly, it is certain that a positive rate of return would have been shown" (1998, 5).

What is clear is that race and gender differences in IRR become confounded with race and gender differences in annual earnings, life expectancies, and household configurations. At the same earnings level, women will have higher IRRs than men, on average, because their life expectancy is longer. Nonwhites have lower incomes than whites, on average, which translates into higher IRR. At the same time, their lower

Figure 4.9   Survivorship to Age Sixty-Five

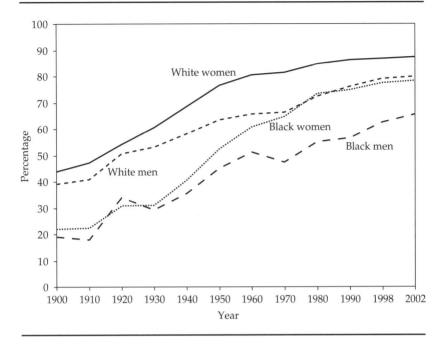

Source: Author's compilation from Arias 2006, table 10.

life expectancies relative to white translates into lower IRRs. Studies of race differences show that African Americans are more likely to be disabled, more likely to die before retirement, and more likely to have dependents than whites are (GAO 1999). Because of these differences, IRRs for African Americans are higher when based on the full range of benefits (retirement, disability, dependents, and survivors) than when based on retirement benefits alone (Duggan, Gillingham, and Greenlees 1993).

Variation in the IRR by earnings level is a more general consequence of the redistributive aspects of the benefits structure. Low-wage workers are therefore more likely than high-wage workers to realize positive and higher IRRs. Based on hypothetical workers at different earnings levels, the SSA provides estimated IRR for different earnings profiles (see figure 4.10). By setting average earnings at the average Social Security covered earnings in each year, low earnings at 45 percent of the average, high earnings at 160 percent of the average, and maximum earnings at the maximum taxable earnings for each year, these profiles provide useful benchmarks even though the earnings histories assume a consistency of earnings that is atypical.

The prominence of adequacy concerns over equity created entirely new categories of beneficiaries, none of whom had made contributions

Figure 4.10   Social Security's Implicit Rates of Return by Earnings Level

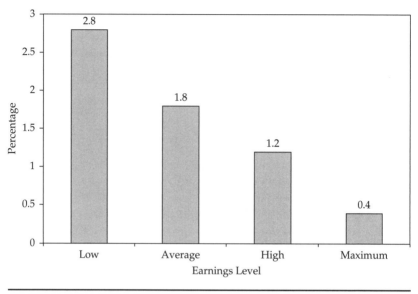

Source: U.S. General Accounting Office 1999, 27.
Note: Inflation-adjusted rates for single women born in 1973; estimates include all
Social Security contributions and benefits, including disability, and reflect tax rates
that would keep the system in actuarial balance on a pay-as-you-go basis; estimates do
not reflect differences in life expectancy, which would make relatively small differences
in overall rates; returns for single men were roughly 0.5 percentage points lower in each
earnings level. Each earnings level is for a specific amount of earnings per year: low
(45 percent of average earnings); average (average Social Security covered earnings);
high (160 percent of average); maximum (maximum taxable earnings in each year).

to the program. Because the 1939 amendments entitled spouses to benefits based on worker earnings histories, many homemakers were able
to collect retirement benefits even though they had never contributed.
One-earner couples being the norm until the latter part of the twentieth
century, early efforts to better incorporate adequacy provisions into the
benefit structure were linked to the number of dependents (unemployed
spouses and children) the worker supported. As more and more women
began to combine work and family, two-earner couples became the
norm. Because married women are automatically entitled to 50 percent
of their husbands' benefits, recent cohorts of working married women
have been making routine contributions to receive benefits they were
already entitled to receive—in whole or in part—as spouses.

Therefore, a given level of contribution can initiate significantly different benefit streams. A single worker who dies just before taking retire-

ment generates no benefit payments. A single worker who survives for twenty years beyond retirement receives twenty years of benefits. A married worker who dies just before retirement, with a wife who never worked for pay and who survives twenty years beyond eligibility age, initiates twenty years of benefits. A married man who survives for twenty years beyond retirement, whose wife never worked for pay and who survives him by ten years, initiates twenty years of benefits for himself, twenty years of 50 percent benefits for his wife, and ten additional years of 100 percent benefits for her as his widow. As a result, one-earner couples receive significantly higher IRRs (see figure 4.8). At average wages, the hypothetical one-earner couple's IRR is more than twice as high as that of the two-earner couple and the single woman, and almost three times that of the single man.

Demographic Imperatives

Privatization proponents argue that, even if we could manage to maintain the solvency of Social Security in the short term, a longer-term view makes clear that the program as it stands is unsustainable. The design of a PAYG program transfers funds from contributors to beneficiaries. In this case, Social Security relies on collecting enough tax income from workers to pay the benefits of retirees. The program therefore involves a huge intergenerational transfer of income from younger to older generations. The earliest cohorts reap the greatest benefits. PAYG programs necessarily rely on favorable demography. As long as those receiving benefits are outnumbered by those paying for the benefits, the program works well: the tax burden on workers can remain relatively small and the benefits received by retirees are satisfactory. But as the demography shifts—as the proportion of retirees increases relative to the proportion of active workers—maintaining benefit levels requires higher and higher taxes, as each retiree is supported by fewer and fewer workers.

During the second half of the twentieth century, fertility rates dropped (women had fewer children, on average), survival rates increased (a higher proportion of people born in a given year survived to old age), life expectancy increased (people lived longer), and the average age of retirement got younger (most retirees claim their Social Security benefits before they're sixty-five years old). In addition, the demographic anomaly known as the Baby Boom cohorts have been working, making contributions to the program, but will soon begin to retire and collect benefits.

There are two ways we can measure this burden. The first is the old-age dependency ratio, which is based on the relative size of the population aged twenty to sixty-four (those most likely to be in the labor force) with the population aged sixty-five and older (those most likely to be collecting retirement benefits). When we compare the growth in these

Figure 4.11   Age Structure of the U.S. Population, 1950 to 2080

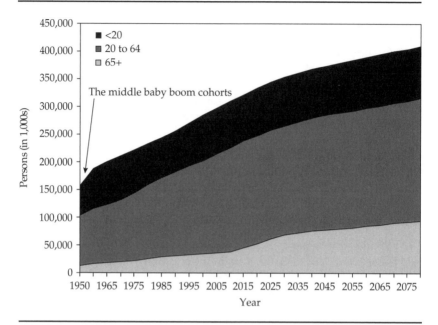

Source: Office of the Actuary 2005, table V.A.2.
Note: 1950 to 2000 is historical data; 2005 to 2080 based on intermediate assumptions.

different aged populations since 1950, we begin to see how our current problem developed. By 2005, the size of the twenty to sixty-four population had almost doubled, whereas the sixty-five and older population had almost tripled. Within the next twenty-five years, the number of people aged sixty-five and older will be almost twice its size in 2005, but the number of twenty- to sixty-four-year-olds will increase by only 10 percent.

The youngest age group, those younger than twenty, is also growing, but at a much slower rate. If we look at the very beginning of the period (the far left of the chart) we see the steep increase associated with the Baby Boom cohorts, those born from 1946 to 1964. Between 1950 and 1965, the population of those younger than twenty increased by almost 50 percent. In contrast, between 1965 and 2005, it increased by less than 5 percent. According to the Trustees' 2005 report, we can anticipate that it will grow less than 14 percent in the next seventy-five years.

If we use this information to construct the aged dependency ratio (ADR)—the ratio of those aged twenty to sixty-four divided by those aged sixty-five and older—we see why the Social Security program is in need of major revision. The left half of the figure illustrates how this ratio has changed since 1950. In 1950, there were more than seven workers

Figure 4.12   Aged Dependency Ratio, 1950 to 2080

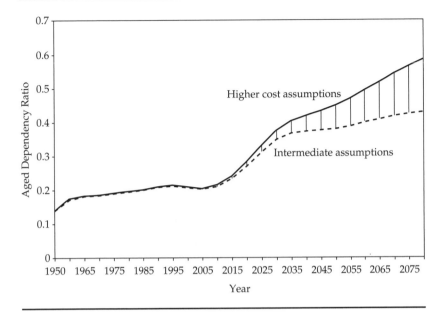

Source: Author's calculations.

(those aged twenty to sixty-four) for each retiree (those aged sixty-five and older). By 2005, the old-age dependency ratio was not quite five.[7] The big change, however, will occur when the Baby Boom cohorts move into retirement, which should begin within the next decade. Projections are that we will have three[8] workers for each retiree by about 2020, and that from that point forward the number will gradually decline to a little more than two.[9]

This trend is based on what the trustees call the intermediate assumptions. Because we do not know what medical breakthroughs the future may hold, we have to make certain assumptions about how long people will live in retirement. During the twentieth century, life expectancy increased dramatically. Suppose the intermediate assumptions underestimate life expectancy. If so, retirees will be collecting benefits for a longer period, which will further stress the system. The report notes substantial disagreement over this issue, however. Some thought we should anticipate significant increases in life expectancy during the twenty-first century. To see what kind of a difference this makes, look again at figure 4.12.

The top line tracks changes in the age dependency ratio that will occur over time if the high cost assumptions turn out to produce the better set of estimates. These assumptions are based, in part, on a future that offers life expectancy and medical breakthroughs that may result in more people surviving to old age and living longer lives, in general. The area between these two lines, hatched by a series of vertical lines, shows us the difference between the two sets of assumptions. Beginning in about 2020, we see increasingly divergent estimates of the ADR. By the early 2060s, we will already have fewer than two workers supporting each retiree. Of even greater concern, however, is the possibility that by the end of the seventy-five-year planning period, if the high cost assumptions are accurate, the aged dependency ratio will be nearing .6, which means that we will have fewer than two workers (one and two-thirds workers, to be precise) supporting each retiree.

A second way to measure the implications of these demographic changes is to look more precisely at those who are contributing benefits relative to those who are collecting benefits. This worker-to-benefit ratio uses information from the Social Security Administration, based on year-by-year information on the number of both covered workers who contribute to the program through payroll taxes and people collecting benefits (from OASDI), which include retirement benefits for workers, for their dependents, surviving spouses, and for those on disability.

In 1940 (not shown in figure 4.13), the first year in which benefits were paid, this ratio was 159:1 because all covered workers were making contributions, but the number of workers qualified to collect benefits was quite small. In 1950, the ratio had shrunk to 16.5:1 and was still strongly influenced by the early stage of the program. Ten years later, in 1960, it was 5:1. In other words, for each person receiving benefits, five workers were paying into the system to cover the cost of those benefits. This ratio has gradually declined. By 2004 it was 3.3:1, which is the same as thirty beneficiaries (receiving retirement, dependent, survivors, or disability benefits) per 100 workers. Based on the intermediate set of assumptions, that ratio will reach two workers per beneficiary by 2040, and drop below two in 2065. If we instead use the high cost assumptions, the ratio reaches two workers per beneficiary in 2030 (ten years earlier), dropping to 1.5 by 2065 (Office of the Actuary 2005, 48).

Which Side is Right?

Proponents of preservation and privatization both find support in the historical record, both cite economic evidence to buttress their positions, and both use demographic projections to attempt to persuade us that their perspective is correct. What is also clear is that these two sides interpret and present their evidence in different ways, using different measures, emphasizing some points and dismissing others. Unfortunately, some attempts to emphasize perceived advantages deteriorate

Figure 4.13   Ratio of Covered Workers to OASDI Beneficiaries, Intermediate Assumptions

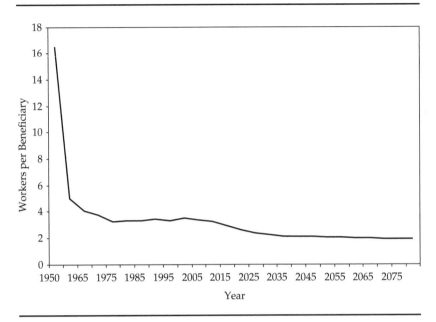

Source: Author's calculations.

into gross misrepresentations, measures offered as evidence are presented without adequate discussion of their limitations, and projections of what we can expect are either filtered through rose-colored lenses or accompanied by warnings of impending doom. However, behind the differences in their arguments are more fundamental differences in priorities, which goals are most important, how people's behavior is influenced by the current program structure, and what sorts of roles government should—or should not—play in helping citizens prepare for old age.

═ Chapter 5 ═

Markets and Social Insurance

I F WE hold the distortions, misstatements, and other political maneuverings to the side of the contemporary discussions, what is left of the
Social Security debate? One large part consists of a set of comparisons
between two organizational models, two ways of trying to maintain some
rationality of organization of processes of exchange and distribution.
Resources and risks are always distributed and exchanged among members of society in some fashion, whether by design or happenstance. In the
Social Security question, the resources and risks of principal interest
have to do with providing retirement income. The relevant distributions
and exchanges unfold over time, between different periods and the age-
specific actors (workers, retirees, children, and so on) living during those
periods. But they also take place across actors of specific age or across
status-defined groups of actors (for example, defined by gender, parental
wealth, personal wealth) during each period. The two models—the market and the hierarchical—were broadly introduced in chapter 2. Each is
actually a class of models—markets and hierarchies come in a variety of
forms—but for present purposes we ignore most of the variations.

Two questions are important to this debate. Which of the two models
offers the better way to provide retirement income? Is one model better
across time and across groups living at the same time? Champions of preserving Social Security in close to its present form answer these questions
differently from those who propose replacing or supplementing it with
a system of private-pension accounts. Champions of the private accounts
obviously and explicitly prefer what they regard as the general superiority of market-based solutions. In contrast, those who favor preserving
the current structure of Social Security are skeptical that the market can
offer the same coverage, level, and predictability of benefits that Social
Security provides.

In this and the following chapter we examine, as carefully and honestly as we can, the relative merits of the two approaches. Our focus here
is primarily on comparative financial rates of return of saving and investment and, toward the end, on the comparative costs of repairing Social
Security versus a transition from Social Security to a system of private-
pension accounts. The focus of chapter 6 shifts more to comparisons of

116

the two models in terms of the distribution and exchange of risks, including political risks.

Returns on FICA Taxes

Since at least 1958 and a now-famous paper by Paul Samuelson, analysts have been aware that the implied rate of return on FICA taxes, which fund Social Security, is the future rate of growth of aggregate cash wages and salaries (subject to a ceiling limit on tax liability, $94,200 in 2006). Based on current projections, this implied rate will continue to be less than 2 percent.

The easy and widespread assumption is that surely the same amount of money as paid in FICA taxes, if invested in private financial assets such as corporate stocks or bonds or real estate, would earn a much better rate of return. Under certain conditions, that assumption can be supported by concrete evidence, though the difference in rate of return is not as high as is sometimes imagined, and those certain conditions must be taken quite seriously. We will turn to this matter of alternative investment avenues shortly. For the moment, let's take as given that the return on private investment instruments is on average significantly greater than 2 percent, even after we make comparable deductions for other costs, such as the expense of trading and managing accounts, or the taxes we must pay on investment returns. What happens to that difference? Is the additional return from markets simply wasted by social insurance, a sum of potential profits that went down the drain? Or does it buy something?

The answer is that the difference is the cost of postretirement income security for the working poor (those lower than average wage workers), the disabled, eligible survivors of workers, and the middle class. Wealthy workers participate in it, too, for reasons described earlier, even though they generally do not depend on the social insurance returns—assuming, of course, that they adequately self-insure by retaining enough wealth for their retirement years. Quickly following that answer is another question, however. Is the price we pay too high? Some argue that it is. They believe there is a more efficient way to use the resource (that is, the difference in rates of return) so that risks can be suitably distributed to satisfy postemployment income security and fairness across both periods and various status-defined groups, but at lower cost. Because these questions are about future periods, and we cannot guarantee what will happen, we are limited to projections, predictions, and other manner of crystal ball gazing. The best we can do is to examine historical records and venture some cautious guesses.

Actual Markets and Rates of Return

Actual markets, such as the financial markets on Wall Street and elsewhere, are considerably more complicated than the idealized or theoretical model presented in chapter 2 and just cited above. The theoretical model that has dominated the discipline of economics emphasizes assumptions of rational expectations—the efficient market hypothesis—and other principles and perspectives that are analytically powerful but descriptively inadequate. Actual markets do not perfectly conform to those assumptions, and often diverge rather widely from the model. For one thing, the distribution of information tends not to be highly efficient, but instead exhibits features of a hierarchical model of organization. For example, some players know more than others, some are more skillful in applying what they know, some players manage to get inside information, and so on.

Another major difficulty is the problem of time. Market action is inherently about expectations of future conditions. A market is a process, not a static state. The very idea of marginal utility—that the key dynamic is change in quantity of a good, or the value of the last or next increment, not the quantity itself—involves the passage of time. A host of elements and relationships therefore need to be addressed in a satisfactory manner. What are the proper time horizons? How are sequences of horizon integrated? To what extent does discounting vary over time, and how much does that matter? Unfortunately, we have no models that include an adequate treatment of the complications that arise when temporality is taken seriously (see, for example, Katzner 1998; Loewenstein and Elster 1992).

To the extent that rational expectations and the efficient-market hypothesis are actualized in complete markets, asset prices would always tend toward the fundamental values of the independent assets, and all information relevant to the market would already be reflected in prices. The price-setting mechanism would generate historical track records that are indistinguishable from the record of a random walk. Future prices would never be predictable beyond the predictions of a random distribution. The trouble with that picture is not that it is entirely wrong, but too many demonstrable and repeatable experiences do not fit it. Two relatively simple ones are the January effect and the weekend effect: Stock market returns are significantly higher in January than in any other month, and returns are lower (and negative) for Monday, on average, than for any other of the five trading days. Both effects have been robustly documented for long periods of time and (at least the former effect) in stock markets other than those of the United States (see Sheffrin 1996, 124–5).[1]

The internal logic of rational expectations is also troubled by serious problems of context sensitivity. A simple illustration of one such problem is the failure to generate a stop signal, which has been presented by Rosemarie Nagel (1995). Imagine a competition in which one rule is specified: guess a number from zero to 100 such that it will most closely approximate two-thirds of the average (that is, the arithmetic mean) guess. A player following rational expectations will think the number thirty-three. But then this same actor will realize that the number thirty-three can be correct only on the assumption that all other responses follow a random distribution. That is, because fifty is the mean value of randomly distributed choices from zero to 100, two-thirds of fifty is thirty-three. Why should a rational actor assume that she or he is the only rational actor in the game? Surely many others, even most others, perhaps all other players, are equally rational actors. If one assumes that all other players are equally rational, in the sense that each will form rational expectations about the decisions and actions of all other players, then the winning answer becomes twenty-two (two-thirds of thirty-three). It is now apparent that we are in an unstoppable regress, however, and that the only stable equilibrium is zero. Yet something is surely awry, because the dynamic just described is surely not, in its own terms alone, translatable into a useful trading strategy.[2]

Because of such difficulties, financial economists have increasingly modified the basic rational-expectations, efficient-market model in several ways. One alternative, for example, allows for different types of market players—those whose behavior closely follows the rational-expectations model and those who are instead what some observers call noise traders (see, for example, DeLong et al. 1990). The noise category is defined residually from the strict information approach of the rational-expectations model, and can be more or less expansive. One of the most important approaches aligns it closely to the underlying dynamic that financial analysts usually call technical analysis or market charting. Following the aggregate behavior of a stock market as if the market were operated by a sole representative agent can be fundamentally misleading when used in the sense that Frank Hahn and Robert Solow criticize (1995, 2). When used as technical analysts do, however, it generates a summary description of the balance of sentiments of active traders, especially sentiments of greed and fear, and this underwrites a number of useful trading strategies (for example, one known as contrarianism: selling one's assets in X when trading sentiment becomes notably greedy about X, and buying assets in X after trading sentiment has become notably fearful about X).[3] In that sense, noise traders attempt to trade on the mistakes made by other traders. Part of the inherent risk in that strategy is that discovering who was actually mistaken is always a future event that can embarrass either side of the trade.

Measuring Growth in Stock Equity

The payout that a person receives from a saving or investment program depends on the selling price and size of the accumulated asset, which in turn depend on the price and size of the principal saved or invested and the rate of growth of the asset. A number of component issues are involved in that simple statement: the rate of change in the asset's nominal value, rates of inflation during the holding period, and the transaction costs of acquiring, holding, and selling or converting the asset. When, as in the case of a pension account, the asset is converted to an annuity,[4] future rates of inflation during the annuity period are also relevant. Some if not all of these component issues are and have been subject to manipulative or dishonest presentations from various quarters.

For example, various experts (self-styled or otherwise) have cited substantially divergent numbers in answer to the question, "What has been the historical rate of change in the value of the U.S. stock market?" Some say 6 percent, others say 8 percent, still others say 11 percent. If you searched the literature diligently enough, you could probably find every number from, say, 4 percent to 12 or even 15 percent cited as the correct answer. Why so much variation?

One reason is that the rate of change differs depending on which collection of stocks one cites—for instance, the 30 stocks of the Dow Jones Industrial Average (DJIA), or the 500 of Standard and Poor's (S&P) broad index, or the Russell 2000 index, or the Wilshire 5000, and so forth.[5] Generally speaking, the more companies included in a stock index, the smaller the proportion with large capitalizations, high visibility, well-established high-quality management, and other characteristics associated with long-term survival and relatively good rates of growth. Thus, the rate of growth in the DJIA tends to exceed the rates in the S&P 500, the Russell 2000, and the Wilshire 5000. During specific periods, however, rates can be higher in small than in large companies. Also, note that the composition of these (and other) index collections changes from time to time, as the fates of specific companies change. Although it is now possible to invest in index funds keyed to a specific index,[6] most investors have either made their own stock selections or have adopted those of a fund manager or personal advisor (neither of whom works for free). In sum, a person can cite this or that index value, or shift from one to another, depending on which value is more favorable to the claim being asserted.

Another reason for the variation in cited rates of return is that different periods of time are used. For instance, the rate of change in the DJIA from 1945 to 2000 is different from that for the 1900 to 1945 period. The historical record looks better if it is calculated for 1930 through 1959 than for 1950 through 1979.

A third reason is the difference in how the rate of change in a given stock or portfolio of stocks is averaged over a given period. It is perfectly simple to calculate the average rate of change in, say, the DJIA for any specified sequence of days or months or years. But even simple averages

Table 5.1   Rates of Return Illustrated

Year	Start Value	Rate of Change	Multiply Factor	End Value
1999	$1,000.00	+.25	1.25	$1,250.00
2000	1,250.00	−.06	0.94	1,175.00
2001	1,175.00	−.07	0.93	1,092.75
2002	1,092.75	−.17	0.83	906.98
2003	906.98	+.25	1.25	1,133.73

Source: Authors' calculation.

can be used improperly or dishonestly to manipulate impressions. Consider the following illustration. During the five years from 1999, the DJIA had two very good years (1999 and 2003, each year increasing by 25 percent) and three years that were not so good (a decline of 6 percent in 2000, followed by a decline of 7 percent in 2001 and then a decline of 17 percent in 2002). The arithmetic average of those five annual rates is 4 percent; that is, the addition of the five numbers (+.25, −.06, −.07, −.17, +.25) gives a total of +.20, which, divided by five, yields the arithmetic average of .04 (that is, 4 percent) a year. This, however, is not the correct average. The arithmetic average is appropriate when quantities are added to achieve a sum. Here, with rates of change, we have quantities multiplied to achieve a product. The correct average for this type of number series is the geometric average (or geometric mean), not the arithmetic. The geometric average of the five annual rates of change is 2.54 percent, not 4 percent.

A simple illustration demonstrates both that point and the importance of the difference. Assume that you invest $1,000 in the stock market. For present purposes, it does not matter whether you invest in a single company or a collection of companies or an index fund. Indeed, the same principle applies even if you invested the $1,000 in a money market fund or a savings account at your local bank, although the rates of return cited below would not be realistic for either. Assume you leave the investment alone for five years and that the annual rates of change are as described for the five years from 1999 to 2003. Again, for present purposes it does not matter whether those rates include or exclude dividends reinvested. The information in table 5.1 tells what happens to your investment.

At the end of the first year (1999), your $1,000 investment has increased by 25 percent. In other words, $1,000 multiplied by 1.25 gives $1,250, which is the value of your investment at the start of the second year (2000). At the end of 2000 the value has declined by 6 percent. In other words, $1,250 multiplied by 0.94 yields $1,175, or, if you prefer, $1,250 multiplied by −6 percent gave you a loss of $75 on the year, which means that your

$1,250 has become $1,175. And so the calculations follow for the third, fourth, and fifth years of your five-year investment period. At the end of the fifth year (2003), your investment is worth $1,133.73. Therefore, your initial investment of $1,000 generated a profit of $133.73 at the end of five years, for an overall rate of return of 13.37 percent.

Now, notice (as before) that the sum of the column of annual rates of change is .20 (that is, +.50 − .30 = .20). That gives an arithmetic average of 4 percent per year (.20/5 = .04). If in fact you had averaged 4 percent a year, you would have ended the fifth year with a total investment value of $1,216.65, not $1,133.73. (In other words: $1000 × 1.04 = 1040; 1040 × 1.04 = 1081.60; 1081.60 × 1.04 = 1124.86; 1124.86 × 1.04 = 1169.86; 1169.86 × 1.04 = 1216.65.) The correct average is given as the geometric mean, which in this case is calculated as

$$G = \left(1.25 \times 0.94 \times 0.93 \times 0.83 \times 1.25\right)^{1/5}$$
$$= \left(0.13373\right)^{1/5}$$
$$= .02542$$

In other words, you actually averaged a 2.5 percent rate of return.[7] The difference between an average of 2.5 percent per year and 4.0 percent per year might seem very small. In the context of the $1,000 investment held for five years, the difference is only $82.93. But remember, we are dealing with a compound rather than a simple interest rate, which means that small discrepancies in the beginning of the period grow at an accelerating rate (that is, grow faster and faster) over time.[8] At the end of twenty years, the difference is $539.02 (that is, $2191.12 − 1652.10), which means that the 4 percent rate produced almost one-third more than the 2.542 percent rate. Or, to put it differently, at the lower rate your $1,000 would grow by almost two-thirds (65.2 percent), but at the higher rate it would more than double.

To repeat, the main point of this illustration has been to urge caution when reading or hearing claims about rates of change or rates of return for any specific stock or collection of stocks or stock index (or, for that matter, any other investment). If the writer-speaker has not been very clear and explicit in stating how the claimed rate was calculated, skepticism is more than usually recommended. We do not argue that the claim is necessarily misleading or dishonestly made.[9] But to the extent that the claim is bound up in a political struggle, caution is especially warranted. Politicians may call it spin. Others may consider it deliberate manipulation. Social scientists and other people who are by profession expected to be evenhanded and straightforward are hardly immune to bias (deliberate as well as not), but social scientists are less likely to use without comment an arithmetic rather than geometric average when calculating averaged rates of return over some period of time. Their bias is more likely to appear in their choices of assumptions, for example, as noted earlier.

Triumph of the Optimists

One of the most accurate, evenhanded, straightforward treatments of the historical record of stock market returns that we have seen is the recent book *Triumph of the Optimists*, written by a team of researchers from the United Kingdom (Dimson, Marsh, and Staunton 2002). As their title suggests, they are hardly a group of blind critics of equity markets. Nor, however, are they apologists. Their title is a judicious statement in proper historical perspective. During the nineteenth century, many generations of people in the United States (as in the United Kingdom, France, and other countries) were heavily skeptical of banks, to say nothing of anything as suspicious-looking as a joint stock company (as such firms were once called) and any market that proposed to engage in trade in anything as immaterial as pieces of paper (stock certificates) and promises to pay at stated future date.

Throughout the 1800s and well into the 1900s, the country experienced one financial crisis after another, some of them extremely severe. People who had placed their trust in banks or in companies that offered public stock often lost some or all of their money—not only its accumulated worth at the time of the crisis but also the future (though unknown) growth that would otherwise have occurred (see, for example, Macdonald 2003; Mann 2002). A stock market, whether the stock in question consists of livestock or pig bellies or pieces of paper and promises to pay, depends on trust, as we observed in chapter 2. Recall the adage attributed to P. T. Barnum[10]—"a sucker is born every minute"—and the observation of the greater fool theory that does apply to segments of market transaction: "If you now believe you paid too much for that item, just wait; a greater fool will come along and buy it from you at an even higher price." But markets will continue to clear, that is, function more or less as they are supposed to function, only if there are enough players who trust that they can count on reasonable fairness in market transactions.

The modern market in publicly offered stock issued by private companies was slow to develop and even slower to gain public acceptance as a reasonable way to invest one's money. The pessimist side of potential investors always remembered the last crisis as sufficient discouragement to recommend against participation. Few readers of this book have personal memory of the crisis that ensued from the series of market crashes in 1929, but for those alive at the time, it was simply the latest and most severe of a long series of similar events. It is against that backdrop that the title Elroy Dimson, Paul Marsh, and Mike Staunton chose for their book has its significance: the optimist, or the optimistic side of potential investors, has indeed triumphed.

So what has the record of the U.S. stock market been? The annualized real rate of total return on equities in the United States from 1900 to 2000, was 6.7 percent (Dimson, Marsh, and Staunton 2002, 52). For purposes of comparison, the annualized real rate of return for bonds during those 101 years was 1.6 percent, for Treasury bills, 0.9 percent.[11]

In view of that real rate of return, 6.7 percent per year, one might ask why there aren't many more millionaires among men and women aged fifty or older. If we assume an average investment in that general equity portfolio of $5,000 per year for thirty years, the 6.7 percent real return per year would yield $525,357 at the end of that time. It is important to note that the end-of-period value is given in constant Year 1 dollars and that each annual realized value was rounded to the whole dollar. Remember, this would be per adult person, not per household, and the investment would be completely untouched during the period. Of course, $5,000 was a lot of money in 1900, and still in 1920. The point here is that an annualized real rate of return of 6.7 percent would generate large wealth over a long period of saving or investment, yet the proportion of the adult population who seem to have benefited from that rate of growth is rather small. Why?

One obvious factor is inadequate saving and investment. If the initial principal is not there to invest, or is there but was consumed in shorter-term uses, growth cannot occur. Another factor is failure to optimally time the conversion from more to less risky assets. Fear and greed are major emotions of market behavior. As many investors learned to their chagrin during the late 1990s and 2000, either withdrawing too soon (excessive fear of loss) or too late (greed for more gain) had its costs. A more charitable view is that turns in the equity market are poorly predictable. One day's notable gain or loss is clearly the start of something big only in retrospect.

Another, more common factor is the failure to persevere over a long holding period. Whatever the annualized real rate of return, early money is worth a lot more than late money, but only if the early money (that is, early investment) is left invested so that compounding can occur. The temptations to draw from a stock of assets for immediate consumption are many and insistent. Therefore, the proposal of private investment accounts as either a supplement or a substitute for Social Security usually includes the promise of some government-mandated rules, an enforced holding period being one of them. If you may not withdraw your assets, the funds in the private account are no more available than contributions to Social Security, and for good reason. The government planners have no more confidence in the average citizen's risk-management abilities than did those who designed the Social Security program.

Equity investment is by definition risky. That is why the rate of return on equities generally exceeds the rates of return on investment options that involve some substantial guarantee of protection, for example, U.S. Treasury bills. This difference is sometimes called the equity risk premium. The core of this risk is volatility, the fact that prices for stocks move up and down more often, and by bigger margins, than do prices of bonds or Treasury bills. This volatility is opportunity—for gains as well as losses (Shiller 1989).

Volatility in the market valuation of stocks was illustrated in the preceding discussion of how to calculate average rates of investment return (table 5.1). The annual rates of return for the five years from 1999 through 2003 were highly diverse, ranging from +25 percent to –17 percent. A more general way of measuring volatility is to calculate the standard deviation around the mean of a distribution of values. The larger the standard deviation[12] the more the individual observations (for example, annual rates) diverge from the average of all the observations. Dimson and his colleagues (2002, 55) estimated this measure of volatility (that is, the standard deviation) of real returns on U.S. equities from 1900 to 2000 as 20.2 percent, which is more than twice the size of the geometric mean of 6.7 percent. Other analysts have reported very similar estimates for different periods (for example, Levy and Gunthorpe 1993; Campbell et al. 2001). That indicates a relatively high degree of volatility in stock prices. Some analysts have detected, relative to the efficient market hypothesis, an excess level of volatility, which reflects not just the fundamentals of market pricing but also a set of social psychological or market psychology factors (Shiller 1989).

If the years that witness unusually high rates of gain or unusually high rates of loss were randomly scattered across the period of years, the main consequences of a high degree of volatility could be managed relatively well. But in fact Dimson and his colleagues (2002, 308) showed that multi-year clustering of extreme rates did occur. In particular, the annualized rates of real return were much better during the 1980s and 1990s than during the 1950s and 1960s. Take out the good years of the 1980s and 1990s and the rate of real return is substantially lower. If one could assume that these very good decades are the wave of the future, so much the better. The record that Dimson, Marsh, and Staunton examined, however, certainly recommends against that view. Furthermore, the evidence suggests that volatility in individual stocks has been increasing. Campbell and his colleagues (2001) disaggregated observed volatility of stocks traded on the New York, American, and NASDAQ stock exchanges into three components: the part common to the market as a whole, the part common to firms within a specific industry sector but variant across sectors, and the part specific to firms within sectors. Whereas the degree of volatility in the market as a whole and in industry sectors was relatively stable, volatility at the level of individual firms followed a positive trend line, doubling from 1962 to 1997. Increasing volatility at the level of the firm is consistent with no trend in the market as a whole because the correlation in price performance across stocks declined. Increased volatility is increased opportunity, of course. At the same time, the increased opportunity of gain is counterbalanced by increased opportunity of loss. Moreover, the increased opportunity has taken place in terms of individual stock selection, not in terms of index or mutual funds (which tend to dampen the peaks and troughs of volatility).

It seems clear that in at least one respect this is not the best of times to be debating major changes in public policy concerning postemployment income insurance, such as replacing Social Security by a program of private investment accounts. The debate gathered steam at the tail end of a record period of growth in the value of common stocks, as represented by such bellwether markers as the Dow Jones Industrial Average, the S&P 500, and the NASDAQ Composite Index. Many people otherwise not known for foolishness began talking about (and apparently believing) a new economy and a new market, suggesting that the fundamental processes governing economic and market behavior had changed in ways that made the old rules no longer applicable. Too many individuals— from paid professional financial analysts, advisors, brokers, and fund managers, to amateur traders and the fifty-five-year-old John Q. Publics who had been happily watching the accumulated fruits of twenty to thirty years of investment in IRAs, 401(k) and 403(b) plans, and mutual fund or direct stock purchases double and then triple or quadruple in value— were happily inclined to believe that they had acquired some late twentieth-century version of the Midas touch. Human actors too often succumb to the view that a welcome outcome better credited to luck—that is, due to random, unpredictable factors—is actually due to their own intelligence, intuition, business acumen, or mystical powers. That tendency can both feed and ride the wave of a collective epiphany about how the rules have changed. In the late 1990s, one could watch numerous instances of professional analysts, advisors, brokers, and fund managers trying to work the wave so that it would send more marginal profits in their directions. Likewise, one could watch numerous instances of John Q. Public letting motivations of greed overpower emotions of fear, and in the process lose sight of the major problem of timing that stared them in the face. Then the bubble burst, and too many individuals lost moderate to huge amounts of accumulated value in their private accounts, with the consequence that their sentiments shifted from the greed pole to the fear pole, and they shifted whatever funds remained into more conservative investments, locking in their losses. It was far too easy in 1999 to believe that the rules had changed. It then became far too easy to forget the main points of the story Dimson, Marsh, and Staunton told about the triumph of the optimists.

The timing problem referred to above has already been discussed, but a revisit is appropriate here. In misleadingly simple terms, this problem is often summed up in the question, "When should I sell?" or, more specifically, "When should I lock in profits, in what amount, and what alternative investment venue will better protect me from the negative risks of the market?" These questions are indeed important, but the terms are misleadingly simple because this version of the timing problem involves inherently unpredictable factors. This version of the timing problem is asking when the market will reach its peak for this bull market. The desired answer to that question—like its bear market counterpart—is a point estimate that has very high probability, if not certainty, of being correct. It seeks a response on the order of "tomorrow" or "next week," not "probably some time within the next year" or "there's a 50 percent chance of a secular turn in the market during the next six months and a 65 percent chance during the next year."[13]

Good financial advisors correctly stress the importance of the difference between time in the market and timing the market. The latter is a fool's play. The former can be a beneficial strategy. Notice that the verb is *can be*, not *will be*. There is simply no guarantee that any particular strategy will yield the desired level of profits, or any profits at all, from investments in the stock market. Time in the market, otherwise known as the buy and hold strategy, is a preferable strategy in the sense that it results in superior outcomes on average in the long run. That is to say—and the point is crucial—this preferable strategy will give superior outcomes for most investors in a large population of investors. Any particular investor in that large population of investors will not necessarily benefit, however. There will be losers as well as winners when following this or any other strategy. The difference is that any particular person's chances of being a winner are better if a time in the market strategy is followed. Time in the market is relatively effective because the length of exposure to market volatility enables one better to manage that volatility in advantageous ways (at least in principle).

As illustration, consider the thirty years from 1963. This period was unlike the twenty years that ended in 2004, for example, in that it did not include a long sequence of years with spectacular rates of increase in stock values, such as we saw in the recent period (annual rates of 20 percent or more for nine of the twenty years, and only four years with net losses). But the thirty years from 1963 nevertheless experienced its own share of market shocks—that is, unexpected events that distressed confidence in future outcomes. These ranged from the assassination of President Kennedy to the oil shocks of the 1970s. The resulting volatility of share prices created opportunities to profit from market gains, and many people did just that. Indeed, the annualized rate of change in the S&P 500 was more than 10 percent (in nominal terms; that is, not net of inflation, transactions costs, and taxation). Now, on the assumption of five trading days

per week for fifty-two weeks of each of the thirty years, that period consisted of 7,800 trading days. (Market holidays are ignored.) Let's subtract
from that market record the ninety best trading days, the ninety days that
had the best returns, only ninety of the 7,800 days. The result? The annualized rate of return drops to a little over 3 percent! Once inflation, transaction costs, and taxes are taken into account, the real return probably
averaged very close to zero or less. If one could have predicted when
those ninety days would occur, one could have taken profits on each of
the following days. That is an ability that no one really has. Some people
make lucky guesses, and some of those then delude themselves (and
others) into the belief that the outcomes were driven by their unusual
skills. Even if a person predicted that somebody was going to shoot
Kennedy or an oil shock was coming, the questions of when and how the
market would react remained to be decided. Market shocks—virtually by
definition negative events because of the triumph of the optimists that
Dimson and his colleagues described—are generally not predictable for a
superficially simple reason. When market traders anticipate a market-
influencing event, they try to factor it into their trading. They do not
always succeed, of course, either in the anticipation or in making the correct adjustments to their trading behavior. But the point is that, to the
extent they do succeed, the potential market shock has been defused; and
to the extent they do not succeed, the realized market shock was not predicted by the very people who probably had the most information and the
greatest vested interest in the market process.[14]

As a final illustration of the difficulty of succeeding with a strategy of
buying low and selling high (that is, a market timing strategy), consider
the structural model that Doyle Farmer, Paolo Patelli, and Ilija Zovko
(2005) developed, a market in which all traders have zero intelligence. In
other words, traders behave randomly in their buy and sell orders. The
model accurately predicted 96 percent of the price difference between the
best buy and sell limit orders (that is, the spread variance; a limit order
places a floor price for selling or a ceiling price for buying) and 76 percent of the variance in the price diffusion rate (a standard measure of
market risk that gauges how quickly the price changes and by how
much). In sum, the actual behavior of stock prices was not much different from the results of a random walk.[15] As a macro-level or aggregate
phenomenon, a market can behave in regular and somewhat predictable
ways over a long period, thus the triumph of optimism that Dimson,
Marsh, and Staunton describe and the January effect, the weekend effect,
and similar patterns described in chapter 2. The component processes,
however, the micro-level phenomena that occur at the level of individual traders, generally do not reveal patterns that can be used to advantage by a trader's strategic action except insofar as that action follows the
time in market approach.

There are major investment alternatives to the stock market. Corporate firms and governmental entities issue various sorts of bonds. The U.S. Treasury sells bonds and bills to creditors, with low risk to either the principal or the guaranteed interest. Other venues, such as real estate, are also options. Investments in the stock market (by the time in market approach) have generally been better in terms of eventual yields, however, because of the greater risk that a stock investor has been willing to assume. This is the equity risk premium referred to earlier.[16] How big is it? That is, how much has the stock investor been rewarded, on average, for assuming the greater risk associated with investment in stocks rather than in, say, the less risky Treasury bills? Dimson and his colleagues (2002, 164–5) estimate the answer from the historical market record: the twentieth-century mean was a very substantial 7.7 percent, not far from the annualized real return on U.S. equities. Volatility in the premium was also quite large, with a standard deviation of 19.6 percent. For about a third of the century, the estimated risk premium was negative, most of those years coming in the 1930s and the 1970s.

It is also possible to estimate a forward-looking risk premium on equities, which is what any investor in the stock market is doing, implicitly if not explicitly, by the very fact of investing in stocks rather than less risky assets. Although past performance is indeed often a poor predictor of future returns, the historical record does offer some useful clues about the future level and direction of change in the equity risk premium. Dimson and his colleagues (2002, 192–3) estimate a future premium of about 5.5 percent. This figure agrees with the differently constructed estimate by Eugene Fama and Kenneth French (2002), which implies that, for an investor to offer money to an equity fund or an individual stock-issuing company, she or he would have to be confident that the fund or company would pay a return at least 5.5 percentage points higher than the prevailing rate paid on U.S. Treasury bills, which are the benchmark.

Bear in mind that an equity premium is volatile for all the reasons that individual stock prices and index prices are volatile, plus the reasons for volatility in Treasury bills and other sorts of assets. Although there are correlations across those factors, they are far from perfect and rarely stable for very long. The inflation-adjusted return on Treasury bills averaged 0.9 percent during the twentieth century, but there were long periods (for example, from 1940 to 1959 and from 1970 to 1979) when the inflation-adjusted returns were actually negative (Dimson, Marsh, and Staunton 2002, 196, figure 14-1). For all decades between 1900 and 2000, the average equity premium ranged from a little less than zero to about 15 percent. For all thirty-year periods during the same interval, the average equity premium ranged from zero to about 13 percent. Note, by the way, that the import of the equity risk premium first assumes an investor who is able and willing to invest in Treasury bills or bonds, and thus would invest in stocks if the equity premium (viewed as an expectation premium) should be met. This is important because, at the very times that inflation-adjusted returns on Treasury bills are at or below zero, potential investors might be less interested in investing in anything, since the low Treasury-bill rate could be signaling that a difficult period lies just ahead (that is, high inflation, churning in the market, unusual political uncertainties, and the like).

Clearly, an equity risk premium is sensitive to the operation of consumer sentiment, especially among that segment of consumers who are actual or potential investors. If, for whatever reason, the majority have come to believe that a particular market has become inherently less (more) risky, they will demand a lower (higher) risk premium, if they are behaving prudently. That does not necessarily mean they are correct in their attribution of change in inherent risk, however. Again, illustrations abound in the experiences of the 1990s in stock markets of all sorts, from those of broadly based index funds to the highly speculative initial public offering (IPO) markets in high-tech start-up companies. Market players can (and did) both fuel and feed off a variety of sorts of moral hazard, analogous to a celebrity believing his or her own hype or politicians believing their own campaign promises (Frankfurt 2005). Consider the hazard that can result if actual and potential market players begin to believe that the Federal Reserve Board (especially as personified by a media-celebrated chairman) has in fact conquered inflation so decisively that it will not be a drag on market performance in the foreseeable future (Sargent 1999). That belief might lower their risk expectation substantially, lower their risk premiums, and lead them into investments that would be, on other grounds, judged as riskier than they perceive (where, note, the concern is chiefly about risk of loss, not risk of gain). It is perhaps odd to think of the Federal Reserve Board as creating moral hazard, but in fact it would not be unusual. Corporations (for example, insurance companies), government agencies, and other organizations that wield great influence over perceptions are often in a position to generate moral hazards.[17]

In reporting some main results of the Dimson, Marsh, and Staunton research, we would be remiss if we did not add to all the usual caveats about predictions of future stock market values one very specific cause for caution, which the researchers emphasize, especially in conjunction with estimates of the future equity risk premium. Dimson and colleagues pointed to two disturbing facts: first, that the yield on corporate dividends in the United States "fell from 7.2 percent in 1950 to just 1.1 percent by end-2000" and, second, that most of that decline can be accounted for by the fact that dividend payments are disappearing (2002, 158). Whereas more than four out of five U.S. firms paid dividends in 1950, that ratio had fallen to one in five by century's end. A small fraction of the decline in dividend payers was due to firms changing policy—

shifting from being dividend payers to paying none—but the bulk of the decline was due to the emergence of firms that never pay dividends. "U.S. firms have become less likely to pay dividends, whatever the company's characteristics," though the explosion of initial public offerings following the end of the 1970s has also been a factor, because these tend to be "small firms with low profitability and strong growth opportunities—characteristics typical of firms that have never paid dividends" (2002, 159). From all present indications, the disappearance of dividends will continue. This can have serious implications for future rates of return on stock investments. To drive that point home, Dimson and his colleagues compared two portfolios of U.S. stocks during the length of the twentieth century. The portfolios were identical in all respects but for the fact that in one portfolio all dividends were always immediately reinvested in the portfolio, whereas in the other portfolio all dividends were always squandered. At the end of the century, the value of the first portfolio was eighty-five times the value of the second portfolio. Dividends were that important. Without them, the portfolio lost almost 99 percent of its potential value.

Inflation, Taxes, and Transaction Costs

The annualized rates of return that Dimson and his colleagues reported (2002) are real rates of return, meaning that they are net of inflation (or expressed in constant dollars). Whereas the annualized real rate for stock equities for the century was 6.7 percent, the nominal rate (that is, not adjusted, as if there were zero inflation during the period) was 10.1 percent. Likewise, whereas the annualized real rate for U.S. Treasury bills was 0.9 percent, the nominal rate was 4.1 percent. Inflation erodes purchasing power value. As the rate of inflation rises, interest rates tend to rise as well, reflecting the increasing nominal cost of money (cost of borrowing money). Using data compiled by Ibbotson Associates in their *2004 Yearbook* (a standard, reliable source for investment markets), the rate of inflation for 2004, based on the consumer price index–urban, was 3.26 percent. Let's assume that rate continues at a constant level. This would mean that $1 in 2004 prices would be equivalent to $1.38 in 2014, $1.90 in 2024, and $2.23 in 2039. In other words, one would need $1.38 in 2014, $1.90 in 2024, and $2.23 in 2039 just to stay even with the purchasing power of the 2004 dollar. An investment in stocks (or any other asset subject to inflation) would have to return 3.26 percent each year to offset the effect of inflation.[18]

Consider an illustration closer to home in terms of actual experience. As we have mentioned before, the twenty years from 1985 to 2004 included an exceptional string of years of growth in the value of the Dow Jones Industrial Average. In nine of the twenty years, the annual rate of growth was 20 percent or more, with a peak rate of 33 percent in 1995;

and in only four was the rate of return negative. Those rates are nominal; they do not reflect the impact of inflation. The annualized nominal rate of return in the DJIA during the period was 11.54 percent. Inflation, measured by the consumer price index–urban, averaged about 3 percent during those twenty years. That reduced the geometric mean (that is, the annualized rate of return) to a real rate of about 8.5 percent—still handsome, and better than the century-long annualized real rate of 6.7 percent, but not quite as impressive as the double-digit nominal rate.

After adjusting for inflation, one should also make some allowances for taxes and for the costs of buying, holding, and selling stocks (or any other investment asset) to determine more precisely how much one's investment has actually gained (or lost) on the principal. Adjustment for taxation is important because federal and some state and local tax rates on income are sensitive to income composition, with higher marginal rates of tax on capital gains and some categories of dividends, and low or zero rates on certain kinds of bonds and Treasury assets. Also, tax rates tend to change over investment periods. Adjustment for transaction costs is important because these vary in size not only between categories of asset (asset classes) but also within an asset class, especially across mutual funds and similar collective asset classes. They also tend to change over the course of an investment period.

Estimates of allowances against investment returns for taxes and transaction costs are sensitive to a number of characteristics of the individual investor. For example, the size of the tax bill will depend on applicable liabilities for state and local taxes, as well as federal taxes, and on the applicable marginal rate of taxation. Moreover, dividends are taxed in the year they are assigned to the investor (whether reinvested or taken as current consumable income), whereas capital gains (which will include reinvested dividends; that is, the notorious double taxation of dividends) are taxed in the year the unit of asset is sold by the investor. With those (among other) reasons for caution in mind, however, the preceding illustration for the 1985 to 2004 period can be continued, using data from Ibbotson Associates' *2004 Yearbook* to calculate additional adjustments for tax liability and transaction costs for a typical investor in stocks. A reasonable estimate for the combined deduction comes to about 2.5 to 3 percentage points. Thus, the nominal annualized return of 11.54 percent reduces to about 5.5 to 6 percent, once inflation, taxes, and transaction costs have been deducted. A return of 6 percent after all deductions is quite good; it means that one's dollar will double in real value—after tax, inflation, and transaction costs—in twelve years. The other important point to remember from this exercise is that it is on the basis of this real value—the value after taxes, inflation, and transaction costs—that one should compare alternative investment classes, including a public insurance program such as Social Security.

Transaction costs include all the costs to an investor of making, maintaining, and realizing an investment. Examples are the fees one pays to a broker who executes trades (the fees are paid to an individual or to a brokerage service) and maintenance fees paid to a broker or account manager for maintaining one's investment account (for example, fees for physically keeping the stock certificates or bonds, fees for reporting to the investor, to the Internal Revenue Service, and to other agencies). Mutual funds are often advertised as no-load, but that does not mean that the fund charges no fees. The no-load typically refers to the absence of a commission on purchases. They often charge fees for selling, however, or for selling prior to a required holding period, and all funds charge maintenance fees that include costs for reporting, as noted, and a 12(b)-1 fee, which is a charge for some of the fund's promotional expenses.

In general, investment accounts are highly sensitive to the frequency of trading, or churning, it is sometimes called. Some account managers who have been authorized by clients to be active managers (that is, to make investment decisions for the client) have been known to engage in churning, to their own benefit. The claim is that by buying and selling strategically they can improve the investor's profit margin. It is usually only, or mainly, the manager's commissions that benefit from the strategy. One of the advantages of the "buy and hold" strategy is that it minimizes transaction costs, though holding too long can be as detrimental as selling too soon.[19]

It is difficult to make meaningful generalizations about transaction costs given the variation by length of holding period, by type of investment asset, and other factors. Perhaps the best review came from an investigation conducted by the U.S. Securities and Exchange Commission (2000), through its Division of Investment Management, even though the study pertained only to mutual funds. The SEC evaluated management fees primarily in terms of an expense ratio, which is the sum of the fund's management expenses divided by the fund's average net assets for the year. Because the ratio varies by asset size of the fund, the SEC mainly examined asset-weighted average expense ratios. These ratios fluctuated between 0.68 percent and 0.75 percent for no-load funds and between 1.12 percent and 1.17 percent for loaded funds. These figures are for management fees alone, including the 12(b)-1 fees. Total ownership costs can be a bit higher, on average. For funds carrying sales charges (loads), and assuming a holding period of five or ten years during which all sales costs are amortized, total ownership costs averaged about 1.85 percent, or 1.50 percent for ten years. An expense charge of 1 to 1.5 percent of asset value might seem very small. It is. Bear in mind, though, that even a fee as small as 1 percent can have a substantial impact on a fund's growth (see figure 5.1).

**Figure 5.1   Illustration of the Impact of Fund Management Fees
on an Investment**

Let's assume you invest $10,000 in a fund of your choice, and you leave it there for twenty years. Let's assume an annual rate of return of 9 percent (whether that rate is net of inflation or not is irrelevant for purposes of the illustration). The following chart tells what would happen under various assumptions about fees and the presence of a deferred sales charge (that is, an end-of-term sales charge). We are assuming the fund is "no load" (that is, does not charge a commission on purchase).

Annual operating expense	2.0%	2.0%	1.5%	1.0%
Deferred sales charge	2.0%	0.0%	0.0%	0.0%
Value at end of period	$37,215	$37,415	$41,424	$45,839
Total cost of fees	$18,828	$18,628	$14,620	$10,205
fees	8,963	8,763	6,976	4,938
forgone earnings	9,865	9,865	7,644	5,267

Growing at 9 percent each year for twenty years, the $10,000 became $56,044. But one-third of that (or $18,628) was paid to the investment fund that charged management fees of 2 percent; had it been in an investment fund that charged management fees of 1 percent, about one-fifth of the $56,044 (or $10,205) would have been lost in fees.

Source: Authors' compilation.

The foregoing estimates are arithmetic averages and conceal considerable variance across funds.[20] The variance around the average for all funds was predicted by rate of portfolio turnover (as noted), by asset size of fund (larger funds tend to have smaller fees), by age of the fund (older funds tend to have higher fees), and by type of fund (higher fees among international and specialty funds, lower fees among institutional and index funds). Retirement-oriented funds—funds favored, for example, by IRA holders, 401(k) holders, 403(b) holders, and so forth—tend to be quite large and have relatively low portfolio turnover, two facts that probably account for their generally lower fees. The average asset-weighted expense ratio for retirement-oriented accounts during the late 1990s was about 25 percent smaller than that for all equity funds.[21]

What is left of a fund's performance after expenses and transaction costs have been deducted is what matters most to investors. On average, not much is left, probably mainly because fund managers are sensitive to two competing, even contrary concerns. On the one hand, they want positive returns; that much is obvious. On the other hand, and this is less obvious, they dislike volatility because customers dislike volatility. The latter interest often gets in the way of the former interest, and on balance it tends to dominate. Thus, Russ Wermers (2000) found that for the period from 1970 to 1999 the performance of mutual funds, net of costs, lagged the market average by about 1 percentage point. During that same period, remember, mutual funds became an increasingly lucrative business, and the number of funds soared.

One final and important aspect of costs, one that has become a basic fact of political-economic life in our society, is the strong incentive to externalize costs. The selfish actor seeks to push costs away, tries to assign them to another actor or, failing that, to the commonwealth, and generally succeeds to the extent that he or she is relatively powerful. One of the functions of government, supposedly, is to regulate the distribution of costs by some publicly agreed principle of distributive justice. Politicians, on the other hand, generally among the more powerful members of society, often succeed in shaping the distribution in ways that accord with their financial sponsors. How we conventionally assess transaction costs in market behavior is a good illustration of the advantage that can be gained by externalizing costs.

In our accounting of transaction costs involved in market behavior, we followed standard practice, which counts only standard costs. Defined in a complete sense, however, transaction costs consist of all expenditures undertaken to negotiate and enforce contracts and protect property rights. For modern societies as a whole, these costs increase substantially as societies become more complexly structured through indirect relationships. Through these circuitous connections, flows of information can be manipulated to partial advantage, interests are often negotiated through multilevel agent-principal networks, and the fairness of enforcements is sometimes difficult to determine. In one of the few efforts to study transaction costs in something closer to this full sense, John Wallis and Douglass North (1986) estimated an increase from about 25 percent of national income in 1870 to more than 50 percent a century later. Partitioning that total amount into portions assignable to this or that venue of transactions is anything but simple, which is one obvious reason why the exercise is seldom attempted. However, we should not be surprised that in certain comparisons of public policy one or another side to a debate will be happy to ignore a large portion of transaction costs. For instance, many advocates of continuing Social Security intact with only necessary modifications to the financing structure cite the program's distinct advantage in having very low management fees, almost surely lower than the fees that would be charged by any for-profit manager of private retirement accounts. The same advocates, though, neglect to mention that the transaction costs of contract enforcement have been increasing, as officials of the second G. W. Bush administration began signaling that the federal government should refuse to enforce the contract unless major renegotiation of its terms could be brought to a satisfactory end. Some of these issues, which recall the fact that risk is a political-economic concept, are addressed in chapter 6.

Market Solutions

Many, perhaps most, problems do have market-based solutions. There have been countless demonstrations, not merely in laboratories but in ordinary, everyday practices everywhere, that the large majority of citizens will not preserve the commons simply because of an ethical or moral principle such as the Golden Rule or normative judgment that it's the right thing to do. Although there is indeed some variation across societies and across individuals within a society in this regard, it is nonetheless generally true that common resources are better protected if they can be appropriately priced in the marketplace. Otherwise, too many members of modern society define the commons as a free good and thus drastically undervalue it. Therefore, for instance, we are much likelier to gain cleaner air if we charge for it (or, conversely, assign prices to polluted air) than if we leave it to the commonwealth, where it can be used as a sump by anyone who wants to externalize costs by dumping pollutants into it.

When someone in a political discussion prefers to begin negotiations with one or another market-based solution, however, one should ask exactly what problem is being addressed. However useful a market model might be, any actual market always exists within a network of hierarchies, or relations of power, and is therefore subject to forces from those hierarchies. Even, or especially, when a market has been deliberately designed to respond in some fashion to problems deriving from a hierarchy, the resulting market-based solution can be little more than an instrument of the interests of that hierarchical organization.[22] Furthermore, market-based solutions are no more cost-free than corresponding solutions from hierarchical organizations are; and markets are no less prone to externalize costs, especially when costs can be externalized onto a hierarchical organization that incorporates some sort of common good. Markets, for example, generally do not pay all of the costs of enforcing property rights, the very rights on which their continued operation depends.

With those cautions in mind, let's look more closely at the comparison between what is purchased by FICA taxes as Social Security and what could be purchased through a market-based solution to the postemployment income security problem. We have already established that the rate of return on FICA taxes, net of all costs, inflation, and so forth, is less than 2 percent for the cohort born circa 1960.[23] What is purchased with that? In 2005, the seventieth anniversary year of Social Security, 10.6 million people, or 22 percent of the 48 million who were receiving Social Security benefits, depended solely on that income as their means of support. The average 2005 payout was $960 a month, or $11,520 a year.

Compare that to the median annual income of people aged sixty-five or older who had any reportable income: for men in 2002 it was $19,436, for women, $11,406. If you think living on $960 a month is difficult, try an income at the poverty threshold for a person aged sixty-five or older, which in 2002 was $719 a month. The same year, nearly one in seven women and nearly one in ten men aged sixty-five or older who did not work had total incomes below the poverty line.[24]

Whereas the average payout was $960 a month, variation around that figure was considerable. The minimum was $577 a month, an amount that is assured by the SSI part of Social Security, which brings low-wage beneficiaries up to $577. The maximum was $1,874. The large majority of beneficiaries were tightly bunched around the average of $960 and the standard deviation was only about $36, meaning that nearly two-thirds of all recipients received some amount between $924 and $996 each month.[25]

How should one evaluate that record? Any answer to that question will depend on one's values. In our view, the record is unsatisfactory for a country that has the largest economy in the world and is one of the richest countries in the world, on a per capita basis, especially when one recognizes that a number of other countries have a better record.

That said, however, we emphasize two other evaluative factors. First, as minimal as it is, the $960 a month was guaranteed. Juggling bills from month to month was no doubt in many cases very difficult, but the juggling did not also have to contend with uncertainties of whether the firm that provided one's pension would enter bankruptcy and shed pension obligations for pennies on the dollar, or of whether one's specific stock investments would significantly worsen, and so forth. As recent rhetoric has been making clear, even government obligations do not carry ironclad guarantees. Until recently, though, those government obligations were in fact one of the few investments one could count on, month after month after month, at a known rate of payment that made household budgeting reasonably stable, even if the rate was quite meager.

The second evaluative factor to be added is that Social Security was not designed to be the sole source of income to a retired person. Just as most insurance policies from private firms do not promise a dollar-for-dollar replacement of lost income due to injury or accident or job termination (and those policies approaching that replacement rate are very expensive), the Old-Age and Survivors Insurance (OASI) component of Social Security was intended to be a fallback, an insured floor that one could count on for future years and build on through private saving and investment and perhaps an employer-sponsored pension plan. Why, then, has OASI been the sole income source for so many people, and for so long? Bear in mind that the large majority of these people had been relatively low-paid workers before retirement. Did they plan to have such a low level of postemployment income as well? The question is virtually nonsensical. They probably did expect that it would be no higher than, and perhaps even not as high as, their employment incomes. To ask whether they intended that outcome or preferred that outcome is tantamount to asking a starving person if he or she prefers being hungry. Granted, persons of some authority have claimed that true preference is revealed by actual outcome. If a person truly preferred a better outcome, then, insofar as that person was or is a free agent, he or she would work hard to achieve the better outcome. (We will meet some of these people in chapter 7.) However that may be as a matter of intentions, it seems gratuitous to expect those low-wage workers to have saved or invested sufficient capital in corporate stocks to have gained greater wealth during their retirement years.

The enthusiast of moral hazard explanations will be quick to disagree. Precisely because it has been a guarantee, OASI has robbed covered workers of the incentive effect of greed and fear. Insurance can be good insofar as it frees a person from fear of failure enough to encourage him or her to be a constructive risk-taker who strives for greater achievement— including in the process, the hope or plan is, an outcome of very secure financial status for future years. But, the argument continues, insurance can stimulate too much freedom from fear of failure, too much greed for ever greater achievement, and thus an increased likelihood of failure, including not just short-term failure from which one can recover, but also that frightful end-state failure that (without any backup insurance payout) would include impoverishment and perhaps chronic morbidity. Of course, one could argue that greed is a good thing in the long run—that is, for a large population of outcomes—because sometimes the highly greedy actor (or, if one prefers, highly ambitious actor) actually does achieve unusually great outcomes, including perhaps those from which all or at least many other members of society will benefit. Indeed, that sort of consequence does happen. The remaining question is twofold, one part particular to the example and the other generalized to the whole of society. First, what happens to those who not only do not succeed in their greed but also utterly fail because of it? Second, the generalized part, what should be the moral obligations of all members of society simply by virtue of that membership? Again, these are issues to be considered in chapter 7.

To summarize, the comparatively low rate of return on FICA tax investments in Social Security has purchased a guaranteed floor for postemployment income. The average level of that income is quite low— roughly 130 percent of the official level of poverty at age sixty-five or older, though that official level is also quite low by comparison to many other countries and to younger households in the United States. It has nonetheless been a guaranteed floor that, until now, workers could count on with about as much certainty as anything can be counted on. What could a market-based solution such as a private retirement account (PRA) offer in place of the OASI provision of Social Security?

The first answer is a higher rate of return. What exactly might that rate be? Whereas with Social Security there has been a regularity and thus predictability to the rate of return, with a PRA a similarly near-exact prediction cannot be offered. That, of course, has been part of the point. The PRA offers less predictability in return for the opportunity of a higher rate of return. The best we can do in that regard is look to the historical record, just as we did with Social Security's rate of less than 2 percent. As we noted earlier, best estimates of the equity risk premium have centered on 5.5 percent.[26] That is, before taking on the additional risk of loss of investment a prudent investor would expect a stock or stock fund to offer about 5.5 percentage points on top of the (very low risk) return of Treasury bills, which averaged about 0.9 percent during the twentieth century. Assuming that the obligation of Social Security was as low in risk of loss as the obligation of a Treasury bill, and at least until very recently it was, it is reasonable to make the same comparative expectation of a PRA return in relation to Social Security. Adding the 5.5 estimated equity risk premium to the estimated 2 percent return on Social Security implies a real PRA rate of less than 7.5 percent—let's say 7.2 percent.[27] In other words, to do as well as low-risk Social Security, a PRA investment should return about 7.2 percent, on average, to cover the premium for higher risk. How does that compare with the real return on stock investments?

Recall that the century-long average rate of return for U.S. stocks was about 6.7 percent, net of inflation. Transaction costs and taxes have not been deducted from that average rate of return, but the rate is already below the benchmark of 7.2 percent. If we base the average rate on a more recent period, the result is not any better. As noted, for example, the rate of return for the twenty years beginning 1984 was between 5.5 and 6.0 percent, net of inflation, transaction costs, and taxes—still below the benchmark of 7.2 percent. Moreover, recall that in recent decades the number of firms paying dividends and the dividend yield among those firms that have paid dividends have both declined significantly. Reinvested dividends have been the major part of the growth potential of investments in stocks. If the decline in dividend payment continues, the expected return on stock investments probably will not improve on the recent record.

These comparisons can be only rough approximations. They nonetheless indicate that the net advantage of private retirement accounts probably would not be significantly better, on average, than Social Security has been in recent years—unless one assumes either that U.S. stocks are not riskier investments than the past record of Social Security or that the added risk has zero market value. The latter position is irrational. Clearly, some people prefer to believe the former, that the stock market is no more risky than government bonds or Treasury bills. We understand the wish behind this belief, but fail to see persuasive evidence—

even though a number of politicians and government officials have seemingly been trying very hard to persuade us to this belief by their words and actions.

The preceding comparisons have focused on the average case in a large population of cases. No doubt some investors would reap a higher rate of return than 7.2 percent, net of inflation, transaction costs, and taxes, over some period of time. Other investors would fare worse. How might the relative winners and losers be distributed cross-sectionally in terms of status-defined groupings? Let's assume that PRA participation is mandatory, that the rate at which earnings are taxed for investment in the PRA is also mandated, and that accumulated assets cannot be withdrawn until a specified eligibility age, at which point the assets are annuitized according to an actuarial formula. In short, assume that the PRA is regulated much as is Social Security. Under that assumption, the cross-sectional distribution of relative winners and losers at the end of any given period would probably not have a very high positive correlation with relevant status-defined groupings.[28] To the extent that the assumption set is loosened, however, PRA investors who fared worse than average would probably look much like the people who fared worse than average in terms of other status characteristics such as parental income or wealth and own education, health, and frequency of unemployment.

What provisions would be made for these people, the PRA investors who fared worse than average, bearing in mind that average would probably not be better than, and during certain periods would almost surely be worse than, the rate of return that has characterized Social Security? By definition, these losers would be market failures.[29] Would there be some sort of secondary market to supply back-up insurance? What would that funding mechanism be? What distorting effect would its existence have on the primary (PRA) market? It seems likely that the funding of any back-up insurance scheme would have to be generated either from an additional payroll tax or from general revenues. This is the conclusion that Antonio Rangel and Richard Zeckhauser reached in their theoretical analysis of risk-sharing models: "[Because] markets cannot generate optimal risk sharing, a system of individual accounts cannot produce an efficient allocation. In a market with a rich-enough asset structure, agents can buy a lot of insurance against events like a stock market crash, but not perfect insurance. The size of the efficiency loss is an open empirical question" (2001, 139).

There is still another, and even larger, unanswered question. The superior returns on stock investments are not a free good. They must be paid for, and are paid from corporate earnings. Part of that payment is in the form of a firm's dividends (or stock buy-backs). The other part, appreciation in the firm's stock price, which is realized as capital gains, is an expectation of growth in the firm's earnings and thus profits. With diminishing dividends, even more of the load must be carried by capital gains, but let's ignore that. Whether paid as dividends or as capital gains, a real rate of return of 7 percent (or even 6 percent, for that matter) in the stock market implies a very healthy record of future earnings growth for the average firm. Although this is possible for some number of years in a row, we are unlikely to see that quality of record, on average, over decades. Indeed, though economic growth in the United States averaged about 3.4 percent for the last seven decades of the twentieth century, projections for the next several decades are considerably lower, at less than 2 percent.[30] The actuaries who predict that the Social Security Trust Fund will be empty before the middle of this century base their prediction on the assumption that economic growth over the next several decades will average 1.9 percent. If that assumption proves accurate, there simply will not be enough growth in earnings to fund an average real rate of return on stocks that is even close to 7 percent.[31] Granted, in some periods it did seem that the marginal cost of capital had declined to zero (for example, the late 1990s in the United States, the late 1980s in Japan), and rates of return ballooned. Those periods do not last long, however, and when they end the volume of losses, some of them very deep, increases quickly.

Finally, we come to the issue of transition. If it is true that Social Security is approaching insolvency and should be supplemented (if not replaced) by a system of private retirement accounts, then the cost of the transition must be paid from some fund other than Social Security itself. The advocates of the PRA approach, remember, have also been the people who have declared the Trust Fund worthless. Not worthless, its assets do consist of U.S. Treasury bonds. Thus the Trust Fund cannot be raided to pay the costs of transition to a PRA system. Several prominent advocates of a PRA system seem to believe that the transition financing can be achieved by the same mechanism as the PRA: switch from investment in bonds to investment in stocks, because the latter give a much higher return (see, for example, Andrews 2004). If financing were that magically simple, any government debt could be swept aside the same way. Surely one wonders, if it were all that easy, why would a bond market even exist? Who would ever be foolish enough to buy bonds when they could buy stocks instead?

On the face of it, one form of asset swap does seem fiscally sound and workable as a means of paying the transition cost (see, for example, Aaron and Reischauer 1998a). The federal government could sell government bonds to the public and invest the proceeds in the stock market. Insofar as the yield on stocks exceeded the cost of servicing the bond debt, the difference could be used to pay transition costs to a PRA system, completely or partially. However, careful analyses by different economists—most of them, it is fair to say, sympathetic to the notion of private accounts—have shown that the asset swap solution is not viable. Thomas MaCurdy and John Shoven used as their evaluation standard the rule that the asset swap is regarded as successful "if the stock portfolio generates sufficient cash to pay off the interest and principal of the bonds and still have money left over; it would be a failure if the stock portfolio is insufficient to do that and the bond repayments require another round of borrowing" (2001, 31). They analyzed different versions of the asset swap. Failure rates ranged from 6 to 29 percent. Moreover, their analyses showed that there would be long strings of possible annual failures; in one version, the asset swap failed fifteen years in a row. According to Martin Feldstein, Ranguelova, and Samwick (2001), the transition cost would be about 3 percent of payroll each year for thirty-five years.[32] They concluded that asset-swap strategies would not work without additional government funding to cover failures. It is worth noting that the analysis by this team of economists was based on assumptions that, if wrong, underestimated risk of loss from investment in stocks, and still they could not avoid the conclusion that additional government taxation would be required to cover costs of a reform that involved use of a PRA system either as substitute for or supplement to the current Social Security system.[33]

Perhaps the most straightforward approach to covering the transition costs is the one Laurence Kotlikoff and Scott Burns (2004) propose. They estimate that, instead of an asset-swap strategy that has the federal government borrowing money (that is, selling bonds) to pay the transition costs, a 12 percent national sales tax would be both adequate and fiscally sound. Their proposal has the added advantage of being crystal clear; no hidden or unknown future costs lurk in any fine print. It warms the hearts, as one might imagine, of very few politicians. Although Kotlikoff and Burns have hardly been champions of Social Security,[34] their proposed solution points to an interesting comparison. In place of a 12 percent national sales tax, adjusting current FICA taxes, both the income ceiling and the payroll rate, would solve Social Security's impending fiscal problem and preserve the risk protection that gives Social Security an advantage over a PRA system.[35] The disadvantage is that the tax could be reduced as the bulk of the transition from the current Social Security system to the PRA system progressed. However, that would still leave the problem of how to insure against periods of failure in the PRA system. Either the victims of failure would be left to fend for themselves or a government-funded insurance program would be needed as a supplement to the PRA system.

Markets could easily be part of the solution to problems in the distribution and exchange of risks. Indeed, they are just that already, in many different realms of activity, including saving and investment. It is not clear, however, that they are an adequate solution. The evidence indicates that they are not. One of the reasons behind that verdict consists in another category of risk, not market risk but political risk. This is a topic of the next chapter.

═ Chapter 6 ═

Politics and Pensions

R ATHER than acknowledge the connections among the social, political, and economic-technical aspects of the debate over Social
Security, and postemployment income insurance more generally,
discussions have too often been divided between two sorts of issues.
First, we consider the economic-technical matters of financing and fiscal
integrity. Separately, we address matters of political-persuasion, of generating popular support for different proposals as well as governmental
policies concerning income inequality and insurance. This practice is a
common analytic approach to problems, and our own chapters reflect it. It
is important to bear in mind, however, that the debate is political-economic,
not just one and the other, but both simultaneously, interactively, and
in some respects indivisibly. The technically defined economic dimensions are defined, presented, and discussed (to the extent that they are
discussed) within a representational democracy in which the people are
supposed to engage, ask questions, defend their interests, negotiate with
each other, and seek the common good. That sort of exchange, though,
has all but disappeared and few expect much of it to occur on any topic.
What we practice as democracy is a far cry from the invention developed
and practiced by Athenian citizens of the fifth and fourth centuries BCE
(see, for example, Stockton 1990).[1] The difference is great enough that one
can wonder why the same word is applied to both systems of governance. As John Dunn and other observers have emphasized, memories
of the word's heritage can still serve as a resource for present concerns
and future projects, including the prospect of a state apparatus that does
not rely on such "a very large measure of compulsory alienation of judgment on the part of [its] citizens" (2005, 19). That prospect will continue
to depend on the citizens far more than on the professionalized politicians,
whose interests are too often narrowed by self-serving goals. Yet the
greater our cynicism and disengagement, the more we abdicate our role
in this democracy, and the more we are at risk of manipulations.

We draw attention in this chapter to some of the political aspects of the
political-economic debate over Social Security and related programs, both
actual (such as defined-benefit pension plans, the Pension Benefit Guaranty Corporation) and potential (such as proposals of private retirement

143

accounts). What are the attitudes of the public regarding key issues in the Social Security debate? How are property rights being revised, and with what effects? Which moral hazards are important, and to whom? Can a government continue to undermine confidence in its own instruments of trust, without undermining also its own future authority both internally and externally? These are some of the questions that circulate through the following pages.

Public Attitudes

On most issues most of the time, public opinion appears to be rather shallow. How much of that is a reflection of the actual belief structure of the adult public and how much is due to poor measurement technique by those in the business of tracking the public mood is not entirely clear. Certainly the latter fault plays a major part in what we think we know about public opinion, as several observers have been demonstrating (for example, Hibbing and Theiss-Morse 1995). Going one step further, how much of the poor measurement is a deliberate effort to get the results one wants and how much is due to carelessness or ignorance is also not entirely clear, though deliberate deception clearly does play some role. One pertinent illustration is the framing of a question about the future of Social Security. If one wants a result that has the public in favor of changing Social Security, one asks simply that, without context, comparison, or notice of probable consequences. If one wants instead a result that has the public not in favor of changing Social Security, ask them if they think that Social Security should be changed, in part or whole, to a program of private accounts.

Although poor measurement technique does play a considerable role in variation of results, evidence is unfortunately abundant that public opinion itself can in fact be shallow, reflecting either ignorance or misunderstanding, and prone to weakly motivated fluctuations. Philip Converse (1964) argued that when public opinion questions are put to adults, the invited respondents know that they are expected to have intelligent responses, even though often they have thought little or nothing about the issue or issues being addressed. They search the interviewer and other aspects of the interview process (for example, signs of a sponsor) for cues as to what an acceptably intelligent answer might be. Sometimes they think they see those cues. Sometimes also, failing to find any, they fall back on the last, vaguely remembered, seemingly relevant statements on the matter by someone—family member, friend, radio or television commentator, politician, celebrity—with whom they identify. Sometimes in the moment of the interview they subtly negotiate their answers with the interviewer. They tend to choose moderate positions in pre-coded response categories (for example, preferring middle categories). They are sensitive to other, often more immediate or vivid stimuli in their daily activities, which sometimes frame the questions they hear in ways that alter meanings. They are also, as noted earlier, influenced by the way questions are worded, either because they fail to think carefully about included versus excluded phrases in possible and probable versions of a sentence or perhaps because they are impatient to be finished with the interview.

One of the most frequently cited instances of this apparent inconsistency of public opinion has to do with the public's very low regard of institutions of government—Congress, the presidency, the courts, and so forth. Ask a national sample of adults whether they think most members of Congress waste a lot of taxpayers' dollars, and more than four of five say yes.[2] Ask them whether they believe that most members of Congress are honest, and barely half say yes. Ask them whether most members are poorly informed on the issues, and nearly half say yes. Ask them whether most members of Congress spend more time trying to get reelected than doing work in Congress, and four of five say yes. Ask them whether they approve of the job that their specific representative is doing as a legislator in Washington, however, and three of four say yes. Further, as many believe that their House member is doing a very good or good job (as opposed to not a good job) of representing "your views," and nearly as many approve of the job their current House member is doing in taking care of specific needs at home in the district. In the 2004 elections, more than 85 percent of incumbents in the House of Representatives were reelected by more than 60 percent of the vote. Five of the twenty-five House members from Florida were reelected without appearing on the ballot—excused, by state law, because they had no opponents. Many people have little or no respect for the institution, but on the whole, view favorably the members of that institution who represent them.

Similar images of disconnection have been documented for other venues on many occasions, indicating that public confidence in institutional leadership in general, not just in politicians, has diminished. One of the notable features of the disconnection is that it tends to align along a local rather than a global dimension. Seymour Lipset and William Schneider noted this in their analysis of public-opinion data: "Americans repeatedly express optimism and confidence about their own lives and their personal futures, even while decrying the terrible mess the country is in" (1987, 8, 399–406). Assuming that people assess their own situations accurately, their assessments of the situation at large, whether that means the United States as a whole or the world as a whole, tend to manifest a negative bias. In other words, they tend to view other persons' situations as worse than their own. As a result, the average of their assessments of their individual situations is usually higher than the average of their assessments of the country as a whole.[3]

Whether that disconnection has become more pronounced over the decades is not known. One would think that, with advances in information media, the average citizen knows more about people in other localities, and thus people in the United States in general (if not the world in general), than ever before. However, this might well have been counteracted by another change. Citizens have always been relatively experienced in institutions of local government. With the increased flows of information through the mass media, however, they can better see the operations, or at least the media window on those operations, of state and federal governmental institutions, and what they often see is less than impressive—cases of corruption, unlawful conduct, pandering, and inconsistency. The media penchant for negative stories acts as a magnifier. The debacle of the war in southeast Asia and the corruption of a presidential administration swept away the notion of a taken-for-granted trust in government office. As Lipset and Schneider (1987) and others noted, the sharp declines in public confidence began during the 1960s.

"The voices of citizens matter, but understanding what those voices are truly saying is difficult" (Hibbing and Theiss-Morse 1995, 1). Indeed. If John Hibbing and Elizabeth Theiss-Morse are correct in their understanding of those voices (based on their study of both survey results and focus-group interviews), the public is highly dissatisfied with Congress as an institution, precisely because of those institutional features that give it some of the character of a democratic institution. The market-like behavior of trading votes, forming coalitions, often rancorous debates between winners and losers, as well as features such as the monopolizing tendencies by very large, wealthy, powerful interest groups—all are part of that character, as are the professionalization of politics and the enormous expense of campaigns because of media and related costs.[4] In our view, if not in Hibbing's and Theiss-Morse's, these are all features that militate against democratic practices. Politicians themselves have become adept at understanding the shallowness of public opinion, and disregard it increasingly often. Lawrence Jacobs and Robert Shapiro pointed out that "one of the most important developments in American politics" in recent decades is "the widening gulf between politicians' policy decisions and the preferences of the American people toward specific issues" (2000, i). Politicians no longer (if they ever did) pander to public opinion, but instead have learned how to more proficiently mold and manipulate public opinions in desired directions. Their efforts are not always successful. Efforts to reshape the public's view of Social Security are an example of that, at least for now. The list of successes, however, is impressive. The most notorious is perhaps the impeachment of President Clinton, which proceeded despite polls indicating that, although more than six of ten adults condemned Clinton's affair with a White House intern, about the same number also opposed impeachment and approved of his overall job performance. Other examples on the Jacobs and Shapiro list include "campaign finance reform, tobacco legislation, Clinton's proposals in his first budget for an energy levy and a high tax on Social Security benefits (despite his campaign promises to cut middle-class taxes), the North American Free Trade Agreement (at its outset), U.S. intervention in Bosnia, as well as House Republican proposals after the 1994 elections for a 'revolution' in policies toward the environment, education, Medicare, and other issues" (i). At least in the short run, congressional members disregarded public opinion with impunity. The manipulations were successful enough that most of the members whose decisions went against public opinion were nonetheless returned to Congress repeatedly.

The exception regarding Social Security is instructive in its own right. There *are* some issues on which public opinion cannot be so easily maneuvered away from its current center of gravity. It remains to be seen whether the second G. W. Bush administration succeeds eventually in its effort to convince a sufficient proportion of the public to support administration proposals. Considering that Social Security was once called the third rail of domestic politics,[5] it is remarkable that members of Congress have been proposing any major revisions, much less offering support to proposals that, by some accounts, would mean the death of Social Security. It is also mistaken to think that the effort to reshape public opinion away from Social Security has been without effect. As Robert Shiller observed (see chapter 5), a great many people now seemingly take for granted that the federal government can do nothing about the revenue side of the Social Security contract, making it captive to the growing weight of expenditures. What makes this shift even stranger is that it occurred when the federal administration that had been promoting that shift also increased the federal deficit, and at an astonishing rate.

Who Favors Private Accounts?

The answer to the question of who favors private accounts also depends on how it is asked, how it is framed, whether and what alternatives are presented, and other sorts of measurement issues. It is clear that lots of people do favor private accounts, judging from the popularity of IRAs, in regular, roll-over, and Roth versions. Calculations from the U.S. Census Bureau's Survey of Income and Program Participation indicate that nearly one of every five workers aged twenty-one through sixty-four owned some sort of IRA at the end of 2002. The median balance was only $10,000, that is, half had less than that amount invested in IRAs.[6] About half of those with an IRA also participated in a 401(k) retirement plan. Among those whose total family income was $75,000 or more, about 29 percent had an IRA. These participation rates are not large, but they do indicate support for private investment accounts, especially given that the IRAs are funded as additions to the worker's FICA tax liability.

The implicit question answered by IRA participation rates is hardly without context or comparison. First, as noted, any contribution to an IRA is made in addition to FICA taxes. Participation in an IRA is voluntary. It is not provided as a substitute or replacement for Social Security. It allows occasional as well as periodic contributions. It offers considerable tax advantage to qualified tax payers (Howard 1997). Considered within the context of the current Social Security debate, the most important modification that must be made to the question of whether people support IRAs is the issue of a mandate. Few in government, business, academia, or the world of NGOs and lobbies are seriously proposing that Social Security benefits should be either reduced enough to restore solvency or abolished and that workers should be free to either store the money saved from FICA taxes in an IRA-type private account (or some other saving-investment venue) or spend it on a shopping spree, on cosmetic surgery, or perhaps on inoculations for children in poor countries.[7] The assumption is that many people will not save or invest enough to cover their postemployment income needs unless they are forced to do so through some sort of taxation program. Granted, as we saw in chapter 2, politicians are selective in how they choose to apply the word *tax*. Whether called a tax, a user's fee, or a personal contribution, however, the outlay amounts to the same thing. When asking about support for personal retirement accounts, it is therefore important to be clear that these accounts would be mandated, not voluntary, and that the withdrawal of funds would be restricted in ways that are comparable to Social Security. Furthermore, because a system of personal retirement accounts is being proposed as supplement or replacement for Social Security (and the solution to its fiscal problems), a survey question should pose some sort of choice set. "Do you prefer this, or do you prefer that?"

As it happens, such questions have been asked of representative samples of U.S. adults aged eighteen or older, in surveys commissioned by the Pew Research Center for the People and the Press, a nonpartisan public-interest organization. Results from some of the surveys were described briefly in chapter 1; we return to those survey data now, with a more detailed examination of information they contain. A question keyed specifically to the controversial proposal from the second G. W. Bush administration asked whether workers should be able to divert some of the FICA taxes into a private account (see figure 6.1). One might argue that the question is not ideally worded in some respects. For instance, it is silent about proportions—the question of how much "some of their own contributions" is unanswered—and other details of the PRA part of the blended program. It is silent about transition costs and procedures, which are important, though complicated, issues that should be taken

Figure 6.1   Interview Question about Social Security and Private Accounts

---

People have different opinions about how the Social Security system might be changed for the future. When decisions about Social Security's future are being made, which do you think is *more* important?

Keeping Social Security as a program with a *guaranteed* monthly benefit based on a person's earnings during their working life?

(or)

Letting younger workers *decide* for *themselves* how some of their own contributions to Social Security are invested, which would cause their future benefits to be higher or lower depending on how well their investments perform?

Source: Pew Research Center for the People and the Press 2005, question 34.

into account in any careful consideration of alternatives. It is silent on the possibility that a blended program could be designed in a way that not only fails to restore Social Security to fiscal health but instead ensures its demise. The survey designers likely concluded, however, that introducing so much detail into the question would likely overtax most respondents, and were probably correct in doing so. Moreover, each of those details involves variables that would require additional questions (for example, "Would you be in favor of letting younger workers decide, if the proportion diverted to the private account were *this* much?").

Responses to related questions help put the question of privatizing Social Security into perspective. For example, about four in five respondents said that Social Security has been good for America (83 percent of Republicans, 80 percent of Democrats). Strong majorities of each of the three political groupings agreed that the program faces a financial deficit, and roughly three of four believed that some sort of change is needed right away or in the next few years. Respondents disagreed about how the program should change, however. The most favored change (60 percent) was to lift the ceiling on employment earnings subject to the FICA tax. This proposal was supported about equally by young, middle-aged, and older adults, by low-income and high-income households, and by Republicans, Democrats, and Independents. On the other hand, clear majorities opposed three other proposals: increasing the FICA tax rate, reducing the rate at which Social Security benefits grow (the cost-of-living adjustments), and raising the retirement age.

The most controversial proposal was the idea of private accounts. In the September 2004 survey, support for the proposal to introduce private retirement accounts was at 58 percent. Three months later support had perhaps fallen very slightly, to 54 percent, although that difference could have been within a margin of sampling error. From December 2004 to January 2005, support had clearly declined, from 54 to 46 percent, with 38 percent opposed to the idea and the remainder (16 percent) undecided or refusing to answer.[8] Not surprisingly, given that this proposal came from a Republican administration, Republicans were the most in favor (68 percent) and Democrats were the least (29 percent), with Independents in the middle (45 percent). The evidence also indicated that as adults learned more about the proposal they were less likely to favor it. Even in January 2005, only one in five had "heard a lot" about the proposal, up from one in ten a month earlier. Of those who had heard a lot, 43 percent favored the proposal, 49 percent opposed it, and 8 percent were undecided. Of those who had heard little or nothing, 49 percent favored the proposal, 30 percent opposed it, and 21 percent were undecided.

People who were in favor of private accounts most often cited reasons of personal control, accountability, responsibility, and options (38 percent). The next most common set cited a general preference for private rather than governmental institutions (13 percent). By contrast, people who were opposed to private accounts most often cited risk, uncertainty, and possibility of loss (34 percent), with concerns about knowledge and ability of people to save and invest the next most often cited reasons for opposition (16 percent). It is worth noting that 15 percent of the proponents and 12 percent of the opponents either said they could not give a reason or did not answer the question. Further, 7 percent of the proponents said simply that the proposal was good, in answer to the question about reasons for support; similarly, 13 percent of the opponents said simply that the proposal was bad. These people tended to be among the respondents who had not heard much about the proposal and responded merely on the basis of party identification.

The issue, though, is not simply whether people think that Social Security has been a good program or that IRAs or private retirement accounts (PRAs) would be a good idea. Rather, it is whether they think a PRA program should be available, at least to younger workers, as at least a partial alternative to Social Security. If given those alternatives, how does the public respond?

In general, the respondents chose Social Security by a margin of more than two to one. Of the 1,503 respondents, 65 percent said that keeping the guaranteed monthly benefit was more important, and 29 percent said that giving younger workers the option of diverting Social Security contributions into a PRA was more important, even though (or perhaps because) the rate of return would be more volatile. The remaining 6 percent were divided between those who did not answer the question

(4 percent) and those who either could not choose between the two or professed that neither choice was important.

What portrait can be drawn of the 29 percent who thought it more important to give younger workers the opportunity to divert some of their FICA taxes to a PRA? A number of demographic characteristics correlate with that choice, all of them in expected ways, though the relationships are very weak. Men were more likely than women to prefer that choice, as were respondents with more rather than less formal education, respondents with higher rather than lower annual (household) income, and younger rather than older respondents. African Americans were less likely to choose this alternative, as were respondents who were employed full-time rather than part-time or not at all. This last result probably reflects the fact that persons employed full time are more sensitive to the greater investment they have already made in FICA taxes. Each of these relationships is statistically significant (that is, it is probably not due to sampling error). However, as already noted, the relationships are weak. Even if we used all of these relationships to predict which of the respondents selected at random from the sample would support giving younger workers the option of diverting some of their FICA taxes into a PRA, we would be correct only one out of eight times.

The results just reported are presented more systematically in table 6.1, which summarizes the outcome of a logistic regression analysis for each of six combinations of variables as predictors of the choice posed in the interview question.[9] The results reported in the preceding paragraph are bivariate—that is, assess the predictive power of each of the variables one at a time. In table 6.1, they are multivariate. That is, all variables in a given combination of variables (for example, column 1) are assessed simultaneously, so that the predictive power of each variable is assessed relative to (or net of) the predictive power of all other variables in the combination. The first combination (column 1) includes a typical array of basic demographic variables. Columns 2 and 3 add different measures of religious identification to the list. Column 4 adds a measure of political ideology, and columns 5 and 6 complete the list with attitudes regarding the current economic situation. This multivariate approach allows a more realistic assessment of strength of relationship between any given predictor variable and the choice of options.[10]

In column 1, the combination of variables includes those described in the previous paragraph, plus a variable called Income Censored, which means that these respondents (coded 1 on Income Censored) did not answer the question about annual household income. By including this binary (yes-no) variable, we can retain all of the respondents who made a choice between options. Note that the top number (the regression coefficient) for Income Censored is positive. Thus, we are reasonably confident that people who refused to divulge their annual household

Table 6.1   Logit Regressions

	1	2	3	4	5	6
Constant	.781	1.096	.629	.676	.478	1.511
	(.194)	(.210)	(.216)	(.230)	(.235)	(.346)
	.000	.0001	.004	.003	.042	.0001
Age	−.017	−.019	−.018	−.020	−.019	−.019
	(.003)	(.003)	(.003)	(.003)	(.003)	(.004)
	.0001	.0001	.0001	.0001	.0001	.0001
Female	−.683	−.710	−.735	−.696	−.684	−.656
	(.086)	(.087)	(.087)	(.089)	(.090)	(.091)
	.0001	.0001	.0001	.0001	.0001	.0001
Black	−.758	−.836	−.832	−.729	−.584	−.592
	(.153)	(.155)	(.155)	(.157)	(.158)	(.162)
	.0001	.0001	.0001	.0001	.0001	.0001
Education						
< HS diploma	−.971	−1.044	−1.132	−1.169	−1.189	−1.110
	(.180)	(.181)	(.184)	(.187)	(.187)	(.190)
	.0001	.0001	.0001	.0001	.0001	.0001
HS diploma	−.647	−.702	−.725	−.745	−.758	−.755
	(.126)	(.127)	(.127)	(.129)	(.131)	(.133)
	.0001	.0001	.0001	.0001	.0001	.0001
Some college	−.303	−.330	−.370	−.395	−.432	−.425
	(.128)	(.128)	(.129)	(.131)	(.133)	(.135)
	.017	.010	.004	.002	.001	.002
Postgraduate	−.367	−.367	−.376	−.325	−.308	−.280
	(.153)	(.153)	(.154)	(.157)	(.159)	(.162)
	.016	.017	.015	.039	.052	.083
Full-time work	−.391	−.403	−.371	−.353	−.404	−.393
	(.092)	(.093)	(.093)	(.095)	(.096)	(.098)
	.0001	.0001	.0001	.0001	.0001	.0001
Family income	.003	.003	.003	.003	.002	.002
	(.001)	(.002)	(.001)	(.001)	(.001)	(.001)
	.003	.005	.002	.002	.033	.148
Income censored	.339	.365	.394	.393	.307	.233
	(.161)	(.161)	(.163)	(.166)	(.168)	(.173)
	.035	.024	.016	.018	.068	.178
Religion						
Roman Catholic		−.189				
		(.105)				
		.072				
Other		−.455				
		(.113)				
		.0001				
Religion 2			.190	.111	.115	.072
			(.133)	(.135)	(.138)	(.140)
			.153	.411	.405	.607

Table 6.1   *Continued*

	1	2	3	4	5	6
Born-again			.323	.134	.130	.120
			(.096)	(.100)	(.101)	(.103)
			.001	.182	.197	.241
Ideology						
Very conservative				1.089	1.014	.879
				(.189)	(.192)	(.197)
				.0001	.0001	.0001
Conservative				.477	.433	.329
				(.102)	(.104)	(.107)
				.0001	.0001	.002
Liberal				−.219	−.151	−.118
				(.130)	(.132)	(.133)
				.094	.252	.377
Very liberal				−.355	−.293	−.279
				(.231)	(.233)	(.236)
				.124	.207	.237
Jobs are plentiful					.680	.515
					(.091)	(.096)
					.0001	.0001
Economy today						
Good						−.566
						(.244)
						.020
Only fair						−1.206
						(.248)
						.0001
Poor						−.938
						(.273)
						.001
Cox & Snell R^2	.070	.076	.079	.098	.115	.131
Nagelkerke R^2	.099	.107	.111	.138	.163	.184
Percent correct prediction:						
Letting workers	12.6	15.5	18.2	23.5	30.2	33.7
Keeping same	95.6	95.7	94.7	93.4	92.5	92.1
All cases	70.0	71.0	71.0	71.8	73.2	73.9
Base n	1405	1405	1391	1391	1391	1378

Source: Authors' calculations.
Note: Religion 2 is coded 1 if Protestant, Roman Catholic, Mormon, and Other; else, 0. Family income is for previous year. Income censored is coded 1 for all cases of don't know or no answer. Reference category for education is baccalaureate; for full-time work, part-time or not employed; for religion, protestant; for ideology, moderate; for economy today, excellent. The cell entries are, from top, the regression coefficient, the standard error of the estimate (in parentheses), and the probability value associated with the t-test.

income (and in general, not just in this survey, many people are reluctant to do so) were more likely to agree that younger workers should be able to choose the PRA option. This result is consistent with the fact that people who refuse to divulge income data tend to have higher incomes.

The results in column 1 generally confirm what we said above about the bivariate relationships. The one clear exception is formal education. We summarized the bivariate relationship by saying that respondents with more rather than less education were likelier to choose the PRA option. That statement must be amended in light of the results in table 6.1. Although it remains generally true that the likelihood of supporting the PRA option increases as one moves up the educational hierarchy, the direction of that relationship reverses at the highest educational level. Recall that the reference category is baccalaureate degree. Persons with postgraduate education were less likely to support the PRA option than those with a bachelor's degree. Any explanation we might offer for that difference would be ad hoc, but it is tempting to speculate that the post-graduate respondents joined those with some college or less because they had less confidence in either the people proposing the program or the ability of the average adult to manage his or her own private retirement account (or perhaps both).

There is a hint of the same difference of effect in the figures for income. The greatest support for letting workers invest in a PRA occurred not among those with highest income but among those whose incomes ranged from about $75,000 to $100,000. This curvilinear result did not hold up in the multivariate analysis, however, suggesting that it was an information effect (that is, the education variable) more than a consumption effect. In any case, the relationship was not all that strong. Whereas 40 percent of the respondents in the $75,000 to $100,000 range and 30 percent of those with incomes above $100,000 agreed that workers should be at liberty to invest in a PRA, the same was true of 20 percent of those with incomes below $20,000. The motivations for these responses cannot be determined from these data. A number of studies, though, have shown that proposed reforms involving private accounts will be regressive and thus increase inequality, whereas Social Security has been mildly progressive (see, for example, Deaton, Gourinchas, and Paxson 2000).[11] We know that individuals do not have the same risks in earnings or in returns on assets; those risks tend to accumulate over time; and Social Security redistributes risk in a way that reduces the transmission of individual risk into inequality. Perhaps the respondents were agreeing with the position that Martin Feldstein (1998a) argued, in conjunction with a PRA system—namely, that an increase in inequality is not important, as long as the poor do not become poorer.[12]

In column 2, we added to the combination of variables a set of three terms that denote the respondent's broad religious confession: Roman

Catholic, Protestant (the reference category), or Other. Finer discriminations of religious confession could have been made (for example, Jew, Muslim, Mormon, Protestant), but the categories either contained too few cases to analyze separately or did not add significant information to the analysis. The result tells us that Roman Catholics were probably neither more nor less likely than Protestants to choose the PRA option, but that Others were almost surely less likely to choose that option than Protestants and therefore also Roman Catholics.

In column 3, the categories of religious confession are redefined in order to add to the combination of variables a term that singles out respondents who defined themselves as born-again Christian. Because this designation is automatically no for some of the categories of religion (Jew, Moslem, and so on), as well as for the respondents who said none to the question about religious confession, a variable named Religion 2 was defined accordingly; it is coded 1 for respondents whose religion recognizes the born again distinction. The result for column 3 indicates that the born-again Christian respondents were more likely to choose the PRA option; however, once we control for political ideology, this preference is not significant.

In column 4, we added categories for respondent's choice of self-description in conventional terms of political ideology. The reference category is moderate. These results indicate that people who described themselves as very conservative (5.7 percent of the total) or as conservative (29.3 percent) were more likely than self-defined moderates (41.9 percent) to support the PRA option. On the other hand, respondents who preferred the labels liberal (14.8 percent) or very liberal (3.9 percent) were neither more nor less likely than moderates to choose the PRA option.

As noted, once differences in political ideology are taken into account, the distinction between born-again Christian respondents and those who said they did not consider themselves to be born-again Christians loses its power to discriminate preference for the PRA option. The regression coefficient remains positive, but is no longer large enough to generalize (with acceptable confidence) to the population. Born-again Christians, whether Protestant or Roman Catholic, were somewhat more likely to put themselves on the conservative end of the political spectrum; still, roughly 50 percent said they were moderate or (seldom) liberal in political ideology, which contrasts to 65 percent of the Protestants, and nearly 75 percent of the Roman Catholics, who did not regard themselves as born-again Christians. Thus, though the born-again religious ideology is certainly relevant to a variety of issues commonly designated cultural values, it is neither identical to political ideology nor (at least as of January 2005) a good predictor of preference for giving younger workers the option of diverting FICA taxes into a private retirement account.

Differences in political ideology were about as strong as differences in formal education in predicting response to the choice question. Table 6.2

Table 6.2   Political Ideology

	VC	C	M	L	VL	total	n^*
Gender							
Women	6.1	27.1	43.4	18.6	4.9	100.1	739
Men	5.4	32.0	43.8	14.8	4.1	100.1	699
Race-ethnicity							
White, non-hisp	6.1	31.8	42.9	15.2	4.1	100.1	1132
Black, non-hisp	7.0	20.1	46.8	23.1	3.0	100.0	142
Asian, non-hisp	0.0	22.2	53.3	24.4	0.0	99.9	18
Other, non-hisp	7.5	21.7	49.2	16.7	5.0	100.1	51
Hispanic	0.8	26.4	41.5	20.4	9.9	100.0	83
Education							
< HS dip	8.2	33.3	36.5	15.4	6.6	100.0	100
HS diploma/GED	6.7	30.4	46.6	13.1	3.2	100.0	386
post-HS trade	7.1	35.7	40.8	9.2	7.1	99.9	42
Some college	5.5	28.5	43.8	17.3	4.8	99.9	386
Baccalaureate	3.9	31.2	42.0	17.9	5.1	100.1	299
Postgraduate	3.7	20.7	45.2	26.7	3.7	100.0	219
Marital status							
Married	6.2	33.3	43.1	14.3	3.2	100.1	842
Divorced	5.1	26.3	48.6	14.5	5.4	99.9	180
Separated	0.0	21.1	38.2	30.3	10.5	100.1	31
Widowed	8.0	31.6	47.6	9.8	3.1	100.1	125
Never married	4.6	21.8	41.7	25.0	7.0	100.1	255
Employment							
Full-time	2.9	28.9	46.0	18.0	4.2	100.0	735
Part-time	10.9	26.3	37.5	20.5	4.8	100.0	173
Not employed	7.8	31.2	42.5	13.7	4.8	100.0	527
Family income (000s $)							
< 10	14.2	25.9	37.1	16.2	6.6	100.0	78
10 to 20	5.3	24.8	48.9	16.4	4.6	100.1	134
20 to 30	6.3	32.2	40.2	17.8	3.5	100.0	179
30 to 40	7.0	32.7	42.3	13.7	4.4	100.1	161
40 to 50	5.8	31.0	42.7	16.4	4.0	99.9	139
50 to 75	4.6	26.5	46.1	18.1	4.6	99.9	238
75 to 100	2.8	31.9	46.4	14.5	4.4	100.0	163
100 to 150	4.4	25.3	43.7	19.2	7.4	100.0	123
150 +	1.4	30.1	47.3	17.8	3.4	100.0	83
No answer	6.2	34.0	39.0	18.1	2.7	100.0	140
Present financial situation							
Excellent	9.1	33.3	34.4	17.2	6.0	100.0	161
Good	6.1	33.1	43.0	12.9	4.8	99.9	634
Fair	3.2	26.0	48.3	20.0	2.4	99.0	459
Poor	8.9	22.8	40.0	20.5	7.8	100.0	166

Table 6.2   *Continued*

	VC	C	M	L	VL	total	*n**
Financial situation year hence							
Improve a lot	9.2	36.7	35.4	14.8	3.9	100.0	144
Improve some	4.6	31.7	43.6	16.7	3.4	100.0	788
Same	6.3	26.9	46.1	15.0	5.8	100.0	228
A little worse	4.5	18.5	48.9	20.1	8.0	100.0	198
A lot worse	13.3	21.4	39.8	19.4	6.1	100.0	46
Political party preference							
Republican	12.1	50.3	31.9	4.6	1.2	100.1	500
Independent	2.0	21.4	53.1	17.9	5.7	100.1	422
Democrat	2.9	17.4	46.0	26.9	6.8	100.0	455
No preference	4.5	27.0	39.3	22.5	6.7	100.0	41
US Response to Tsunami							
More than fair	9.4	35.0	43.5	9.8	2.2	99.9	515
Fair share	3.3	28.4	47.1	16.8	4.4	100.0	693
Less than fair	1.9	17.5	34.7	34.4	11.5	100.0	150
Age: mean	49.4	47.7	45.9	39.7	39.7		
SD	19.2	17.6	17.1	16.6	16.7		

Source: Authors' tabulations.
Note: VC = Very Conservative, C = Conservative, M = Moderate, L = Liberal, and VL = Very Liberal.
*unweighted sample *n*.

offers insight into the ideology categories by comparing them in terms of various other characteristics. Overall, support for letting younger workers divert FICA money into private accounts ranged from 50 percent among the very conservative to 37.4 percent among the conservative, 25.6 percent among the moderate, 21.1 percent among the liberal, and 17.2 percent among the very liberal respondents.

Perhaps the most notable conclusion to be drawn from table 6.2 is that while there were some differences in the distribution of ideological labels in terms of basic demographic variables such as gender, race-ethnicity, formal education, and marital or employment status, the differences were generally quite small. One often reads or hears about how sharply polarized the adult U.S. public is on any number of issues of the day. Such polarization does exist on several hot button issues, such as abortion, evolution, and respect for human differences, but it is driven mainly from the extremes of U.S. culture. The fact that the ideological labels relate so poorly to variables such as formal education, employment status, family income, and even perceptions of the state of one's present and future financial situation is consistent with the claim that the issues that today drive such ideological distinctions are not economic or financial self-interest but cultural—that is, chiefly beliefs, and especially beliefs with high emotional and cathectic content. These issues are often labeled issues of cultural values. The intended distinction can be superficial and misleading if it is taken to mean the alignment of conservatism with the market model, religious evangelism or intolerance of human diversity, and liberalism with the opposite beliefs and practices. In fact, liberalism has a long heritage of promoting applications of the market model and especially its core value, the liberty of the individual. Conservatism has as often voiced caution about corrosive effects of the market model. Neither political view has had a monopoly on religious evangelism or on a preference to respect others' privacy of belief. Rather, the labels were long ago hijacked in the perennial market for electoral advantage. They now have only the thinnest of links to their historical roots. Insofar as the contrast between conservative and liberal now invokes a debate at the level of cultural values, it aligns far more with the culture of fear and loathing that we described in chapter 1. Insofar as it is religious-ideological, it harnesses the enormous cathectic energy of Manichaean dualism,[13] which is as potent in secular as in religious dressing. "You are either with me—and thus on the side of the Good, God, Light—or you are against me—and thus on the side of Evil, Satan, Darkness" remains a potent rallying cry in a culture of fear and loathing. Neither conservatism nor liberalism (nor the blend of the two known as libertarianism), and far older than modern capitalism, this ideology expresses the coercive simplicities of the demagogue, who, contrary to the modern market model, sees only permanent winners and permanent losers.

The largest proportion of respondents describing themselves as very conservative or conservative occurred at low and middle levels of family income: 40 percent among those with incomes below $10,000 and 38 percent among those with incomes from $20,000 to $50,000, versus 30 to 31 percent among those with incomes above $100,000. A politics designed to exploit the energy of a Manichaean world view quickly tunes in to reservoirs of fear and loathing that cannot or have not found expression in more constructive avenues. Even a party whose practical programs will make the material conditions of low-income people worse, relatively if not absolutely, can nonetheless gain their allegiance by making them feel better about themselves, for example, as important warriors in a contest of good against evil.

The sharpest division occurred in connection with political party identification, of course, reflecting the polarization of party politics. Whereas only 6 percent of the respondents who were Republicans described themselves as liberal or very liberal, the corresponding figure for Independents was about 24 percent and for Democrats about 34 percent.

More informative is the next panel of table 6.2, which compares the categories of political ideology by respondent's view of U.S. generosity in response to the huge tsunami disaster that struck coastal areas of southern and southeastern Asia in 2004. The question asked, "compared with other major countries, do you think the U.S. government has given more than its fair share to the relief effort, less than its fair share, or about its fair share?"[14] This question could very well have been an instance of a problem that analysts of attitude surveys often face, discussed earlier in this chapter: respondents who know little or nothing about the topic nonetheless responding to the expectation that they should have an intelligent response. In assessing answers, we have no way of knowing whether the respondents had actually heard about the disaster in question. But let's ignore that problem and move to the next level of assumption. The question assumed that the respondent knew how much the U.S. government had in fact donated to the relief effort, necessary information if the respondent were to evaluate whether it was too much, not enough, or about right. Did the respondents know those figures? Probably not. Moreover, the evaluative question was expressly stated as a relative evaluation—the U.S. government relative to other major countries. Did the respondents know how much other countries had donated? That's even less likely than knowing the size of the U.S. contribution. In fact, Washington generally donates far less than many other wealthy countries in GDP-proportionate terms. Did the respondents know that comparative fact? Perhaps more likely this than either of the others, but probably a substantial portion of the respondents did not, or assumed otherwise. Given that probable lack of information on which to base the requested evaluation, one might expect a high proportion of the respondents to say that they didn't know, or words to that effect. People generally do not like to admit they don't know the answer to a factual question, and in this case, rather than being asked to report the factual basis for their opinions, they were asked to simply evaluate (state an opinion about) the U.S. response in terms of fairness. For some respondents, labeling as fair whatever Washington's response had been was a simple matter of country loyalty. Whatever we did, it must have been what was called for.

It is this latter aspect that makes the question of particular interest for present purposes. Only 6 percent of the respondents said that they did not know in response to the evaluative question; some of them might have been saying also that they had no opinion on the matter, or preferred not to divulge it.[15] The plurality of respondents (48 percent), and the majority of those who chose one of the three offered response categories, chose the middle category, saying that the United States had given roughly its fair share. This was mainly an opinion, either a way of saying "my country usually does the right thing" or a veiled admission of ignorance about the factual aspects of the question (that is, "I really don't know, so I'll guess somewhere in the middle"), or a little of both. Of the minority who did not sit in the middle, more than three times as many said "more" as said "less than its fair share" (36 versus 10 percent). If our suspicion is correct, and these responses are mainly expressions not of factual knowledge but of political opinion parading as factual knowledge, they provide some rationale for the often-noted stinginess or prudence, depending on your point of view, of the U.S. government's contributions to foreign aid. As the panel in table 6.2 indicates, the polarization is about as sharp on the aid question as on the party identification question (and with greater clarity at the extremes).

We assume that the conservative respondents were neither more nor less likely than the liberal or moderate respondents to know how much money Washington had promised in relief of the tsunami victims, but they were much more likely to think that the amount was too much, whereas the liberal respondents were much more likely to think that the amount was too little. Fully 60 percent of the very conservative, versus 16 percent of the very liberal, respondents thought the United States had committed more than its fair share. Two percent of the very conservative, but 35 percent of the very liberal, respondents thought it had committed less than its fair share.

Further insight can be gleaned from table 6.3. The same survey commissioned by the Pew Research Center asked respondents to assess how well a number of institutional systems were working. Three response categories were provided: "works pretty well," "needs major changes," and "needs to be completely rebuilt." With regard to Social Security, the most notable conclusion is that the ideological categories differed little. About half thought that the system works pretty well. Liberals were about as likely as conservatives to think that it needs to be completely rebuilt or at least needs major changes. By contrast, with regard to the health-care system and the education system, two institutional arenas that have been under fire from many quarters in recent years, conservatives were more likely than liberals to be satisfied.[16] Granted, there was undoubtedly a lot of unmeasured variation in the focus of respondents when considering this or that system, and at least some of that variation probably correlated with political ideology. For instance, liberals were about as unlikely as conservatives to think that the tax system works pretty well. It would not be surprising that the dissatisfied liberals focused on, say, the regressive character of the tax system, and the dissatisfied conservatives on some of its progressive features. That same sort of unmeasured variation could be hidden in the response distributions for the Social Security system in table 6.3. Given that the controversy over Social Security in recent years has been defined largely in terms of a constellation of interests involving privatization, rates of return, and fiscal stability, it seems likely that the distribution of responses regarding Social Security can be taken more nearly at face value than the other distributions.

Returning to table 6.1 and columns 5 and 6, we can also see that the impact of political ideology of the choice of options was barely affected

Table 6.3   What Works Well and What Doesn't, by Ideology

	VC	C	M	L	VL
Social Security system					
Works pretty well	51.8	46.6	47.0	46.8	46.6
Major changes	36.9	34.3	35.7	33.2	38.3
Completely rebuilt	10.1	15.8	14.7	16.3	5.3
DK, NA	1.2	3.3	2.6	3.7	9.8
Health care system					
Works pretty well	40.0	33.4	24.6	17.5	28.0
Major changes	44.1	48.4	54.0	50.9	41.7
Completely rebuilt	11.8	16.3	20.7	27.5	30.3
DK, NA	4.1	1.8	0.6	4.1	0.0
Education system					
Works pretty well	33.7	43.5	37.5	25.5	27.1
Major changes	47.9	42.2	44.5	54.2	44.4
Completely rebuilt	16.0	12.9	15.6	19.8	28.6
DK, NA	2.4	1.4	2.4	0.6	0.0
Tax system					
Works pretty well	40.8	51.6	51.8	49.2	35.3
Major changes	34.9	28.3	29.6	32.5	27.1
Completely rebuilt	17.2	17.0	15.7	14.8	27.1
DK, NA	7.1	3.2	3.0	3.5	10.5
Legal system					
Works pretty well	35.1	41.5	48.1	48.8	35.3
Major changes	42.3	41.9	34.9	32.3	39.1
Completely rebuilt	16.7	14.8	13.1	15.4	23.3
DK, NA	6.0	1.8	3.8	3.5	2.3
unweighted n	86	441	630	223	58

Source: Authors' tabulations.

by the respondent's perception of the availability of jobs or of the state of the economy in general. These two variables did relate to the likelihood of agreeing that younger workers should have the PRA option. Respondents who thought jobs were plentiful were more likely to support the proposal, as were those who believed the economy was in excellent shape rather than in good, only fair, or poor shape. Both of these relationships are what one would expect. Evidence of the sort of optimism that Dimson, Marsh, and Staunton documented within the specific context of stock-market behavior is considerable (2002). As shown in figure 6.2, respondents' expectations of future conditions, especially for their own personal economic situations, were decidedly positive, even if they thought present conditions were not so good. Moreover, whatever their assessments of

Figure 6.2   Comparison of Current Assessments with Expected Direction of Change

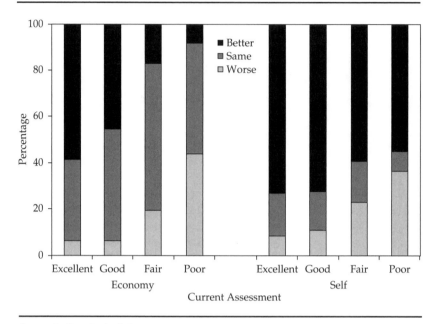

Source: Authors' calculations.

present conditions of self or economy as a whole, the optimists were more likely to support the PRA option for younger workers.

It is notable, however, that controlling for assessments of economic conditions (as in columns 5 and 6 of table 6.1, for instance) makes very little if any difference in the impact of the political ideology variable. This finding is consistent with other observations that adults in unfavorable economic or financial circumstances are often about as likely as their wealthier counterparts—and sometimes more likely—to support public policies that add to their economic disadvantage and to their wealthier compatriots' benefits. Although such behavior might be described as reflecting a false consciousness in a deeper, structural sense, at the surface of personal experience it is clear that the people who do behave against their own economic interests to the benefit of the wealthy often indicate that they know what they are doing. Moreover, just to drive the point home, they often justify those decisions by invoking some set of cultural values.

Unfortunately, the Pew survey, like virtually all surveys on the Social Security debate, was silent about issues involved in the procedures and costs of transition from the current system to an alternative that includes some sort of PRA option. It might be interesting to hear the distribution of public opinion on those issues. More important, it would surely contribute to the education of the public, if that is possible through survey questions. Unfortunately also, the very people who had been proposing the PRA alternative to the current Social Security were conspicuously silent about the costs and procedures related to the transition. In fact, one of the serious limitations of the Pew survey, and the preceding analyses of those survey data, stems from the fact that the question about choice of options, precisely because it was keyed to the proposal advertised by the G. W. Bush administration, was probably corrupted by a suspicion that one of the hidden motives of the proposal was to hasten the end of the Social Security system in any form. After all, if Social Security is in serious fiscal straits because too little revenue is coming in as the volume of expenditures increases, it might seem unreasonable to propose that we can save Social Security by reducing its revenue flow even more by encouraging younger workers to divert some of their FICA taxes into private accounts. Yet proponents of the proposal were persistently quiet in response to the request, "Please tell us how that would save Social Security?" Is it possible that, had citizens been presented with a proposal that demonstrated compatibility between the use of private accounts (as a supplement to or a gradual replacement of the current system) and preservation of the social-insurance features of the current system (at least until the same function could be fulfilled by other means), a larger proportion of the respondents to a survey question like the one featured in the Pew survey would have voiced support for the PRA option? Perhaps. We cannot answer this counterfactual question, and even it omits transaction costs. The same reasoning also suggests, however, that the responses in favor of the PRA option in the data just analyzed were made despite the ambiguity or uncertainty pertaining to costs and procedures of transition and suspicions of hidden motives. Or perhaps for some the choice reflects insight into those motives.

An Ownership Society: Slogan or Reality?

Walt Whitman expressed an already popular sentiment when he said that democracy "looks with suspicious, ill-satisfied eye upon the very poor, the ignorant, and on those out of business. She asks for men and women with occupations, well-off, owners of houses and acres, and with cash in the bank—and with some cravings for literature, too; and must have them, and hastens to make them" (1871/1982, 950–1). The idea of ownership had been socialized, was still being socialized. Not only barons and bishops could own land and fine buildings and have money in the bank, not only men had that right, and not only persons of European background had that right. These last two inclusions were still being contested, hotly contested in some quarters, but Whitman's confidence was that an inclusiveness of democracy would prevail. The Constitution began as a privilege of property ownership, but it was full of promises of the free pursuit of happiness (that is to say, commerce) and opportunities of success—even to pursue the fine arts. Whitman had certainly grasped that ownership is an economic category, and his confidence was that economic forces, those great energies of commerce among diverse people, would gradually press for more and more inclusion. He also knew, however, that ownership is fundamentally a political category, a matter of property rights. He knew that fundamentally economic markets trade in property rights. His confidence was that politics would follow the economic exuberance of his still new, and reunifying, nation-state of states. Democracy must have it, and will make it. Perhaps only intuitively, Whitman understood the intimacy between a democracy of the marketplace and the political conditions of citizenship in a representative-democratic polity.

When Social Security was being constructed during the 1930s, it was deliberately designed as a program in which every worker, ultimately every citizen, would participate, rather than as one for the poor and near-poor only. It was designed to be not a welfare program but an insurance program. The architects of the Social Security Act of 1935 knew that the core provisions of social insurance against old-age poverty should emphasize individual ownership of accounts, because they understood that a sense of ownership in every citizen would give them a stake in the future well-being of the common good. The architects also understood that, to gain business support for, or at least acquiescence in, the insurance program, individual ownership would be vital.

There is more than a touch of irony in the fact that recent federal administrations, less friendly to broad-based social insurance programs, have sometimes tried to build support for decisions and actions that erode or eventually displace such programs by arguing that "America is an ownership society, and that's why Americans prefer my proposal of X, Y, and Z." Well, individuals who are enrolled in Social Security do indeed own their rights to postemployment income (whether in retirement or because of disability), unless a federal administration changes the contract and takes those rights away. As the economist and Nobel prize winner Robert Shiller wrote in his commentary on the paper by Feldstein, Ranguelova, and Samwick, there is a striking "sense in which the Social Security system has been presented to us as promising future benefits but not future contributions" (Feldstein, Ranguelova, and Samwick 2001, 86). It is as if someone has dictated that the contribution side cannot be fixed, so the benefit side will only exhaust the system, leaving an empty shell.

In the industrial sectors of heavy manufacturing (for example, automotive production), generations of U.S. workers purchased postemployment income insurance with their own dollars, in the form of deferred compensation packages that had been organized through negotiations between the workers' unions and the firms' managerial employees. The labor contracts governing current working conditions, including wage rates and health benefits (for often very dangerous jobs), were also contracts across time, something like the more implicit contracts that, in an earlier time, bound grandparents to their children and grandchildren, and vice versa. The principal difference was that these new, more explicit contracts were designed to preserve each worker's liberty and relative independence even during those years when infirmities, the erosive effects of decades of very hard labor in very difficult surroundings, made continued employment increasingly unlikely to impossible. Formally free to accept or reject negotiated contracts defining the terms of labor and compensation, the workers agreed to assign part of their employment earnings to an investment fund managed by specialists contracted by management. These specialists were typically banks and investment houses. Management then realized that the specialists had been risk averse, with the result that the company's investment fund—known otherwise as its defined-benefit pension plan—was not growing as quickly as management thought it could. If the fund were to grow more rapidly, the company could reduce the amount of its contribution while still covering future liabilities.

As U.S. manufacturing lost its ability to compete with new, more advanced manufacturing firms in other countries, firms have shrunk their payrolls, merged with or been acquired by other firms, and in many instances entered bankruptcy protection against creditors. The credits against which they seek shelter include those future obligations of past labor contracts. Sometimes, defined benefit plans were replaced by defined contribution plans; this strategy transferred to individual accounts the sum necessary to generate the benefits to which workers were currently entitled. Because expected benefits in DB plans grew most quickly in the years immediately before retirement, older workers found they were unable to grow their DC accounts quickly enough to preserve the level of benefits at retirement they had been promised under the DB plans. When bankruptcy occurred, the bankruptcy in and of itself did not abrogate the contract. It can in principle nonetheless severely reduce the size and terms of liability, leaving workers with partly emptied rights to their deferred compensation.

Perhaps the message has been that the phrase ownership society should not be taken too seriously after all. Markets must respect property rights, which are necessary condition and currency of market transactions. Market transactions may diminish the value of the property rights of an uninformed, inexperienced or otherwise vulnerable market player. Nevertheless, these transactions depend on and therefore honor the right itself. The freedom of contract, and of players, is primarily formal, not substantive. It is in the realm of politics, electoral politics and governance, that property rights are optional. Even before the Orwellian world of doublespeak, it was clear that property rights were no better than the politicians and governmental officials who would (or would not) respect them.

The legal as well as political record makes quite clear that the composition of property rights, or ownership, changes from time to time. As very recent illustration, consider the case, Kelo et al. v. City of New London et al. The city of New London (Connecticut) had proposed an urban-redevelopment project that involved ninety acres of waterfront land, some of which included private homeowners. The plan was to promote the land for new office buildings, upscale housing, a marina, and special-purpose facilities near a $300 million research center being built by the pharmaceutical company Pfizer. The plan promised an infusion of jobs and capital spending for an area that had reeled from economic setbacks, including loss of the U.S. Naval Undersea Warfare Center and its 1,500 jobs. Several of the residential homeowners resisted sale of their lower-income housing, so the city initiated legal proceedings under the power of eminent domain. Filing suit in state court, the homeowners argued that the city's action amounted to a violation of the takings clause of the Fifth Amendment to the Constitution. The Connecticut Supreme Court upheld the city's plan. The homeowners then appealed to the U.S. Supreme Court, which, in a 5 to 4 ruling announced on June 23, 2005 (No. 04-108), upheld the state decision (268 Conn. 1, 843 A. 2d 500), on the grounds that the city's plan did qualify as a public use within the meaning of the takings clause.

Rights to particular property have always been open to renegotiations, and even in specific cases the renegotiations take place across the balance between efficiency and fairness. Much depends on which property, or whose property, is at stake. Owners of expensive beachfront real estate are better able to afford flood insurance and more likely to receive special federal relief when a hurricane hits than were the residents of the Lower Ninth Ward of New Orleans after the devastating hurricane of 2005. Property rights more generally are often up for renegotiation. These more general cases almost always involve shifting current equilibriums in the trade-offs between efficiency and fairness. For instance, federal administrations that disapprove of broadly based social insurance programs such as Social Security nonetheless support narrowly based social insurance programs such as farm subsidies, the percentage depletion allowance, and the intangible drilling cost deduction for certain producers of fossil fuels and uranium, which draw from tax accounts to protect the interests of a few against failure. Of course, those same politicians and government officials prefer not to call these and similar other narrowly based programs social insurance. Risk is being distributed from the few to the many—that is, from the oil companies, farmers, and so on to the general taxpayers. That, though, does not count as social insurance but is instead known as investing in our future or as investing in America.

Political Trust, Political Risk

During all the debates about Social Security's future, little attention has been given to a number of important political risks. As noted in the preceding section, one of the largest of these risks is the likelihood that federal administrations will withdraw enforcement support of existing implicit contracts and lobby hard for renegotiations. John McHale (2001) has demonstrated that this risk has already been realized with regard to Social Security systems in a number of countries, including the United States, and his expectation that forced renegotiations of contracts have only just begun is certainly plausible. The economic risk of inadequate postemployment income for large segments of the population has to be covered somehow. It has become clear that the two-period model used for decades to analyze the distribution of that risk—one period of paid employment followed by a period of postemployment income, with contemporaneous transfers of money—gives a misleading picture of the problem not simply because a larger proportion of the population (that is, the Baby Boomers) will be entering the second period at any given time. The picture is misleading because it assumes a distinct sequencing of the periods, when in fact for purposes of risk distribution they heavily overlap. This means that the risk of inadequate postemployment income cannot be shifted to another, more risk-tolerant future group of workers. It can be shifted contemporaneously, within cohorts of workers, between those who succeed less well at generating income and private personal saving-investment and those who succeed very well at those tasks. However, these transfers have become increasingly unpalatable in terms of certain political risks, because ideological battles over the proper ethics and morality of what it means to be a mature, responsible member of society have reinvigorated issues such as moral hazard. The main alternatives are, as McHale describes them, "large-scale cuts in benefits to the currently or soon to be retired" (which is rarely considered), "prefund (using current taxes) future defined-benefit [that is, Social Security] obligations, or substitute privately prefunded defined-contribution accounts for these obligations" (2001, 278). The last two options force current workers to pay for themselves what future workers were to have paid for them, but whereas that shift is transparent when current tax liability is used as the vehicle, it is more obscure when the privatized accounts option is used. Obviously politicians prefer the more obscure route, especially when they ride back to office on slogans of "No new taxes!"

Political risk attaches to current promises to pay future as well as present retirees within the Social Security system, but also to any investment-based system of private accounts. Imagine the political pressures from multiple directions that would be brought to bear on investment decisions by the managers of private accounts, whether the managers were employees of a government agency or of a private firm contracted by government agency. How likely, under those circumstances, would investment risks be managed efficiently in a financial as opposed to an electoral sense (see, for example, MaCurdy and Shoven 2001, 30; McHale 2001)? Given the huge size of the total monetary value of the private accounts, investment decisions would have major impact on the general market, and many special interests (including the campaigns and ideological interests of politicians and political action organizations) would be energetic in efforts to sway the decisions. This possibility raises a number of questions. Would investments in companies that directly or indirectly involve uses of biogenetic cloning or stem-cell techniques, for example, be allowed? What about publishers whose biology textbooks give emphasis to scientific theories of evolution? Or a company that makes or retails automatic firearms, or dumps tons of pollutants into the atmosphere of a nearby river or bay? What about companies that give large sums of money to organizations not on the approved list maintained by the party in power? Would investment decisions become an instrument of foreign policy?

Whereas the political risks stemming from specific interests would constitute one type of management problem, another, more general risk would be built into the management process itself. The accounts manager, whether government agency or contracted private firm, would tend to be conservative in investment decisions in order to minimize the risk of financial loss. Not wanting to be blamed when things go wrong, decisions about portfolio composition and perhaps decisions about timing (when to take profits in stocks, when and how much to move into bonds, for example) would favor aversion of risk of loss over tolerance of risk of gain. That preference tends to be typical of individuals when acting on their own account (see, for example, Kahneman and Tversky 2000). Imagine how much stronger that preference would be when the agent is responsible for huge accounts representing so many people. It is well to remember, as mentioned, that corporate firms such as General Motors sought to bring in-house the investment decisions in their own pension funds because of the banks' so-called overly conservative investment strategies.

Corporate pension funds have been a relatively new conduit—added to banks, insurance companies, and old-line investment firms (for example, Merrill Lynch, Fidelity, and the like, most of which then established their own funds)—for siphoning huge sums of capital from huge numbers of relatively small savers and investors. That is, what was sold to employees as a deferred compensation package of postemployment benefits was also a mechanism for winnowing relatively small sums of investment asset into concentrated pools that could be used for corporate ends. This means of capital accumulation for purposes of corporations' investments in their own development and growth has been an important marginal addition to other sources of capital accumulation.

It is easy to overestimate the influence of general pension funds because of their great size in valuation and membership. The stocks owned by a fund are typically highly diversified across companies, which dilutes the fund's influence on any given company. Even more, pension funds concentrate on large-capitalization companies, and these firms rarely obtain more than 2 to 3 percent of their capital financing for new investment from the sale of stocks. The vast majority of their new investment is financed from current revenues; more is gained from the issuing of corporate bonds, usually, than from stock sales.

Corporate pension funds have become another matter, however, in their influence both on the mother company and on their employees' future well-being. Many grew to be very large in valuation, even larger in some instances than the market value of the firm. General Motors is a case in point. Depending on which day of the week and whose accountant is running the totals, GM's pension funds (it has more than one) are collectively worth anywhere from two and a half to six times the market value of GM.[17] Increasingly often, corporate pension funds have been underfunded, leaving large deficits on the books of future liabilities. Various accounting maneuvers obscured those deficits until a wave of corporate bankruptcies exposed the shortfalls and corrupt practices behind them. One of the components of the Employees' Retirement Income Security Act (ERISA) of 1974 authorized formation of the Pension Benefit Guaranty Corporation (PBGC), a quasi-governmental insurer of corporate pension plans and supposedly funded by insurance premiums paid the PBGC.[18] Both ERISA and the PBGC were responses to increasing concerns about the financial health of pension accounts, concerns stimulated in part by discoveries that corporate management had been raiding pension accounts of their assets (for a nicely contextualized review, see Blackburn 2002, 101–72). Through the latter half of the 1990s, the PBGC had accumulated a modest cushion of net assets, but conditions deteriorated rapidly after 2000. Near the end of 2005, the PBGC's total liabilities exceeded its total assets by $23.1 billion (see the PBGC's *2005 Annual Report*, 4). New defaults on corporate pension plans were lurking on the horizon, given that several very large firms—such as Delta Airlines, Northwest Airlines, General Motors, and Ford Motor Company—looked increasingly as if they might settle accounts through bankruptcy courts.[19]

The PBGC had become the trustee and administrator of nearly 3,500 corporate pension plans that had failed as of year-end 2004.[20] During the first nine months of 2005, it terminated another 120 plans, with an average funded ratio of about 50 percent, in the single-employer program. With changing circumstances of competition for product markets and low-cost labor, companies have increasingly sought to discontinue their defined-benefit pension plans, which carry funding obligations far into future periods, and replace them with defined-contribution plans, which place all of the investment risk on the individual employee. Most of those 3,500 failed plans had been the liabilities of relatively small companies. Since 1999, however, more and more very large firms have learned to use the PBGC to their advantage through corporate bankruptcy proceedings. It is interesting to observe, in that regard, that many of the politicians and commentators who profess great worry about moral hazard relative to the individual in terms of, say, health-care insurance and postemployment income insurance have been reluctant to acknowledge the far more obvious moral hazard of the PBGC relative to large corporations. The political risks of failure to enforce original contracts are startlingly explicit in the world of failed corporate pension plans. Employees who had been encouraged to believe that their labor contracts included adequate protection of deferred compensation, that is, future income through the defined-benefit pension plans, find years later that those obligations have been reduced to quarters on the dollar. For single-employer pension plans that fail during 2005, for instance, qualified employees who retire at age sixty-five can receive no more than $3,801 a month ($45,614 a year). For many employees, that is half or less than the sum they thought they would receive from their company pensions.

The PBGC is already saddled with a deficit, but the situation is likely to become worse, both because of new corporate bankruptcies and because other firms will have increasing incentive to shed their defined-benefit pension plans in favor of defined-contribution plans or none at all.[21] As noted, accounting practices have been extraordinarily lax, to the substantial advantage of company management. For example, companies have been allowed to use an averaging or smoothing technique in their quarterly earnings reports, which means that the reported net income reflects the average assumed performance of the firm's pension assets. Any discrepancy between that and the actual performance figure cannot be dismissed, but can be slowly melded into future earnings data. The practice has greatly reduced the reliability of corporate earnings reports. In wake of the accounting scandals involved in the collapse of Enron and other large-capitalization corporations in recent years, pressure has built to prohibit that practice. If the Financial Accounting Standards Board, the overseer of accounting practices in the United States, makes that change, the pace at which firms drop their defined-benefit plans may well accelerate. Regardless, we face an increasing likelihood that the PBGC will need a congressional bailout, which could easily exceed the scale of the bailout during the savings and loan debacle in the 1980s, also a result of inadequate regulation and political dishonesty.

How might the management of investments in a system of private retirement accounts be handled? Presumably, it would be contracted by a government agency with oversight to some number of private firms, in much the same way that government issues service contracts with private firms to operate prisons, build and repair highways, supply equipment, and run the office canteen. In the now-preferred vocabulary of privatizing government activities, this is known as outsourcing. There is an important difference, however. The management of PRAs would have features partly reminiscent of tax farming.

Tax farming is a system of tax collection in which private contractors are employed by the central government to collect some specified types of taxes from either the general population or a particular segment of it. The contractors are allowed to keep a portion of the collection as profit, turning the bulk of the collection over to the Treasury. This system reached its peak of development in the Royal General Farms of eighteenth-century France (see Matthews 1958). The management system for a PRA program would undoubtedly be a far cry from those tax farmers, but some of the abuses that infected the French tax farmers also could occur in the PRA management.

One of the lessons of the Chilean system of private retirement accounts—a system often touted by U.S. champions of the PRA approach—demonstrates how easy it is for pension administration to emulate one of the worst features of tax farming. The French king, distant from grass-roots information, was never quite sure how much his tax farmers were skimming from the top. As the first cohorts of Chilean participants in their system of private retirement accounts retired after twenty or more years of investment, they are finding that as much as 30 percent of the expected proceeds were diverted into transaction costs, leaving them with far less than they had expected in retirement income. Chile's minister of labor and social security, Ricardo Scolari, agreed that "the system requires reform," but also noted that "it is absolutely impossible to think that a system of this nature is going to resolve the income needs of Chileans when they retire" (see Rohter 2005, A1).[22]

The U.S. electorate has been remarkably influenced by the cultural value assaults against government. Recall that this was the primary vehicle by which regulation of the savings and loan industry was reduced to the point that corruption became encouraged (see Blackburn 2002, 130–32). Similar assaults have been effective in political maneuvers that use Social Security's fiscal problems as weapons in other battles. Corrosive effects of those maneuvers have already exacted a toll on public trust, and more is probably on the horizon. Jeff Dominitz, Charles Manski, and Jordan Heinz (2003) find that adults younger than about forty are far more likely to be doubtful, and to be more doubtful, that Social Security will be there for them when they are seventy. The same age correlation can be seen in the Pew data analyzed earlier, as well as in other surveys of public attitudes toward Social Security. Of course, it may well be that younger adults are likelier to doubt the occurrence of most feasible events, when the timeframe extends thirty years or more into their future. As Dominitz and his colleagues (2003) point out, however, much of the public discussion of Social Security's future condition could surely be expected to erode public trust in that future, and the more distant the future the greater that erosive effect.

That erosion is central to any serious attempt to undermine Social Security. Recall from chapter 2 our discussion of Antonio Rangel's (2003) analysis of the forward- and backward-looking components of intertemporal exchanges (see also Rangel and Zeckhauser 2001). The forward-looking component is not self-sustaining in its own terms, because present donors have already benefited from investments by previous donors; if present recipients in turn donate to future beneficiaries, they will do so from altruistic rather than selfish motives. In contrast, the backward-looking component is self-sustaining even with purely selfish actors because the donor pays first, benefiting older recipients, and benefits later from future donors. However—and this caution is critical—that relationship is self-sustaining only to the extent that the intertemporal actors are linked in trust. When these actors are the present and future versions of the same person, the trust can be maintained from within, but when they are different persons—and especially different persons who do not know one another and might have no other interests in common—the trust must be maintained by institutions of political authority that do more than mouth platitudes about compassion and harmony.

As Rangel and Richard Zeckhauser (2001, 116–7) put it, government not only has the power to conduct transfers of resource and risk across generations; it also uses that power often and continually. Government has the capacity to use that power to achieve optimal risk sharing across periods and generations. Governments can thereby address the failures of market-based solutions to problems of exchange and distribution. It can also use that power to enforce exchanges and distributions that are biased in favor of specific groups at any period and in favor of some periods (generations) over others. Rangel and Zeckhauser could only acknowledge the obvious: government failure is as much a problem as market failure. Further, the two institutional sources of failure tend not to be complementary in their successful applications; instead, they are similar in the effects of their failures. Persons who lose in one arena are also likely to be among the losers in the other. Like many other studies, the economic analyses Rangel and Zeckhauser undertook demonstrate that the underlying processes of exchange and distribution have multiple balancing points (or equilibriums). As Kenneth Arrow (1986) pointed out in an argument reminiscent of Adam Smith, in games with multiple equilibriums the required budget of rationality cannot be satisfied by any number of individual players who transact as isolates in the anonymity of market exchange. Rather, a social structure of moral sentiments must establish both the capabilities and the directions of market and government institutions alike.

Trust is a principal ingredient of the glue of human relations whether in market or hierarchical models of organization. In an essay on trust written during the 1960s, Niklas Luhmann repeated an observation that many previous writers had made—namely, that under conditions of increasing complexity, as networks of interests, interactions, and information become both denser and more widespread across space and time, human beings "can and must develop more effective ways of reducing complexity" (1979, 7) to manage long-term expectations, uncertainties, and risks—even to manage ordinary day-to-day affairs (see also Arrow 1974, 22–24).

Luhmann's key insight was that trust is a prime means of reducing complexity directly and an essential condition behind all other means of reducing complexity. Imagine how difficult daily life would be if we could not trust, did not trust, that food on the grocer's shelf is safe, wheels on our cars will not fly off when rounding a corner, our workspace at the office will not be randomly shuffled among coworkers next month, the health insurance company will not cancel coverage if we begin to file claims, our pension assets will be protected from theft or mismanagement or change in regulations, and so forth. Instead of having to do all the tasks that are performed by a bank's employees, bank examiners, and officers of the Federal Deposit Insurance Corporation to protect our savings accounts at the local First Federal Bank and Trust, we trust all of that complexity of action to anonymous (at least to us) actors in many interlinked organizations to carry out many technical transactions for a very large number of people with efficiency and fairness. This complexity is not as much a master plan drawn up as an accumulation of expectations, means-end relationships, and trial and error evaluations as it is a response to accomplish important functions, which, if left to each individual to accomplish anew each time, would be quickly overwhelming in complexity and in the amount of time and energy required. Trust is the chief ingredient that holds it all together. Granted, there are rules and regulations, some of which are enforced with both prescriptive and proscriptive sanctions. But all of this works because of an underlying trust. Regardless of how skillful, brilliant, devious, or conniving, no individual can maintain mastery of more than a handful of the needed tasks in modern society. Self-preservation requires trust in the complexity-reducing properties of complex organizations. This is the mechanism of the invisible hand routinely invoked along with its author Adam Smith by many of the same actors who strive to erode trust in unwanted agreements or contracts.

Governmental Incapacity or Incompetence?

The hierarchical principle has generally been associated with an ideology of benevolence, compassion, care giving, and general welfare. After all, the descending thesis of authority that animates the morality of the hierarchy has traditionally been based in religious texts. Divine authority is at the pinnacle, and a great chain of beings extends downward through various grades of heavenly beings (archangels, angels, for example) through the monarch down to the lowliest peasants and "the dumb beasts." Republicanism altered that notion insofar as authority was grounded in the people, but it did not displace the descending thesis of authority. Just as parental authority continued to reign supreme in socializing children, and patriarchal-patrimonial authority was the basis of the marital bond and kinship bonds, government was looked on as a set of instruments of power to do good. The contrary and to some extent antihierarchical principles of market organization have steadily worked against those limits, in favor of liberty of the individual as individual regardless of parentage, gender or other traits. Along the way, efforts to bind the economic rights of citizenship to republicanism's political rights of citizenship (and thereby to the nation-state) gained some momentum and programmatic successes. One of these successes has been Social Security. The rise of the social sciences as instruments of policy making has been another. But, to borrow a biting phrase, "the poverty of social science and the social science of poverty" (Schram 1995) have not been a match for the neo-liberal discourse of deregulation and a reduced state apparatus (see, for example, Peck 2001).

At the same time, citizens' confidence in the instruments of government has seldom been so low. This is not because of the changing character of the discourse (which is far more a symptom than a cause of anything). What citizens increasingly grasp is a growing incapacity of government, although often it looks as much like incompetence as incapacity. That is to say, government agency has been losing its capacity to act as a complexity-reducing organization, and especially as one with democratic intention. Government agency now often finds itself in the odd position of being led and staffed by persons who are relatively wealthy, powerful by virtue of the resources needed to attain office and then by virtue of the resources of office itself, and professing antigovernment sentiments, sometimes genuinely and sometimes cynically but with such strongly manipulative force that it is difficult for members of the public to know the difference as fact based, rather than as a point of ideological loyalty.

The evidence of that growing incapacity has become increasingly stark. The evidence is not new. For example, a breakdown in the important governmental function of educating the public has long been evident. Because education demands much of its pupils, however, overlooking that evidence has been easier than doing the work of education, such as confronting and reexamining one's ignorance and prejudice. Politicians and officials have become so adept at mixing pieces of factual information with deliberate deceptions that members of the public are often at a loss to know the difference. One result is that more and more people abandon the effort and either resort to ideological postures or drop out of the process of trust altogether.

Some of the recent evidence has been so stark as to leave many members of the public astonished, sometimes embarrassed, and yet even more bewildered as to what they should do. The catastrophe of a hurricane in New Orleans and surrounding areas in 2005 brought home with startling clarity the incapacity of government, at all levels, to respond effectively to a disaster that had been forecast not merely days but months and years in advance. Furthermore, the plight of New Orleans and neighbors is only one in a long list of signs of governmental incapacity. Consider the continuing, repeated failures of governmental response to its citizens' needs of health care, its ineffectiveness in handling issues of border crossings and international migration, its unwillingness to enforce its own regulations concerning the general welfare, and its lack of coherence in policies and practices of economic management—indeed, even its abdication of responsibilities in those areas.

Analysts and policy makers in international organizations such as the World Bank and in academic institutions have often lamented the heavy costs of governmental incapacity in poorer countries—not only Zimbabwe and other so-called failed states but also in countries typically regarded as developing or nearly rich. What they only recently have begun to see is that governmental incapacity has also infected the health and well-being of an increasing number of wealthy countries, including the United States. Imagine the spectacle of a government actually taking steps to reduce the general welfare of its citizens. Until recently this was assumed to occur only in distant lands, places where tin horn dictators have monopolized power. Gradually, however, those pictures are being recognized as mirrors of daily life in wealthy lands. Market forces are reducing some of the long-standing disparities between the rich and the poorer countries of the world, and governments of the rich have done less and less to manage effects of those leveling forces across nation-state boundaries.

This is rich terrain for conspiracy theorists. In fact, however, it is usually difficult to determine whether the failures are due to deliberate decisions and lack of planning or to forces external to government's decisive control. The disastrous lack of preparation for and response to the devastation of New Orleans and coastal areas to the east can be attributed mainly and primarily to decisions taken, including decisions of inaction and other failures of rational decision making and planning. On the other hand, governments generally do not willingly relinquish control of economic processes vital to the long-term stability of the nation-state. Incapacities in that arena, as well as that of incarcerating its own citizens and waging war on others, are typically the most strongly resisted. A government that deliberately reduces the welfare of its current citizens could be genuinely assuming that the short-term loss will result in a proportionately larger long-term gain. That assumes, of course, that the government has been right in its assumption that the external economic forces cannot be controlled to the benefit of both short-term and long-term gain. In the nature of the case, these assumptions and the gamble that follows from them (in either direction) can be proven one way or the other only with the passage of time. In the short run, it is clear that recent U.S. administrations have gambled that greater risk taking, and greater individuation of risk taking, must be the correct approach.

When half or more of all new labor contracts are temporary, with no health or pension benefits and (sometimes) with relatively low wage rates, we know that more of the burden of risk has been shifted from the concentrated stores of capital to the individual worker. The increasingly popular use of actuarially individualized contracts has been part of that same shift (Laffont 1986/1989, 128–33). The upshot of these trends is that individual workers find it harder to realize the benefits of the law of large numbers. When, for instance, a person's insurance premium is calibrated sensitively to his or her specific location in the various probability distributions that describe the odds of needing a particular type of health care—a calibration that will become still more sensitive as genomic (and then proteomic) information is added—opportunities to benefit from a pooling of diversified risk are greatly reduced. Similar actuarial specificity can be achieved with postemployment income policies, whether enacted as public or as private programs. Note that wealthy and powerful persons have far less need of the benefits that are being actuarially individualized. Those with little or no wealth or power are the ones who suffer the loss of benefits of the law of large numbers.

It is clear that components of that gamble have included deliberate efforts to redefine the meaning of welfare, security, and the moral obligations of one citizen to another. It is also clear that instruments of government have been used to manipulate public perceptions, on behalf

Figure 6.3   Social Security and Medicare Cost as a Percentage of GDP

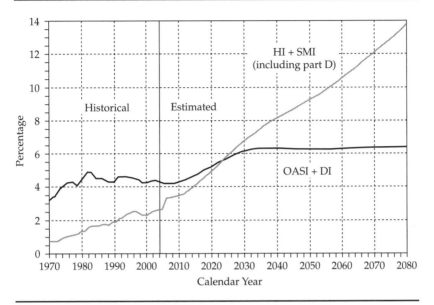

Source: This figure is chart C of the summary published by the Board of Trustees (see note 25 in chapter 6).

of those efforts. The most recent annual report of the Social Security Administration offers a case in point.

SSA's summary of its 2005 annual report presents two trend lines, one for the combination of the Old-Age and Survivors Insurance (OASI) and Disability Insurance (DI) components of Social Security and the other for the Hospital Insurance (HI) and the Supplemental Medical Insurance (SMI) components of Medicare (see figure 6.3).[23] The cost of each of those combinations is measured as a percentage of the gross domestic product, first using historical data for the years from 1970 through 2004 and then using the SSA's intermediate projections for years from 2005 to 2079. The proportionate cost of OASI and DI increased from a little more than 3 percent in 1970 to a high of about 5 percent in 1983, following which (and the 1983 amendments, which restored the fiscal health of Social Security) the cost declined to 4.3 percent in 2004. The cost is projected to increase to a little over 6 percent after 2030 (assuming no new restoration of Social Security's fiscal health) and remain at roughly that level at least until 2079. By contrast, the proportionate cost of Medicare will increase from less than 1 percent in 1970, and 2.6 percent in 2004, to 13.6 percent in 2079. As if anyone had not been paying attention, it is clear there is a very serious crisis in health care in the United States, and it is quite separate from the small problem facing Social Security.[24]

Of course, because the GDP will grow during the next several decades (although perhaps only at the rate of recent decades, not the higher rates of the 1950s and 1960s), the trend lines in figure 6.3 are also saying that total costs of Social Security and, more so Medicare, will become larger. It is to the SSA's credit that it put those projected increases in cost in proper perspective, by stating them relative to the projected increase in volume of GDP—which is and will be the basis from which any internal costs will be paid, whether Social Security or Homeland Security, unless they are paid by debt, which is simply pushing the costs onto the GDP growth of future periods and excluding the possibility of debt default.

Then we come to this statement in the SSA's summary report.

> Because their primary source of income is the payroll tax, it is customary to compare HI and Social Security income and cost rates as a percentage of payroll tax, as in Chart C [here shown as figure 6.3]. Note that the income rate lines do not rise substantially over the long run. This is because *payroll taxes are not scheduled to change* and income from other tax sources to these programs, taxation of OASDI benefits, will rise only gradually from a greater proportion of beneficiaries being subject to taxation in future years. [emphasis added][25]

Costs of OASDI and, especially, of HI continue to increase from present levels, as a proportion of taxable payroll. In the case of OASDI, the increase is because the Baby Boomers are beginning to retire. In the case of the health insurance portion of Medicare, the growth is because health-care costs continue to increase far in excess of the rate of inflation and more people will be entering the age range of increased demand for health care. In these figures, the income for those programs does not increase as a proportion of taxable payroll because, as SSA states, "payroll tax rates are not scheduled to change" ("Status of the Social Security and Medicare Programs," pp. 6–7; see note 25). That is correct: no legislation has authorized an increase in the rate of the FICA tax, for example. But that is also subject to change. After all, the trend lines to the right of 2004 are projections, based on certain assumptions. Why maintain the same payroll tax rates, rather than projecting an increase in rates in the same way that SSA projected an increase in GDP? Ironically, projections are used for quantities we recognize we cannot unilaterally control. In contrast, because tax rates are something we can directly control, we assume a constant rate unless or until legislation authorizes a change. Moreover, there is another assumption hidden in that discussion. The income side of OASDI could also change because of a change in the size of the taxable payroll—either in the size of employment earnings or in the proportion of any worker's employment earnings that is subject to the FICA tax. Why does the discussion, and the graphic presentation behind it, quietly assume that the earnings ceiling for FICA taxation cannot be lifted or even removed or that the rate of FICA taxation cannot increase, but without remark? As for the size of total employment earnings, with or without a ceiling limit on the part subject to FICA taxation, why does the discussion, and the graphic presentation, assume no growth there? After all, both the tax rate and the ceiling could remain constant, yet if a larger proportion of workers have earnings at or above the ceiling, or if the size of the work-force subject to FICA taxation increases, the proceeds for OASDI will be greater. As we saw earlier, most demographic assumptions in the Social Security debates hold that the total workforce as a percentage of total pop-ulation will not grow and more likely will decline. Given that assumption, what will drive the assumed growth in GDP? The answer is that we assume continuing increases in the rate of productivity per worker—getting more product from each worker for the same amount of wages, or at least getting added product per worker at a rate greater than the marginal cost of that addition. Did the SSA assume either that there would be no future increase in worker productivity or that future increases would come without any increase in wages or perhaps even with a decrease in wages?

Something of the sort would account for the fact that the SSA report apparently assumed that OASDI income cannot increase because the tax rate cannot increase and because the base on which the tax rate is applied cannot increase. Perhaps this is exactly what SSA wanted to say. If so, they could have stated more clearly all of their assumptions. After all, the SSA officials end their summary report by drawing attention to "the major sources of uncertainty in the projections," and they include among the relevant factors "the size and characteristics of the popu-lation receiving program benefits, the size of the American workforce, and the level of workers' earnings," as well as "productivity gains, wage increases," and many other factors ("Status of the Social Security and Medicare Programs," pp. 6–7; see note 25). Then they proceed to illustrate how the projections are sensitive to assumptions about some of those factors. However, they do so only with regard to the cost rates. The income rate is set at a constant level all the way to 2079, as if some law of nature—Newton's first law of motion, perhaps, the law of inertia—had been put in charge of that part of the world.

Chapter 7

Changing Actors for Changing Times

W
E BEGAN chapter 1 by pointing to the obvious, that the fiscal problem facing Social Security—and it is a very real problem— can be fixed by either or a combination of two adjustments. The outflow of benefit expenditures can be reduced, the inflow of revenues can be increased, or some combination of the two can be devised. Any path we choose involves a few admittedly difficult choices. Achieving any sense of balance between benefit cuts and revenue growth will necessarily entail some negotiated settlements across cohorts—those already born and those yet to be born. In part, these negotiations strike a settlement between the present (and the relatively certain benefits to current and near-future retirees) and the future (and the relatively uncertain revenue from taxed earnings or expenditures on benefits for distant-future retirees, who will begin to collect their benefits after 2025 or 2030). The choices, though, would be manageable. After all, future periods are always a work in progress.

When are solutions to current problems ever final solutions? We look as far into the future as we can, make judgments, settle on a plan, but expect to revisit our solution at some point down the road, when what was the near-future has been revealed and what was very distant-future has come into somewhat better focus. To be effective, a solution must not last forever. Keep in mind that the current fiscal problems facing Social Security are understood through a rather complicated weave of assumptions and projections about quantities and relationships that will not be known facts for years to come. It is perfectly normal to design solutions to current problems with the expectation that, as conditions change, the solutions will need to be reworked. To repeat, choices that could lead to straightforward solutions of Social Security's fiscal problem would be manageable choices. At least they are manageable choices if the field of trust among the citizens and policy makers has not already suffered so much damage that no government official or politician nor the solutions they propose would have credibility.

How, then, did the relatively straightforward technical-fiscal problem of Social Security become transformed into political fuel to deepen animosities? How did issues that ordinarily would occupy the attentions of few persons outside the arcane worlds of academic and professional policy analysts and other experts on fiscal matters become kindling for the culture of fear and loathing that has resurfaced to dominate so much of the public scene? How has the daily life of politics in the United States been deflected from its traditional mandate—to resolve conflicts of interest short of open civil strife or civil war—and become instead a generator of conflicts by feeding the culture of fear and intolerance?

These are questions that motivate this chapter. Those that preceded it have contained bits and pieces of our argument. Here we try to pull them together in a larger more coherent framework, and in the process we display some of the long historical roots of ideological contests associated with many features of American culture, which have sometimes degenerated into regrettable episodes of fear and loathing.

The routine activities of economics and financial management are usually performed by their various practitioners as technical processes and addressed by technical sciences. These practitioners are not oblivious to the ethical, moral, and political issues. As mentioned earlier (see Fuchs, Krueger, and Poterba 1998), economists are about as likely as anyone else not only to have ethical, moral, and political values, but to express those values in their perceptions of the processes, structures, and events that they study. However, they generally do not approach their studies as ethicists, moralists, or politicians, but instead as economists and financial management experts, and that is to our benefit. Even so, these technical issues have important ethical, moral, and political dimensions (Hausman and McPherson 1996, 6–7, 209, 220).

In *Democratic Vistas,* first published close on the heels of the U.S. Civil War, Walt Whitman said that the mission of government is primarily

> to train communities through all their grades, beginning with individuals and ending there again, to rule themselves. . . . To be a voter with the rest is not so much; and this, like every institute, will have its imperfections. But to become an enfranchised man and now, impediments removed, to stand and start without humiliation, and equal with the rest; to commence, or have the road clear'd to commence, the grand experiment of development, whose end (perhaps requiring several generations) may be the forming of a full-grown man or woman—that *is* something. (1871/1982, 947–48)

This is a singularly American version of what a century earlier Immanuel Kant (1784/1983) had called the project of enlightenment—humans' eventual attainment of maturity and autonomy or self-rule. It was an enthusiastic acknowledgment of the work, the hard work, of democracy, as distinguished especially from works of demagoguery. Whitman's criticism of the age was romantic—though no more so than Mark Twain's critique of the Gilded Age. It did not, however, display that same distrust of the individual that had been part of the romanticist reaction against the Age of Enlightenment at the turn of the nineteenth century, a criticism that would soon circulate through public discourse as concerns about a cult of individualism (for example, Durkheim 1902/1984).

As we have seen repeatedly, the functions of market organization presuppose some political agreements as condition. Most important among these are the rule of law, which provides predictability and a minimal coherence of fairness and trust, a freedom of individual actors to engage freely in agreements among themselves about the exchange of goods and services, and a respect of property rights, or rights of use of particular goods and services. These political agreements take the form of government instruments to regulate conflicts and promote cooperation among diverse and changing interests, with the intent to serve the commonwealth, the common good. But those agreements and the effectiveness of instruments issuing from them also presuppose some community of moral obligations—some understanding that describes the boundaries and some of the content of obligations that each member owes to other members merely by virtue of their shared membership in that we. Integral to all of that is an ethical project, some notion of who the so-called proper actor is. What kind of person, a person with what qualities, should each member strive to be, or become, in order to fulfill those moral obligations and achieve the good society we hope to create?

Making Persons

Histories of modernity, modern society, and "modern man" often invoke a simplification—a binary contrast between the old or traditional and the new or modern. Late in the nineteenth century, scholars seemed to compete to see who could better encapsulate that contrast by unearthing its first or most basic principle. One such candidate invoked a conceptual distinction between status and contract. This distinction provides us with a useful shorthand because so many other of the candidate claims can be folded into it, or, as a foundationalist might say, discovered within it.

In the old order, identity was based on who one is; in the new order, on what one can do and how well. That distinction was meant by its nineteenth-century authors to differentiate types of society, but the vocabulary itself makes it plain that different types of persons, different models of what might be called the ideal actor, were also intended. A change in modal personality, in character formation, in the very process by which the character or nature of self is produced, was being described in the contrast between status and contract, between the "who is" and the "what one can do well."

The old order emphasized the status-defined characteristics of the person—one's location in an elaborate network of positions (stations in life), most of them defined as accidents of birth (gender, ethnicity, and so on). Parentage accounted for many of them. Born to a peasant couple, one was very likely to live out the life of a peasant. Born to the manor, one lived a rather different life, though slipping to a lower rank was always a risk for sons younger than the heir and the spare, and for daughters more generally. One was born to a place, to a geographic area, and the manorial system of organizing territory meant that leaving that place was a big gamble. Younger sons and daughters occasionally attempted to relocate (especially to the towns and cities), sometimes successfully but sometimes with dire results. Urban poverty was experienced differently from rural poverty. Position was also defined by gender. Ethnicity and racial categories gave advantage or disadvantage that was about as automatic as that of gender. Religious confession did as well. Even before the revolt of radical Catholics who became Protestants, various schisms within the church of Christianity marked the pathways of families; after the Reformation those markings became deeper and engendered their own set of mutual sentiments of disdain, in some ways similar to those attaching to distinctions of ethnicity and race.

Although a bare sketch of what was much more complex as well as variable across place and time, this depiction of the old order is adequate for our purposes. In contrast, the new model emphasized the skills and abilities of individual persons—not the family, not the community, much less the court and church of authority, but the individual person taken as such. Skills and abilities had value in the old order as well, but the valuations, even the conceptions of what could count as important skill and ability, had been constrained by considerations of one's place in the larger scheme of positions or stations in the proper order of society. The important difference of the new order was to liberate the skills and abilities of the person from those constraints. Freeing the skills and abilities allowed their development in new ways and to greater extent, all of which set free the individual who was the bearer of skills and abilities.

This development had the liberal professions as its forerunner. These professions of special authority were free to regulate access to and content of the special training in their arcane arts (law, medicine, ministry, teaching), their workplace, and some aspects of their markets. To be sure, free must be read as a relative term. The difference was no less striking for being so. For one thing, the practitioners of these professions were free of the constraints of the manorial system. They were of the city, not the land. For another, with the recovery of city life after the twelfth century and the growing importance of urban crafts, their professions of special authority were becoming increasingly useful to wealthy and powerful persons.[1]

To take the free professions as something of a general template for a new modern citizen was a radical step, in the sense that the difference went to the very root of social relations, identities, and order. What mattered did not, or ought not to, attach to family but to the individual member of a family, the individual member of a society. This shift was a challenge to, an assault upon, patriarchal-patrimonial principle at its roots and had ramifications all the way up what was referred to as the great chain of being, through the manorial system of land barons, to the monarch, with implications that moved still higher in the hierarchy of authority. The worldly implications were slow to work out. Many of them are still in process (for example, the erosion not only of biases of gender, race and ethnicity, religious confession but more important also of the practical reality of those status distinctions as significant). Skepticism toward traditional authority and the notion that one should be bound to the roots of the past joined, sometimes uneasily, with a renewed republicanism—that is, an emphasis on "the public thing," a public realm of the common good, independent of private interests, the host of which (remembered from the ancient Greeks) had been the agora, the market place. It would be an exaggeration to say that prior history was not admissible there; current history could not re-invent all. Pride of place nonetheless looked increasingly forward, to the pursuit of new goals in new ways.

Memories of ancient Greece were far weaker than echoes within Christian doctrine. Renegotiating relations between the one and the many—between "the individual" as a new force in the world and "the community" with its long-entrenched practices and claims of authority—took place in politics and in religion at about the same time. In Christian doctrine, the Christ figure is simultaneously the one and the many, a principle carried over to the duality of the earthly king.[2] Christians who revolted against their church (that is, what was then the Church) and became known as Puritans, Calvinists, and so forth, understood the different meaning of "the one" in "the many." A question of composition as well as unity, it was more significantly an assertion of agency of individual conscience. These debates of revolt, defense, reformation, and counter-reformation during the late sixteenth and seventeenth centuries were highly intense, rancorous, life-and-death struggles for most of the participants, for whom sin and salvation were far from academic exercises. In some respects, current debates behind and surrounding Social Security—debates otherwise known as the culture wars—are oddly reminiscent of the contests among such eminent figures as Christopher Potter, Edward Knott (pseudonym of Matthias Wilson), William Chillingworth, Arthur Hesilrige, John Whitgift, Thomas Cartwright, and Bishop Laud (now mostly forgotten names, as will be the names of today's personalities). Although conducted in a language of decorum that muted much of the emotional charge, their exchanges about governance, sovereignty, individual responsibility, and God's will were often filled with harsh invective, as the adversaries worked their way to and through events later depicted as the English Revolution (see, for example, Zaret 1985; Denton 1997).

Regardless of their orientation toward republicanism, the Puritans shared with other Christians-in-revolt a severe ethical and moral position because of their commitment to a new, liberal order, orchestrated around the free conscience of the individual person. How could a person accept salvation, they asked, unless he or she was free to choose Satan? Believing protection was conferred because of being born into a believing family (both household and Church, or household, monarchal realm, and Church) was a conceit. Freedom of choice had to be fundamental to the meaning of having chosen to follow "the Christian way." That freedom was essential to each and every person's conscience, and the essence included the possibility of choosing wrongly. The emphasis on austerity of moral code was in part a response to Church practices viewed as corrupt, but even more a testimony to the profound discipline of freedom that each liberated person was expected to practice assiduously and with great clarity of soul.[3] There was in that coda to new liberty more than a hint of worry about the free individual getting out of hand, running amok.[4] John Whitgift, archbishop of Canterbury, accused the Puritan reformers (Thomas Cartwright in particular) of proposing "such a perfection in men as though they needed no laws or magistrates to govern them but that every man might be as it were a law unto himself" (1853, 3: 31; see Block 2002, 48). Whitgift was speaking well before the republican cause in England had even begun to coalesce, which occurred (where it did) as a consequence, not a cause, of Puritan revolt against bishops and then the crown.

It was not only in England that such turmoil of faith signaled still stronger, deeper, and more tumultuous changes in behavior and expectation, although perhaps the timetable was more advanced in England than on the European continent.[5] Champions of a new age of reason, such as the French encyclopedist Condorcet, also sought the release of individual energies as a means of improving human society. Our notions of better living through chemistry and the next technological advance, so commonplace that they are barely noticed commercial slogans, were fresh currency in eighteenth-century France, England, Scotland, British North America, Holland and the Low Lands, and elsewhere. Condorcet proposed, of all things, that a model devised by commercial insurance houses could be adopted by government as a way of advancing the quality of life of the infirm, the ill, and the old. This venture was stimulated in part by observations that more and more people, having left the countryside for life in the growing commercial centers of French cities, had been suffering ill effects of isolation and anonymity. In Britain, too, Adam Smith was observing and arguing much the same, although he more than Condorcet or their mutual friend Turgot thought that government should only set standards, goals and limits, draw up broad designs of improvement, and then wherever possible leave to public markets of private interests the innovations and enactments (for example, 1776/1976, 794–7).

Adam Smith, often extolled as a champion of the market, was indeed an advocate of free enterprise as evidenced in his major works, *The Theory of Moral Sentiments* and *The Wealth of Nations*. Some commentators have argued that the former was an early effort and superseded by the latter. But Smith continued to revise and elaborate *The Theory of Moral Sentiments* from its first edition in 1759 through the sixth, published the year of his death, 1790. That long project bracketed *The Wealth of Nations*, published in 1776. Moreover, the two works fit together quite well. Both were fundamentally about an economy of moral sentiments. The modern market was in principle a high expression of this moral economy, but its seat was in what is best called the natural interiority of the person. Contrary to common assertion, Smith was not the author of the phrase, laissez faire (apparently coined by Turgot or Quesney), he rarely used the phrase invisible hand, and he was not an opponent of government. To the contrary, Smith thought government's role to be vital and varied. From providing and enforcing property rights and individual liberty to guiding the directions of improvement in and of society, good government served as the necessary complement to market forces. Although commercial actors act "not from benevolence" but from "regard to their own interest," and rightly so, they also "seldom meet together" without their talk ending "in a conspiracy against the public, or in some contrivance to raise prices," and they exercise great effort to avoid competition over prices or wages. His conclusion: the proper discipline of government is needed where self-discipline does not serve the ends of virtue (1776/1976, 26–27, 45, 471–2).

The key to all of Smith's argument is his view of the natural condition that favors virtue in life—virtuous goals and virtuous conduct. Although sympathetic to arguments of utility, Smith subordinated utility to virtue, to a sense of propriety, to the importance of self-discipline, and to the cultivation of understanding (that is, faculty of mind). "What institution of government could tend so much to promote happiness of mankind as the general prevalence of wisdom and virtue? All government is but an imperfect remedy for the deficiency of these" (1790/1976, 253). Persons of all stations in life seek to build self-esteem and gain the approval of others, approval that responds to virtuous conduct but they often do not succeed in attaining high levels of virtue. Reason is vital, but it is no substitute for virtue. One must apply intellect to gain understanding, "by which we are capable of discerning the remote consequences of all our actions, and of foreseeing the advantage or detriment which is likely to result from them" (255). That expectation, Smith was well aware, was a very tall order, and all the more challenging, given his so-called complex view of "the regular and harmonious movement of the system, the machine or economy," of modern society (247–8). Prudence, the result of understanding combined with self-command, was among the highest virtues, but limits of achievement affected all persons, sometimes as a result of perfectly natural dispositions, such as the admiration of success. Thus, for example, "the corruption of our moral sentiments, which is occasioned by the disposition to admire the rich and the great, and to despise or neglect persons of poor and mean condition"—a corruption that visits those who are in "the middling and inferiour stations of life" as well as those in "superiour stations"—flows from the same impulses that stimulate the need of approval (78, 81).

Smith strongly objected to Thomas Hobbes's view that there is no natural distinction between right and wrong, or that such distinction is changeable and depends on the arbitrary will of civil magistrates or other high figures in society. Nor do market transactions necessarily follow, much less yield, correct distinctions of right and wrong. One should not ask too much of Smith in that regard, however. The ultimate source of virtue, of the sense of propriety, of the distinction between right and wrong—all of which were experienced in the complexity of social, economic, and political relations—lay simply in what was natural in life and behind that in Providence. It was that same unexciting premise in what (to us) is obviously a circularity of argument that lent a general optimism to Smith's complex view of the hidden aspects of modern society, including his version of a "looking-glass self"[6] (that is, "principle of self-approbation and disapprobation"; 1790/1976,150). Smith's work does not support the notion that beneficial outcomes result only or primarily or most importantly from the selfish intentions of actors. He did assert that praise and blame can be assessed only in terms of an actor's "intention or affection of the heart" (123). He also recognized that both good and bad outcomes result from no intentionality, and from good intentions inadequately informed by an understanding of long chains of consequences (for example, 138–9). Beneficial outcomes result from virtuous conduct as well as from vice. Lack of virtue leads to negative results, but "the regular and harmonious movement of the system" also follows from intentions that are less than virtuous, even destructive, and from actions that soon outrun any intentions whatsoever.

Smith's insight was neither that selfish interest is a vice (or contrary to virtue) nor that the best outcomes of human actions result from the pursuit of selfish interest. There is no simple syllogism of automatic relationships to be had in these matters. Rather, Smith's chief insight, though not original to him, was about the complexity of system. Individual actions, whatever the intentions behind them, percolate through the complex relations of modern society and produce results that very often no one intended or anticipated or, sometimes, after the fact, wants or understands. Smith tends to attribute this to nothing more than natural condition and clearly did not see anything magical or mystical in it, as in the peculiar intelligence of some "invisible hand." To say that it is a perfectly natural consequence of complex relationships does not explain anything. Even so, Smith was too much a naturalist to refer the explanatory problem to anything as mystical as a claim that the market knows best.[7] His insight was that transactions of freely contracting individuals will produce outcomes that cannot be obtained, or obtained as efficiently, via other means. To borrow James Surowiecki's (2004) title, the wisdom of crowds depends on the freedom of individuals to pursue different goals in different ways through public transactions. These massively variable behaviors (again, the law of large numbers) are the material on which selection processes operate, often with unexpected, novel results. Left to itself, this process can yield very desirable or undesirable outcomes.

It is the task of government not only to ensure the necessary condition of liberty of contract, of trial and error, of experimentation, but also to guide selections of outcomes toward the continued moral improvement of society and its members.[8] The crowd is not always wise. Often it is merely incoherent, but sometimes it is terribly destructive. Smith recognized that failures occur as failures of that necessary condition (individual liberty and respect of property rights), as failures of guidance (government incompetence or worse), but also as failures of the market process itself (too much greed, too much fear, price-fixing, collusion). Virtue and the desire for approval can extend only so far. Government is "but an imperfect remedy" (Smith 1790/1976, 253), but it is a remedy; it must be, given that virtue and wisdom, though prevalent, encounter limits.

These brief passages provide a background to later debates about what it means to be, or to describe another person as, a mature and responsible person.[9] The point is certainly not the power of ideas; to the contrary. The drivers of history are far likelier to be found in material conditions, the topics of economics and some parts of politics, than in ideas and ideologies. Insofar as material factors operate through the consciousness of human actors, however, they tend to be molded to the paths laid out in ideological proclamations, as well as in subtler perceptions, as when fervid religious ideals direct believers to work hard and live austerely, or to destroy Mammon's palaces,[10] or to disrupt the supply lines of an infidel. The poor and downtrodden occasionally strike against those above them, because of material deprivations, and a few of those revolts have had lasting consequences. Most of the enduring contests, however, have taken place between and among well-off groups who have the material means to sustain hostilities, mostly of the mind (as in culture wars), though now and then also hostilities of the body, brutal and bloody. Persons who worry about their daily sustenance usually lack discretionary time and means for these battles over such causes as right thinking and the right way of life.

The thought that a latest generation of subjects or citizens differs, on average, from those who came before is not novel to the eighteenth or nineteenth century, but what had become more noticeable was the pace and the degree of difference from one time to a later time. This heightened sensitivity to change was not only about material conditions, or what would later be distinguished as technological change. It was also about change in the interiority of a person—change in mind, in character, in will. Condorcet's optimism was in celebration of this latter site of change most especially. Smith's more cautious view, and his concern that indirection be given its due (that is, that the greater part of what happens does so despite or in ignorance of intentionalities), represented a more disquieting understanding of the limits of natural condition as well as Providence. The lament voiced by Washington in a letter to John Jay reflected the optimism of principle as well as the disappointment with practice which he shared with others: "We have probably had too good an opinion of human nature in forming our confederation. Experience has taught us that men will not adopt and carry into execution, measures the best calculated for their own good without the intervention of a coercive power" (1786/1997, 605). There was general agreement that education matters, that the constitution of personhood, of citizen, of worker and boss, was to some extent a process of forming, shaping, even making something of malleable materials. The main disagreements were about extent, safety of pace, and desirability of consequence.

The main venues of these developments were two rather different marketplaces. One was trade in goods and services. It was becoming much faster, more extensive in penetration both spatially and personally, and more powerful relative to other institutions of society. The other, generally not yet noticed as being market-style in organization, was citizenship in political organizations with republican, quasi-republican, or parliamentarian ambitions if not much practical experience. The design of new government was to a substantial degree direct, as leading figures in France, England, and British North America (later, the United States) sought to create new instruments for a new contract of governance—in some (highly variable) sense, a contract of self-governance. The design of a new actor, a new producer-trader-consumer and a new citizen all bound together in one indivisible person, was as much by indirection as by the direct means of education and public training. It is clear from documents of the times though that this project too, like that of designing new government, both exercised and troubled the thinking of many people. It was, after all, an audacious undertaking. The more interests one had, the more one had to defend against unwelcome, perhaps unforeseen, consequences of these new experiments.

The road to public education and the mandated lessons during the nineteenth and early twentieth century followed less directly from the closely bridled optimism of Smith than from a different mix of sentiments, better represented by a voice from the generation after Smith. In fact, Thomas Malthus's two essays on population contain phrases that voice sentiments one hears repeated today by politicians' speech writers, and in some cases directly from the politicians themselves. A prime example is one of the motivating principles in all of Malthus's thinking—namely, that evil does exist in the world, that it is an independent determinant presence, and that it has purpose, which is not to cause despair but to stimulate action. Life, Malthus says explicitly, is a struggle for existence, an essential struggle, which both depends on ever-present obstacles and produces superior character among those who survive. The Darwinian imagery is unmistakable, though, as already noted, Darwin borrowed from Malthus and other early economists, not the other way around.

Malthus constructed an argument of supply and demand that begins with two observations, neither unique to him: people were becoming plentiful, and so, too, were the plans and consequences of wrong-headed government. According to Malthus, it followed that an excessive supply of people would result in an excessive demand for food relative to any conceivable rate of supply. The proposed solution to this dilemma was part technical and part moral. The technical part could be achieved by better public policies—in particular, policies that encouraged delay of marriage, which Malthus took to mean delay of childbearing and thus a reduction in the total number of births per woman. (Contraception within marriage was not an option.) The moral part also had two components. One was individual self-restraint, a virtue that good government could sustain and encourage. The other was a natural consequence of failure of self-restraint, which good government would not attempt to overturn—namely, too many children for a family to sustain. Malthus would have understood Washington's lament as foretold in its premise. Reacting to what he explicitly rejected as the utopian projects of men such as Condorcet, Malthus believed that too much was often expected of human nature. He also believed that poorly conceived government would do more harm even, and especially, where it intended to do good. Policies that attempt to stay "the 'killing frost' of misery" (for example, the poor laws of his day) are misguided at best, for they do not accord with "the lessons of Nature and Providence" (1798/1890, 523, 525). A century before Bismarck's introduction of a program that served as model for the U.S. plan of Social Security, Blackburn (2002, 40–42) has reminded us, Condorcet proposed that a modern state should establish a risk-pooling fund that would supply insurance of old-age income. This was just the sort of "establishments and calculation," Malthus (1798/1890, 299) maintained, that might "appear promising on paper, but when applied to real life . . . will be found to be absolutely nugatory"[11] (compare Rothschild 1995).

Too much security is unhealthy for the moral economy of the individual person, as for that of society as a whole. This verdict became commonplace during the nineteenth century, a time when the modern social sciences were developing as several distinct disciplines for the promotion of improvements of the economy, the body politic, the social realms of family, friendship, and private as well as public order. At the center of it all was that "economy of the soul" that animated the diversities, the capabilities, and the ambitions of individual persons (Sklansky 2002). There was similarly a great deal of nagging, from the pulpit and an army of circuit-riding preachers, in the lyceum, the mechanic's institute and the chautauqua,[12] in newspapers and public addresses, in poets' readings and museums' displays, and nearly everywhere else that moral uplift might have effect.

During the first four decades of the nineteenth century another Great Awakening occurred in the United States, with a storm of urgency to save souls, stiffen moral fiber, and democratize institutions of religious belief. Improving the economy of the soul was not just a matter of organized religion and the itinerant preachers. Francis Grund, professor of mathematics, newspaperman, and diplomat, published (among other works) a fascinating portrait of "Americans in their moral, social, and political relations" in 1837, which included the observation that "discredit must attach itself to those who are unfortunate and poor. A man, in America, is not despised for being poor in the outset . . . but every year which passes, without adding to his prosperity, is a reproach to his understanding or industry" (172–3). No doubt this verdict was intended to be as much prescriptive as descriptive. Grund was not the first in what would continue as a long line of immigrants (he was from Bohemia) who found their new country remarkably prosperous and open.

Often overlooking the self-selection process that favors initiative and perseverance, immigrants were likely to be impressed by signs of lethargy and sloth when they surveyed their new fellow citizens. But much the same sentiments were prevalent among natives, too. Henry Ward Beecher, prominent minister in New York City, asserted that "no man in this land suffers from poverty unless it be more than his fault—unless it be his sin." The "general truth," Beecher declared, is that "if men have not enough, it is owing to the want of provident care, and foresight, and industry, and frugality and wise saving" (see Sandage 2005). Henry's sisters, Catharine and Harriet, were life-long champions of the improvement of women through education, though not the suffrage, and self-help books the two sisters wrote for popular consumption.[13]

One of the peculiar tensions running through those composites of advice and urgent care stemmed from an uncertain relationship between what one should do and what one could do, and how some proper balance between the two should be measured.

That tension is still very much with us, of course, and not only in the specific debate over Social Security. Frugality and saving, correlate and consequence of individual ability, hard work, and self-discipline, were understood as pure goods, to be encouraged at every opportunity. This nineteenth-century society was not yet a place in which the only measure of value, and therefore of public policy, was the growth of goods and services, both in volume and in currency of trade. It was already a consumer society in some respects, though, and for all the nostalgia of images such as the yeoman farmer, it was also rapidly becoming a society of employees.

About two-fifths of all U.S. workers in 1860 were employees, the proportion had more than doubled ten years later. The condition of employment—wage slavery, in one popular image of the day—ran counter to republican ideals of independence and autonomy. How should one measure personal responsibility and personal success under these new conditions? The core liberal principle—to free the creative action of the individual, with full access to market transactions—seemed to be stymied, even reversed, by the clockwork regime of new employment contracts for millwork, factory work, railroad transport, and the like. The same principles of individual independence and autonomy also recommended great caution in designs of improvement by government agency; yet the prescriptive force of pulpit, school, and other private venues seemed clearly no match for the moral regulations of these new engines of production and commerce.

Intellectual clarity—the sort that appears in published works—typically occurs late in the day, in part because another selection mechanism delineates the terms and connections of what becomes remembered as a definite assignable idea or insight. A century after the American Civil War, a Russian immigrant-scholar, Isaiah Berlin, clarified some of the tension that had then been experienced in that relationship between the prescriptive and the permissive. The problem, Berlin (1958) said, was that two different concepts had been traveling under the same name—liberty.

John Stuart Mill's famous treatise *On Liberty*, published in 1859, illustrates some of the confusion. Mill's core preference was not just individual liberty but also personal autonomy and responsibility. The aim of liberty is to be autonomous (self-governing) but also to be responsible in that liberty and autonomy. Responsibility entails self-restraint, which presupposes a liberal education, a formation of self-reflection that understands that a tyranny of the majority will undermine the authority of democracy, which rests in the consent of the people. Although Mill's emphasis on liberty and autonomy was an endorsement of self-governance at the root level and the capabilities of the individual person (that is, decentralization of authority to the smallest feasible units), it was easily confused with a mission of public moralists improving society.

The Emersonian notions of self-reliance seemed to bridge the permissive and the prescriptive, as if they invoked a single theme of liberty. In fact, two different notions were at work, and one of them tended to be antithetical to the other. On the one hand, liberty means to be free to do something (where that something can be specified in any number of ways). On the other hand, liberty means to be free of restraint; nothing more, treating liberty as an end in itself. In contrast, the former treats liberty as a means to something else. Of course, one may also notice that the latter (the so-called negative concept of liberty) is silent on the follow-up question: when free of restraint, then what? To the extent that the liberated person is free of restraint, what then regulates his or her behaviors, choices, or perceptions? How does this interior self-regulation and responsibility occur, if not by training and reward-punishment schedules deriving from . . . whom, with what intentions and aims?

Thrift and saving are behaviors that benefit the individual actor. They also benefit the larger society, however, both because the individual actor has provided for his or her own security and because the frugality and saving serve as a model for others and as a means to the accumulation of large and concentrated sums of capital. Is the individual actor free to fail sufficiently (by whatever standard of sufficiency one might propose), or is there sufficient basis in public morality (whether measured by church or government or some other collective authority) to train or to distribute reward and punishment in such a way that the responsibly autonomous actor will be sufficiently frugal? We can see here why the idioms "born to fail" and "born loser" have been popular. To the extent it is believed that failure follows from something (or the lack of something) interior to the individual, persons in positions of authority are relieved of unwanted responsibility for that failure. The optimism of Condorcet's *Sketch for a Historical Picture of the Progress of the Human Mind,* with its conviction that we could achieve goals of betterment through application of the scientific method, and especially the new mathematics of probability and analysis, was an invitation to disappointment from this idiomatic point of view.

Writing at a time when U.S. culture was enmeshed in another exercise of fear and loathing, the Red Scare and McCarthyism of the 1940s and 1950s, Berlin addressed some of the terms of those debates, as well. In part, he was responding to a position like that of the nineteenth-century

Tories, which was dominant in U.S. politics during that time as well as now. Although they professed strong support for economic liberalism (free markets), they disliked individual liberty in other realms of life. Eric Dodds drew a parallel to distant events in another famous experiment in democracy. At the end of the fourth century BCE, when it appeared that further advances in rational discourse, self-governance, and self-enlightenment were on the horizon, Greek society succumbed to a reactionary wave of fear and distrust—a "fear of freedom" in Dodds's words, "an unconscious flight from the heavy burden of individual choice which an open society lays upon its members" (1951, 252, 254). Fear of the liberal or free individual became widespread in ancient Greece, as illustrated by reactions to Athenian democracy by a decidedly undemocratic Plato. However, Dodds's real point, as he openly declared, was current: "We too have experienced a great age of rationalism, marked by scientific advances beyond anything that earlier times had thought possible, and confronting [humankind] with the prospect of a society more open than any it has ever known. And in the last forty years we have also experienced something else—the unmistakable symptoms of a recoil from that prospect" (254).

In one of the celebrated cases of the Red Scare era, Dennis v. U.S., eleven members of the Communist Party of the United States had been convicted in 1949 of violating the Smith Act by advocating forcible overthrow of the U.S. government. On appeal, the eleven argued that their political doctrine did not call for the use of force and that their speeches did not constitute a clear and present danger. The appeal was heard and denied by the Second Federal Circuit of the Court of Appeals (183 F.2d, 201) in 1949, a denial upheld later by the U.S. Supreme Court (341 US 494) in 1951. Of interest here is the appellate opinion written by the Second Circuit's chief judge, the famed Learned Hand, who is usually recalled as a staunch defender of liberty.[14] In this opinion, Judge Hand formulated what became the new standard for the clear and present danger test—namely, "whether the gravity of the 'evil,' discounted by its improbability, justifies such an invasion of free speech as is necessary to avoid the danger" (183 F.2d, 212). This rational calculus of risk assessment made rather specific claims on, as well as on behalf of, the free individual as legal subject. Hand was recognizing the commonly held emotionally based perspective on threat, which in the new era of atomic weapons had become seemingly open-ended in scale, and this, by comparison to the 40 million fatalities of World War II. Because the potential loss resulting from the gravest threats is so great, the threshold of evidence governing evaluations of the threat and the probability of loss from it should be lowered. Or, in Hand's terms, the graver the evil, the higher the degree of improbability we reasonably require to not worry about it. This is an invitation to rule by ignorance or worse.[15]

It should also be clear that Hand's test carries the expectation that the ordinary citizen should judge actions by an exacting rational calculus of risk and uncertainty. In fact, in a prior decision (U.S. v. Carroll Towing, 159 F.2d 1969 [1947]), Hand had already laid out the terms of that expectation. The case had been a claim of tort liability against a boat owner who had allegedly caused damage to another's property rights by failing to secure his boat adequately. Hand explained it this way:

> The owner's duty, as in other similar situations, to provide against resulting injuries is a function of three variables: (1) The probability that she [the boat] will break away; (2) the gravity of the resulting injury, if she does; (3) the burden of adequate precautions. Possibly it serves to bring this notion into relief to state it in algebraic . . . terms: if the probability be called P; the injury, L; and the burden, B; liability depends on whether B is less than L multiplied by P; i.e., whether B less than PL (183 F.2d, 212).

Thus, financial liability for a tort should be imposed only if the burden of preventing injury does not exceed the magnitude of the injury multiplied by its likelihood of occurring. Notice the expectation that is made of individual actors. Before any of an unknown range of potentially damaging events occurs, we must calculate the magnitude of damage that would result from each of those potential events, plus calculate the probability of occurrence of each such event. Note also that in this test it could have been reasonable to assume that foresight was an acceptable condition, that the calculation should be made before the occurrence of any range of foreseeable potentially damaging events. The coda added by the 1951 decision removes that expectation of foresight, at least under circumstances when the threat is so severe that it could not even be reasonably foreseen but (perhaps) only vaguely imagined.

Certainly we have come to the domain of market behavior where sentiments of fear and greed often rule—and are viewed as beneficial forces, at least in the long run. We can see some signs of progress along the way. Hand's tests say absolutely nothing, for example, about the actor's gender or ethnicity or body type or sexual preference; about the actor's mother or father, or whether the actor might be considered good looking or not, young or old, daring or timid, atheist or agnostic or deist, or Christian or Moslem or Hindu. The tests demand simply a certain minimal competence in specific calculations and behavior in accordance with the results of those calculations.

The competence demanded of the modern market player is at least as high as that demanded of the citizen. Both venues of the liberated individual share in the idea that history is a narrative of progress shaped by the human will. In parallel to that, however, is another view, which is skeptical of and contrary to that narrative of progress. It is not the view of Malthus, which, for all its austerity and doubt, was a variant of the progressive reading. Rather, it involves what might be called an exchange between "romantic violence and utopia" (Pfaff 2005). It extends from Edmund Burke's critique of the French Revolution's high ideals to the conservative pole of early twentieth-century liberals such as Max Weber and Emile Durkheim, and beyond (Burke 1989).

As we presented in chapter 2, the central action of a market is price setting. A market transaction results in an agreement between buyer and seller on a fair price, whether the trade is one tangible object for another or for a sum of money or a promise to pay, or a service of labor for a tangible object, sum of money, or promise to pay. Some commentators have focused on the price-setting feature as a criticism of the market model. Any exchange relation, however, involves an agreement about equivalence, whether the equated objects are gift and obligation, knightly servitude and lordly hosting, or some other pair. Instead, the focus of this critique is on the highly abstracted means by which the modern market achieves equilibration of values—monetary pricing. The basic expression of monetary exchange is one dollar is as good as another, which generalizes to the players as one buyer (seller) is as good as any other, as long as they play by the rules of the market. This abstract essence of market transaction highlights a democratization, of access, of the application of rules, and of the execution of trades. The resulting test is a test of competence: how well can you play the game, win at the bargaining, and deal with buyer's regret, winner's curse, selling too low, and losing one's shirt.

For traditional society, and for those areas of modern society that retained much of their traditional heritages, the increasing presence and power of this modern market form was a jolt to local sensibilities and a site of dangerous temptations, typically likened to gambling. Insofar as they were associated with long-distance trading, even the market place of traditional (that is, pre-modern) society could be a site of the exotic and the alien, thus of potential contaminants. For most people, though, the market was a physical place to take one's goods, to trade for needed supplies, to visit with neighbors as well as newcomers and the occasional stranger, and exchange reports, weigh opinions, build or rejuvenate bonds of trust and interdependence. A person's credentials mattered; these credentials were the whole of his or her being. To put that in its proper order, the whole of a person was what mattered, and that whole included all of the integrity of characteristics that mattered in society— gender, parental heritage and place, religious confession, station in the order of things, as well as competence in specific skills. The new market model stripped all away but the skill, leaving a bare individual and the contents of his or her mind and embodied capabilities. It seemed, whether as market player or as citizen, anemic, alienated, much too abstract, and, in a phrase made popular by a liberal diagnostician, Max Weber, a "parceling-out of the soul" (1909/1956, 128).

During the late nineteenth and early twentieth century a growing number of religious leaders in the United States turned against this modernism of market society. They extolled the virtues of a fundamentalism, in which moral certainties were defined and judged in opposition to the free agency of liberal man. The language of these pulpits, revival tents, books, and pamphlets differed from the moral boosterism of Beecher, Smiles, Emerson, and kindred liberals. A culture war had been joined within religion as well as against what were referred to as liberalism and secular humanism and Godless capitalists. On one side were figures such as William Jennings Bryan and J. Gresham Machen, swords drawn against the impurities sown by people such as Harry Emerson Fosdick and John D. Rockefeller (see, for example, Machen 1923).

Granted, those battles were to a large extent rearguard actions—nostalgia for lost worlds—similar to aspects of the current debates surrounding Social Security. Not that the component issues within that nostalgic reaction were unreal. As markets became more abstract and anonymous, very real people were losing more often than not because the balance of market power was shifting heavily toward highly abstract instruments of trade. Some defenders of the market model shy away from any sorting of winners and losers, arguing that in a free market everyone wins. No one forces a person to sell at a price he or she does not like; no one forces a person to buy at a price thought too high. At junctures such as these, economists invoke the notion of revealed preference (Harsanyi 1955).

Though not irrelevant, the practice is often more complicated than that, because the freedom of a free market is not independent of residual distributions of power that are as much situational as personal. A rancher wants to take cattle to market when they are at maximum readiness, neither too soon nor too late. A dairy farmer must sell milk more or less as it is produced. In other words, some tradable goods have properties of liquidity very different from those of more abstract goods such as corporate bonds and stocks and commodity futures. Ranchers and dairy farmers, residuals of the mythical yeoman farmer, no longer had much leverage in their markets; the power had shifted to professional traders whose contracts were primarily about options and futures and derivatives.

More generally, there were concerns that market actions were too often ignoring, even disregarding, the noncontractual bases of contract—trust, property rights, moral character. Both the modern market player and the citizen had become too much like the bureaucratic office-holder: a procedural functionary, abstracted of all qualities other than ability to perform the assigned task, which itself was increasingly fragmented, atomized, and specialized. The human person was becoming much like the currency of trade, the monetary unit one of which is as good as any other, so long as it performs its sole task. The informational part of organization is mostly objectified in the office as a set of rules, regulations, and task functions. The individual person who occupies the office acts as a battery that energizes that objectified information by supplying a few pieces of technical skill and a well of endurance.[16] All of the particularities of group membership, constraints from the past such as ethnic tradition or family heritage or community spirit count for nothing. What is left, then, critics were asking (then as now), to be a source of character? How does character emerge?

As a set of twentieth-century critics put it, the framers of the Constitution agreed with Montesquieu. "The virtuous citizen was one who understood that personal welfare is dependent on the general welfare and could be expected to act accordingly; forming such character requires the context of practices in which the coincidence of personal concern and the common welfare can be experienced" (Bellah et al. 1985, 254). What happens when these contexts that marry personal concern with common welfare become difficult to sustain? Building such character becomes even more difficult as politicians seek to dissolve that coincidence still more, by separating personal concern for one's future well being from the common welfare of citizens arrayed across different generations, yet united in the pooling of individual risks?

Education of the Investor

One good reason for giving people control of their investment decisions is that they could align their decisions with whatever value preferences might be of foremost concern. At present, banks, investment houses, and other financial institutions make those decisions as hired agents for pension holders, mutual-fund shareholders, and retail bank customers. But because the investment money does belong to the individual worker, as champions of private retirement accounts frequently declare, why not let individual workers decide where their money should go? If people want to invest in real estate development, why not let them? Likewise, the person who wants to invest in tobacco or medical research and the person who wants to invest in alternative energy or a Broadway production, let them as well. As Robin Blackburn (2002) has argued, people should have the opportunity to direct all of their investment money into firms that they regard as socially responsible companies. If they liked, individuals could form investment consortia, or use their union or church membership as a similar collective vehicle, with the aim not only of making money but also of combining forces to influence the uses to which all that money is put.

The foremost value consideration for most workers when planning retirement income security is, however, security. This is financial security, to be sure, but the basis on which it is built is psychic security. At the postemployment stage, whether by design in retirement or by mishap in disability, a person has very limited options to improve resources; the inertial trend favors steadily diminishing opportunities to access new resources. The facts of past decisions and behaviors will dominate present and future financial options. Some investors might choose their investments on the basis of values such as those described in the preceding paragraph, but probably the majority will have the value of a secure future uppermost in mind.

Can the typical person of the twenty-first century become the skilled manager of risk and uncertainty that reliance on markets in corporate stock and bonds, options, derivatives, and other investment instruments will continue to require? Can people be at least skillful enough to know which reputed expert to hire and how to monitor decisions and practices? Perhaps. Certainly the possibility should not be dismissed out of hand. Anyone who learned to drive on a tractor, the top speed of which was ten to fifteen miles per hour (and dangerous at that), remembers the jump some years later to an automobile and the sometimes unexpected lessons of angular momentum at forty or fifty miles an hour. Imagine, too, the transition from being practiced at driving an automobile to landing an airplane on an aircraft carrier, one of those activities that a person does either very well or not at all.

Much work is required to make each citizen adequately informed about risk and uncertainty to manage their own consumption and investment decisions. The task facing the individual investor is complex, requiring successful responses to two rather different and difficult sequences of decisions. The first sequence has to do with the accumulation of assets. That seemingly simple phrase translates into not-so-simple negotiations between present and anticipated future selves about the optimum distribution of categories of consumption (that is, immediate or delayed, and so on) across periods of a lifetime. Much of what present self would like to know, to make well-informed decisions, cannot be known in advance but only estimated within a sea of uncertain future events. Determinations of optimum distribution can be revised, but only for present and future periods, and previous decisions can cast long shadows. Eventually a future self reaches the point of converting delayed consumption—those accumulated assets—into a chain of immediate consumptions; now the sequence of decisions has to do with optimum divestiture. It is at this stage that the dimensions of security become starkly clear.

As we suggested throughout, the economic or financial behaviors of an individual through time are fundamentally about psychic security, whether approached as a social or as a radically individualized good. Decisions about divestiture are obviously constrained by how well those prior selves succeeded in preparing for their successors' needs at a time (postemployment years) when flexibility of personal resource acquisitions and allocations are significantly diminished. Poverty or near poverty in old age is much more likely an end state from which there is no prospect of escape.

Deciding how to annuitize assets can be difficult. Those who have accumulated too little must deal with that limitation. Those who have apparently adequate assets must decide on a distribution across an unknown number of remaining years with unknown but potentially very costly problems of health. Of course, one can hire an expert, but that adds expense. In any case, it would be prudent to know how to evaluate the expert judgments being made supposedly in her or his behalf.

How well prepared are today's investors? In general, the answer is not promising. First, levels of ignorance are rather high, as many studies have demonstrated. Successful management of risk and uncertainty, whether in investment markets or elsewhere, requires basic skills of mathematical logic that far too many people do not have. Imagine how easy it would be for someone who does not know the difference between an arithmetic mean and a geometric mean to be misled by an account manager's report of average returns.

The ignorance extends to options actually available and decisions already made. Alan Gustman and Thomas Steinmeier (1999) estimated, for instance, that only about half of workers in employer-sponsored pension plans knew whether it was a defined benefit (DB) or a defined contribution (DC) plan. Fewer than half knew (within a margin of a year) the dates of eligibility of normal and early retirement benefits, and those within three years of their desired retirement were not more likely to know them. Workers enrolled in DC plans knew a little more about their plans than did the workers enrolled in DB plans. The direction of that difference is good, because DC plans expect their holders to assume more of the risk of decision making; but the margin of difference is trivial in comparison to what is needed. Whereas 45 percent of the workers with a DC plan knew that their employers offered matching contributions, and 14 percent knew that their employers did not, the remaining 41 percent professed incorrect knowledge—most of them claimed incorrectly that matching contributions were not available.

When not mandated as in a DB plan, individual contribution rates are rather low. Of the 31 percent of workers who participated in a 401(k) plan, the median (mean) balance at end of year 2002 was about $14,000 ($34,000).[17] Fewer than one in five owned an IRA (regular, roll-over, or Roth), and of these the median (mean) balance was about $10,000 ($27,000). Participation rates are higher among workers in families with total income of $75,000 or more: 17 percent had both a 401(k) plan and an IRA, 27 percent had a 401(k) only, and 12 percent had an IRA only. But still, close to half (44 percent) had neither. Compulsory participation and a mandated minimum contribution rate are features that do not accord well with the notion of a new model actor. As a free agent, this new actor is supposed to be astute about matters of financial investment, responsible toward future selves (and thus toward the common good) in designing an investment plan that will likely result in a secure income flow during post-employment years. He or she is also well disciplined enough to implement that carefully conceived plan of action through all the ups and downs of conditions of life, economic and otherwise.

Can internal habits be reformed and sharpened to a degree that they can substitute for mandated behaviors and requirements? Some existing habits blocking the way are quite resilient. For instance, a proposition from the theory of discounting says that a person tends to behave as if his or her future discount rate will be lower than at present. Thus, experimental evidence shows that many people, on being asked to choose between taking $1,000 now and $1,100 a year from now, will be too impatient to wait for the 10 percent reward and thus take the $1,000 now. But many of these same persons, when asked to choose between taking $1,000 ten years from now and $1,100 eleven years from now, will opt for the $1,100 payoff. It is tempting to believe that, though we do not save in the present, we will become savers in the future—that our saving and investment behavior will improve with time. If our goal is to accumulate a certain amount of money over the next thirty years, however, we can accomplish that goal with the lowest level of contribution from our current income if we begin saving early, even relatively small amounts, because those small amounts will have a long time to grow into bigger amounts. Can people be trained to believe that early dollars saved or invested are worth far more than late dollars and to act accordingly? The distance from here to there is substantial, and has been growing. One illustration of this is that so much more of the accounting mentality of economic, political, and managerial realities has been emphasizing short-term results, quick turnaround times, and persistently high rates of reward.

Evidence concerning actual experiences with stock markets is also not promising. As we observed in chapter 5, one of the perennial problems associated with market behavior is that many investors are not as adept as they should be at managing the emotional charge of the investment process. For instance, a patch of success can delude a person into believing that only exceptional skill has led to that success; in fact, it is more sensible to view the successes as events in a probability distribution that recognizes that many outcomes occur at random. There is no doubt that some persons have won more often than they have lost, and won much larger amounts than they have lost, from their market decisions—in some cases with the uncommon result that they have been or are relieved of much of the stress of uncertainty about postemployment income. (They are relieved mostly, but not completely, because there is always some lingering chance of a fiscal collapse that wipes out the personal assets even of billionaires.) The problem is that no one has been able to distill that individual experience of success into a proven formula that can be generalized as an educational tool, for at least two reasons. First, if in fact the successes are due to a proven formula (perhaps more than one), the information is carefully guarded by successful investors, for obvious reasons. Second, if such a formula should become known and efforts made to generalize its use, the information would be incorporated into market dynamics very quickly, thus nullifying future success from the formula.

There is probably another, still more basic reason that the uncommon records of success have not provided us with how-to instructions to replicate the outcomes we desire—namely, that those individual successes have been a consequence far more of chance (luck, in the vernacular) than of deliberately calculated strategy. Professional investment managers, financial economists, and related professionals offer their expert advice about investment strategies with a healthy dose of caution about any strategy that they might recommend. The caution is certainly in order. Different experts have been known to suggest contrary strategies, and sometimes the same expert will switch between contrary strategies. Perhaps all of these experts have some chance of doing respectably better than the market average, but it is doubtful that they convert the chance into actual riches except by the fees they charge for the privilege of using other people's money. For example, probably the most commonly voiced recommendation says that, if the task is to optimize the balance between return (expected value) and volatility (risk as volatility), the preferred approach is to invest in a diversified portfolio that gives center stage to common stocks, and the longer the intended holding period, the larger the proportion of stocks should be. Some evidence of actual market performance is rather inconvenient for that preferred approach, however. If the task is to optimize the balance between return and volatility, says this contrary stack of evidence (see, for example, Levy and Gunthorpe 1993), common stocks are inferior to a particular class of government bonds, and the longer the intended holding period, the worse stocks are, because "the rate of increase in the standard deviation [that is, volatility] is much faster for assets with high mean returns" (that is, common stocks and especially growth stocks) than for certain other assets that have lower average levels of return (Levy and Gunthorpe 1993, 32; see also MaCurdy and Shoven 2001, 33–35). What is the typical investor to make of that? Whose advice should the prudent investor follow?

Many people become quite impatient with what they are hearing or reading at this juncture in discussions of market strategy. Their impatience is understandable. People expect or hope to hear or read solutions and recommendations that they can count on. They prefer to stake their hoped-for fortunes on gambles that are heavily loaded in their favor or, better, that are sure things. But that is the point: the nearest to a sure thing in the arena of postemployment income security has been Social Security. Market investment is not and never will be even close to a sure thing. The skills needed by a prudent investor are skills of managing risk and uncertainty, not driving them to zero. Markets live on risk and uncertainty. Fortunes are made because of risk and uncertainty. Fortunes are lost because of risk and uncertainty. Although the Reverend Thomas Malthus was the only figure we've mentioned in this chapter who sang the praises of the withering frost, he was far from the only figure who argued that sure things, or even insurance against the failure of a highly likely thing, have unhealthy effects on individuals and societies.

Impatience can interfere with even the most finely developed rational calculus. Robert Shiller's analysis of survey data about the perceptions and actions of individual and institutional investors before and after the stock market crash of October 1987 suggests that emotions dominate rational decision making even among some investment managers, although more so among individual investors (1989, 372–3, 379–402).[18] For instance, a plurality thought the market was in a bullish rather than a neutral or bearish phase before the crash; after the crash the plurality chose bearish as the best description. The reaction is understandable. But, again, that is the point: attitudes were reactive to what had happened, not forward-looking to what would likely happen next. Nearly 75 percent of the individual investors and 84 percent of the institutional investment managers said that they thought the market was overpriced before the October 19 crash; the proportion was about the same whether the particular investors had themselves been buyers or sellers. Presumably the buyers thought they could be sufficiently skillful at timing the expected correction that they could take their profits just before that event. Perhaps some were, but that gamble is generally a loser's game.

The crash generated lots of emotion—anxiety, nervousness, fear. But the main behavioral consequence of that emotional reaction seemed to be added passivity. During the month leading up to October 19, nearly 75 percent of the individual investors had not changed their stock holdings. That proportion increased to 86 percent during the interval from the twelfth to the nineteenth and stayed at that level on the nineteenth and the twentieth, then dropped back to 77 percent the next few days. Of the minority who changed their holdings at some point during the period, about twice as many increased as decreased their numbers of shares during the month prior to the twelfth; about twice as many decreased as increased during the twelfth to the nineteenth and twentieth; and then the ratio shifted back to twice as many increasing as decreasing their holdings during the few days after the twentieth. It is easy to say in retrospect that the correct response would have been (whatever one's behavior before the twelfth) to buy more and more heavily as the market went down—to buy carefully selected firms for which the evidence had been indicating sound fundamental characteristics of the firm's business model and management. That would have been deciding in the face of strong contrary emotional factors, to be sure, but for anyone who had already been comfortable with the general level of risk taking in stock investments, that would have been the rational choice.

As we noted in chapter 5, the historical record shows very decisively that opportunities of significant returns on investment capital in common stocks occur on a tiny fraction of all trading days. The period from October 19, 1987, included a handful of that small number of days. It was apparent on the nineteenth, if not before, that economic fundamentals had not changed, that the market crash was entirely a phenomenon of investor psychology on top of inertial effects of what was then known as program trading (computer programs based on factors of technical analysis for deciding buy and sell decisions). The nineteenth and twentieth were prime days for buying stocks; a very small fraction of individual investors did just that. The fraction tripled in size during the next few days as stock prices began signs of recovery and the chances of big returns diminished accordingly. Even so, according to Shiller's data, no more than one in six individual investors took advantage of the opportunity.

Investment managers for institutional funds were better at the game, on average, although not greatly so. During the month prior to the twelfth, for instance, more of them were reducing (45 percent) than increasing (11 percent) their holdings. That pattern continued during the twelfth to the nineteenth (27 versus 8 percent); but then on the nineteenth and twentieth more managers were adding than subtracting stocks (21 versus 13 percent), as they were also later in that week (34 versus 16 percent). From the standpoint of rational account management, one might wonder why more of the managers were not buying into the declining market. Surely they understood the opportunity? The answer is that, yes, on the margin, the investment managers probably did understand the opportunity better than did the average individual investor. This rational decision model is not the only one, or even the primary one, that applies to the manager's situation, however. Fund managers are in competition with one another for shares of the consumers' investment dollars, and the best advertisement in that competition tends to be short-term results. Which fund can boast the highest rate of return during the latest quarter or the year to date?

The company's profits are heavily influenced by such statistics, and managers are judged accordingly. It is very difficult to beat the average, and it is even more difficult to beat the average two or more reporting periods in a row. Managers' decisions reflect those facts and concerns of short-term performance in the marketplace of competing funds. A manager whose fund has performed better than average, or even at the average, during the last few weeks or months or a reporting period is strongly tempted to lock in that superior record and become more risk averse. Conversely, a manager whose fund has performed well below average during the early part of a reporting period is tempted to shift to a more risk-seeking approach, in hopes of getting at least to the average before the end of the period. For managers, too, it is more difficult to win than it is to lose. When the few opportunities to win handsomely come along—and we have seen that they are rare and not always easy to recognize—the countervailing pressures can easily result in delay or in hurried foreclosure.

In addition to the emphasis on short-term results, the tendency to emulate others' best behaviors generates more inertial pressure in favor of investment outcomes that pull the average down. It is not unusual for individuals to rely on existing organizational rationalities for clues about their own best options. One of the most common of these resources is the perception of how other people, who are facing a similar need to decide, made their choices and with what consequences. Rather than reinvent the wheel each time, why not learn from others' experiences and decide or behave accordingly? In fact, modeling the successful behaviors of other can be a very useful instrument of efficiency. Unfortunately, it can also lead to decisions that virtually ensure poor performance. Shiller's analysis of responses during and after the October 1987 stock market crash shows some signs of that lesson, but a simpler and more direct illustration is found in an analysis featured in *The Economist* (February 12, 2000, p. 81).

Assume that an unusually perceptive person—call her Felicity Foresight—has successfully predicted at the beginning of each new year since 1899 the one asset, "in any established market in the world, that would experience the highest total dollar return (income plus capital gain) over the following twelve months" (81). Confident in her skill, she would invest all of her wealth in that one asset and leave it untouched for the duration of the year. Of very modest means initially, she began with $1. But by her hundredth year, "Ms Foresight had turned her initial $1 into $9.6 quintillion ([that is], $96 followed by 17 zeros). Even after deducting taxes and dealing costs, she would still be worth $1.3 quadrillion (a mere 14 zeros)—making her 15,000 times richer than Bill Gates" (81). So much for perfect knowledge! The truly interesting aspect of the story comes with the second part. Ms Foresight's former companion, Henry Hindsight, began with the same initial investment, $1, and at the beginning of each new year he invested his total wealth in the one asset that had been the single best performer over the preceding twelve months. His initial $1 grew to $783 during the 100 years—or, with costs subtracted, $290.

The typical real-world investor is neither Felicity nor Henry but unfortunately much nearer Henry than Felicity. The problem is not a new one. We celebrate the Titan Prometheus (foresight, forethought), not his brother Epimetheus (hindsight, after thought).

One would think that the average adult today is better prepared to manage financial accounts than the average adult a century ago was. The difference in experience should mean that much: the proportion of adults today having that experience is much higher than was true in 1900. If the comparison is restricted to the subset of adults who did or do have financial accounts then and now, however, the picture is not so clear. For one thing, the private personal saving rate has plummeted in recent decades. Does that suggest a loss or an increase of sophistication? One could argue either way—loss, for obvious reasons; gain, because the average adult today understands that some saving is built into socioeconomic organizations of employment, government taxation, and so forth (that is, forced saving).

Other recent evidence gives a similarly mixed picture. Consider the record for a large retirement fund, TIAA-CREF. Men and women who enroll in those saving and investment programs are not exactly a microcosm of all U.S. adults, not only because they are active savers but also because they are predominantly educators. This latter fact does not necessarily mean that they are, on average, financially more astute than the average adult. It surely does mean that they are situated in occupations that appreciate the value of information, fresh information especially, and they are more likely to be experienced than the average U.S. adult in how to search for and analyze information. With that in mind, consider a recent analysis of how participants have been allocating their premiums across classes of investment in the TIAA-CREF funds (Rugh 2004). The four classes of asset are guaranteed assets (TIAA traditional annuity), equity (a set of stock and stock-index funds), fixed income (bond and money-market funds), and real estate. Historically, the first two classes were the only options available. As of the end of March 2004, they still accounted for 49.0 percent and 44.4 percent, respectively, of all assets in TIAA-CREF pension accounts and retirement-class mutual funds, with fixed income adding 4.9 percent and real estate the remaining 1.7 percent.

Jacob Rugh's analysis considered the balance of premium allocations at the end of each year from 1992 to 2003 and then at the end of March 2004. For present purposes, these data are summarized in figure 7.1, which displays for each of three of the asset classes the annual average premium allocation by premium-active participants, and in figure 7.2, which displays the allocations of participants who invested 100 percent of premiums to the equity class or to the guaranteed class.[19] Clearly, there has been a long-term increase in tolerance of risk and uncertainty. In 1992, half of all premiums invested that year were put in the guaranteed

Figure 7.1   Average Premium Allocations by Asset Class, TIAA-CREF

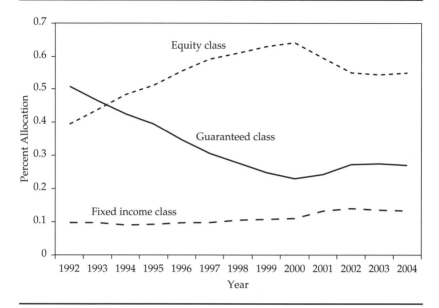

Source: Author's calculations from Rugh 2004.

asset class, about 10 percent were put in fixed income, and about 40 percent in the equity class. At century's end, the proportionate allocation between the guaranteed and the equity classes had flipped. Likewise, the proportion of allocations that were given entirely to the equity class grew from 8.4 percent in 1992 to 30.5 percent at the end of 2000, and the proportion of allocations that were given entirely to the guaranteed class dropped from 18.1 percent to 6.1 percent during that same period. Possible conclusions from that picture are mixed. On the one hand, one can infer, as stated, that the participants were becoming more tolerant of risk and uncertainty. On the other hand, however, one can also see evidence of the tendency of some people—those who are more resistant to risk and uncertainty—to jump onto the bandwagon just as the music is about to stop.

The bull market in stocks during the 1990s, in some aspects so extraordinary that some enthusiasts began to believe "that the rules have changed," came to a close and has been followed by a period in which, judging from the main stock-index gauges, equity values sharply declined, gradually rebounded, but then fluctuated around a relatively flat trend line (in market jargon, moving sideways). This raises an interesting question:

**Figure 7.2   Premium Allocations Among Participants Who Allocated
100 Percent to Equity or to Guaranteed Asset Class, TIAA-CREF**

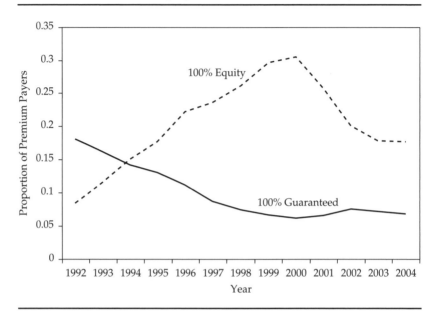

Source: Author's calculations from Rugh 2004.

how have investors responded to that volatility? As shown in figures 7.1
and 7.2, the participants did alter their premium allocations, both on average and, more especially, in the propensity to put all of their money in
equity assets. Again, the patterns observed in the data yield mixed mes-
sages (not all of which can be seen in our summary figure). Obviously the
participants sought to shelter more of their assets in more secure investments. Part of that response reflects a tendency to buy high and sell
low—just the opposite of what a rational calculus of financial planning
recommends. Granted, one cannot predict the timing of a market turnaround. As the bull market got "longer in its whiskers," however, one
could then (as some did) gradually take profits and shift them into less
risky (less volatile) asset classes. Unfortunately, it is at such times that
greed dominates fear and drives prudence out the door.

A somewhat clearer picture of this tendency can be seen by disaggre-
gating the participants into age groups, which Rugh did. One would
expect that participants aged fifty-five to sixty-four, for example, would
want to shift new premiums to guaranteed assets, and indeed to shift
more of their current accumulations also to guaranteed assets. Hindsight
makes obvious that the time to enact those shifts was late 1999 and dur-

ing 2000. If one cannot be Prometheus, one can at least try to avoid being Epimetheus and enact the shifts soon after the evidence of declining market support becomes clear. In fact, the active (that is, premium-paying) participants aged fifty-five to sixty-four, along with those aged sixty-five, did just that, on average. From December 2000 to March 2004, premium allocations by the fifty-five to sixty-four age group to equity assets declined from 62 percent to 51 percent, on average, allocations to guaranteed assets grew from 30 percent to 34 percent, and allocations to fixed income assets grew from 7 to 11 percent. These shifts are not large, to be sure, and these data are part of the evidence Rugh cited in support of the general thesis that the average investor is too strongly influenced by inertia. Once a specific allocation formula has been set (at the beginning of plan participation), the tendency is not to change it or, if to change it, to do so rather timidly. Several factors probably lie behind the tendency to inertia, but one is that the average adult does not behave as a financial planner, using a rational calculus of decision making, when making choices of financial (and related) conditions of his or her own future selves. Rather, the average adult usually emulates the decisions observed for others, either by direct choice and inspection of the relevant other (Whose situation is like mine, and what did they do?) or by following a template of organizational rationality that is signaled from a personnel office (for example, one's employer or union or professional association) or from a track of habituated behaviors laid down by preceding cohorts (see Hardy, Hazelrigg, and Quadagno 1996, 124–7; Madrian and Shea 2001).[20]

Investors aged fifty-five to sixty-four and older are relatively close to retirement age (at least first retirement) and therefore are wise to become more protective of accumulated assets. Young investors are wise to resist the sentiments of pessimism that attend strong declines in equity markets, such as occurred in 2000, precisely because they have relatively long horizons to retirement. Unfortunately, as already noted on a number of occasions, the typical behavioral tendency is in the opposite direction, at least in part because losses of a given amount are evaluated more heavily, and more sternly in a (loosely defined) moral sense, than gains of that same amount (Loewenstein and Prelec 2000, 580–2; Sandage 2005). Rugh thus reported that among the premium-paying participants who were under thirty-five, as well as among those who were thirty-five to forty-four years old, there was also a shift away from the equity and toward the guaranteed and the fixed income asset classes from the end of 2000 through the first quarter of 2004. In 2000, the difference in equity allocations between the youngest (under thirty-five) and the oldest group (sixty-five or older) was 18 percentage points; by 2004, that gap had narrowed to 13 percentage points. Had the youngest group been willing to take advantage of the declining prices of equities, they would have expanded their equity holdings, thus increasing the gap between their behavior and the appropriate behavior of the oldest group.[21]

To return to the initially motivating question, evidence is abundant that the modal adult today is much likelier than was her or his grandparents to be a directly active saver or investor. Because of that, the modal adult actor today is better prepared to manage financial accounts. One should not overestimate the level of skill, however, or for that matter the amount of deliberation involved in that saving or investing activity. Much of the actual saving or investing is at others' direction, and inertial patterns are prominent. Very few savers and investors today behave as a highly competent financial analyst would recommend; and not many today avail themselves of the (for pay) services of a highly competent financial analyst.

What about future generations? Judging by surveys of the results of our educational institutions, future generations might be no more skillful when it comes to financial planning than present generations. As noted, the requisite skills include a modest facility in mathematical logic and numerical analysis. However—and to cite just one example of studies that have reported dire conclusions—the National Center for Education Statistics (2005) recently issued a report of results from the Education Longitudinal Study showing that nearly two-thirds of high school seniors had not acquired an understanding of intermediate-level mathematical concepts and could not convert verbally stated logical problems into mathematical problems that could be solved through numerical analysis. Nearly two of every five seniors did not have the ability to solve even simple problems that required elementary mathematical concepts. Whether these results represent a decline in level of mathematical ability is unknown, because comparable data for national samples of high school seniors in, say, the 1960s are not available. If the expectation is that young adults will become increasingly capable in those skills, so that they can make individually tailored solutions to their own long-term financial planning problems, or at least are capable enough to sort through the market variety of advertised experts in financial planning and choose competent and reliable agents, recent studies of educational quality are hardly reassuring.

And?

Of course we can take away another message from all that evidence. A variant of the Reverend Malthus approach, it has been a strong undercurrent of sentiment in the United States from its beginnings; occasionally, as in recent years, this view has become explicit in particular debates. Keep in mind that markets are transactions between players who are continually sorted into winners and losers. In the ideal market, no one is a permanent winner, no one is a permanent loser, and if all works efficiently everyone is better off eventually—that is, in the long run (which sometimes is very long). Actual markets are not perfect, which means that long strings of losses can and do show up in the account books of specific persons, including persons who are merely unlucky rather than undeserving or lacking merit. The persistence of loss can create severe problems of civic order, as Adam Smith (among many others) observed. Such problems are greatly mitigated, even forestalled, if most people, most especially the persistent losers, simply believe in a consistent human nature, one in which there are, as Scott Sandage (2005) has recalled, an abundance of born losers.

With that as backdrop, then, perhaps we should not worry that a market model, as manifested in the proposed substitution of private retirement accounts for Social Security, will restore the long left tail, the loser's tail, of the distribution of winners and losers in life, to what it was before governmental intervention in the form of Social Security. If that prospect is not enough to awaken people to their own interests, and to take action accordingly, why should any of the winners seek to rouse them from their slumbers? Where do the moral obligations arising from the ethical project of that new model actor—or for that matter any actor—begin and end? These questions are still at issue, early in this twenty-first century, although they are rarely as such the explicit topic of any general public discussion.

Early in the twentieth century much the same questions were raised, without any satisfactory results. Emile Durkheim, for example, had long been occupied with a question:

> How does it come about that the individual, while becoming more autonomous, depends ever more closely upon society . . . at the same time more of an individual yet more linked to society? For it is indisputable that these two movements, however contradictory they appear to be, are carried out in tandem. . . . It has seemed to us that what resolved this apparent antinomy was the transformation of social solidarity which arises from the ever-increasing division of labor. (1902/1984, xxx)

He referred to differentiation and specialization of tasks, not only but especially in the workplace and commerce. There was anxiety behind that search for answers. Durkheim, like many others, was not convinced of the outcome, nor was he reconciled to the view that the contradiction was only apparent. Issues of morality, of the obligations that individuals have (and should have) to one another, carried some urgency even if one did not suspect that the progressives were incorrect in their assumptions about human behavior—that people expended more energy, more eagerly in acts of destruction, cruelty and brutality than in actions of enlightenment and tolerance and improvement. Listen again to Durkheim, this time from the preface to the second edition of the same book, this later view published the same year he was delivering his lectures on *L'Education morale* at the Sorbonne:

> If we attempted to express in somewhat more precise terms contemporary ideas of what should be the relationship between employer and white-collar worker, between the industrial worker and the factory boss, between industrialists in competition with one another or between industrialists and the public, how imprecise would be the statements that we could formulate! Some vague generalities about the loyalty and commitment that employees of every kind owe to those who employ them, or about the moderation that employers should manifest in exercising their economic superiority, a certain condemnation of any competition that is too blatantly unfair, or of any too glaring exploitation of the consumer: this is almost the sum total of what the ethical consciousness of these professions [i.e., those "vague generalities"] comprises. Moreover, most of these precepts lack any juridical character. They are backed only by public opinion and not by the law—and it is well known how indulgent that opinion shows itself to be about the way in which such vague obligations are fulfilled. Those actions most blameworthy are so often excused by success that the boundary between the permissible and the prohibited, between what is just and what is unjust, is no longer fixed in any way, but seems capable of being shifted by individuals in an almost arbitrary fashion. (1902/1984, xxxii)

Durkheim's concerns over "the continually recurring conflicts and disorders of every kind of which the economic world affords so sorry a spectacle" (xxxii) were an expression of his view that the liberation of the individual, so extensively carried forth in and by market relations of organization, had spun out of control. There is another major thread uniting those concerns, then and now; for Durkheim it consisted of a missing middle that has been so anemic for so long that we have largely forgotten it. This missing middle was the fabric of civic organizations and functions that tied top and bottom, central government and grassroots politics together in an extended network of intersecting interests and supports, conflicts, and cooperative behaviors. Durkheim sorted through the possibilities of several different methods to restore and strengthen those vital connections, only to find that each was inadequate. The resulting evacuation of political capacities and capabilities was disturbing, to say the least.

A similar judgment, which Durkheim would surely recognize and understand, has been made by John Dunn at a time when, at least in the United States, civic engagement has been hobbled by the realization that the citizens' government has specialized mostly in waging war (with all the enormous apparatus perpetually in place for that), pork-barrel legislation that representatives of the people hand out to each other and to other, already wealthy persons and organizations, and a perpetual-motion machine dedicated to the next contest of electoral politics. The economic model of "a single economically frictionless world market in goods and services," Dunn (2005, 352, 353) points out, now prevails as our principal, virtually sole, expectation and explanation of what is in store for the world's population. The entire world will be a consumer society, each individual most importantly a shopper. In wake of the terror of episodes such as that of September 11, 2001, the best advice a president can give to his citizens is to go about your ordinary day; go shopping. As Dunn says of the dominant model of this world market, "there is no corresponding unifying conception, of remotely comparable intellectual power or clarity of outline, of what is at stake in how we organize the sustaining or the enhancement of our productive powers, or of the range of patterns of distribution within a given territory or population which might prove to be sustainable socially or politically" (353). This would be an astounding recognition were we not already so accustomed to the state of affairs it describes.

Implications of the state of affairs have generally not been faced, however, and sometimes it seems a willful shortsightedness—or perhaps it is a will-less drowsiness—enforces that neglect. The notion that this sole unifying conception now available to us can be brought to its promised fruition through existing instruments of political agreement does seem, as Dunn pronounced it, fantastical. In the United States, after all, our political capacities have failed, at least for the moment, to solve much simpler problems such as Social Security's fiscal stability or an adequate provision of health care for all citizens. Culture wars, our carnivals of fear and loathing, are more entertaining, as we try to figure out who we ought to be—or at least who we want to be, other than a free rider.

= Chapter 8 =

Questions of Principal
and Principle

IN SPITE of the many important program features involved in this
debate, much of the analysis and discussion of alternative approaches
to postemployment income security has focused on comparative
rates of return on investment, often with some sort of standard of fairness of distribution implied if not explicitly included. The comparisons
are not always evenhanded; in fact, some of these discussions reflect
deliberate dishonesty more than a straightforward difference of opinion. For example, sometimes arithmetic means are used when geometric
means (which tend to have smaller values) would be more appropriate.
On occasion, differences in transaction costs are understated or excluded.
Too often differences of vocabulary are called on in place of careful argument; a major example is that contributions to Social Security are called
a tax (that is, the FICA tax), whereas contributions to an occupationally
based pension are called personal contributions, as are contributions to
a personally defined portfolio of investments as in an IRA. Moreover,
the evaluations of investment returns are often truncated comparisons
between the slightly progressive redistribution built into Social Security
and the less predictable but often higher returns from market-based
redistributions between winners and losers. Some of the truncations are
qualitative—for example, the politically loaded difference in names such
as tax versus contribution. Others are quantitative—for example, focusing on average rates of return but neglecting differences in the variance
of return. Still others are both qualitative and quantitative—for example, ignoring that market transactions are no less redistributive than a
program such as Social Security, usually redistributive to a much greater
degree, and usually regressive rather than progressive or neutral.

Another difference when comparing alternative approaches has to do
with the knowledge base on which comparisons of outcome are built.
We have reasonably good knowledge of what past performance has
been for the alternative programs of income security (or would have
been, in the case of programs not actually implemented). That said,
our present concerns are to design an optimal program—not for past

214

conditions—but rather for future conditions. Although there is a large empirical base of forward-looking knowledge about the distribution of winners and losers in the allocation of Social Security benefits—for instance, longer-lived beneficiaries, one-earner married couples, and low-income earners fare better in terms of replacement rates than their counterparts do—building a comparable empirical base of forward-looking knowledge about the distribution of returns for private accounts faces some serious obstacles and limitations.

First, for any reasonable future period of time, market returns are uncertain and that uncertainty cannot be brushed aside by assumption. Projected distributions of market returns will necessarily be less reliable than the same distributions for Social Security.[1] We can estimate how different patterns of savings might accumulate over time, but unless we assume the lowest risk portfolio—something like total investment in Treasury bonds—the range of possible outcomes for a given long-term horizon can be quite wide.

The second limitation pertains to another aspect of that uncertainty. Whereas the empirical base of knowledge for Social Security is tied to specifically identified persons in future as well as present periods, empirical knowledge of market returns can be projected into future periods only on a statistical basis—that is, for the average case, typical cases, and the like. There are techniques for predicting where individuals with specified characteristics will probably be located in any future-period distributions of winners and losers, but they are also statistical, and the uncertainty is much greater when predicting outcomes for specific individuals than when predicting for typical cases. This uncertainty translates into a range of possible values, and the width of this range (the difference between the minimum and maximum values) gets wider and wider as uncertainty grows.

Too often in the ongoing debates over alternative approaches to income security, proponents of a particular proposal gloss over these differences in what we know about different approaches (and what each can promise) and invoke the word *market* as if it were a magical talisman. Markets are not magical, yet simply using the term seems to persuade many listeners that no evidence is needed. Markets are indeed very powerful forms of organization but, like any form of organization, create problems even as they solve others. Markets are good at some things, not at all things. Likewise, of course, government is good at some but not all things.

An often cited advantage of markets is their efficiency, but the specific meaning of efficiency in this context is not necessarily the one that comes to the mind of the typical citizen. One of the deceits sometimes practiced in these debates relies on the specific concept of efficiency, and the assertion that markets are efficient and governments are not. The trickery intersects with a specific understanding of and assumptions about redistributive effects: market redistributions are good, government redistributions are bad. Although the word *redistributive* is not often associated with markets, any market transaction is in fact inherently redistributive. The basic event of a transaction involves reassigning a good or service from one market player who values the good or service less (and is therefore willing to sell) to another market player who values it more (and is therefore willing to buy). That statement is definitional of the pricing mechanism, an assumption of equilibrium theory. That assumption does indeed point to the efficiency of the market, but it is also important to note that the contrast between "values less" and "values more" can conceal enormous differences in the conditions of the players at the time of the transaction. The good or service might be valued less by the seller because she or he is simply tired of it and wants proceeds from the sale to apply elsewhere, is poorer and thus less able to maintain the good, less knowledgeable and thus less likely to understand any number of factors relevant to the present value of the good's future worth, more gullible and thus more likely to fall victim to sharp trading, in poor health and thus less attentive to transactions, or any number of other possibilities. These conditions are readily connected to transactions we've experienced. The piece of junk turns out to be a more valuable antique; the property was sold just before the site for the new housing development was chosen; the tickets we couldn't use we had to sell at a discount. Market efficiency cares nothing about such conditions. Market redistributive process—the movement of a good or service from where it is less valued to where it is more valued—does not inquire about such varied needs or circumstances of the players.

We are not suggesting here that expected returns provide worthless information. Whether used to estimate an investor's expected return for a private account or for Social Security, a mean rate of return is informative. By definition, the mean of a distribution is the preferred summary statistic, conveying more of the information contained in that distribution than any other single number. Not all means provide equally good information, however, and the difference in how good a summary measure it is involves the amount of variation around the mean. Thus, when evaluating the probable future outcomes of alternative investment programs, one should give as much attention to the variance of outcomes as to the mean outcome. As inequality increases (Gottschalk and Smeeding 2000)—that is, as individual experiences diverge more from the typical case—the mean becomes less useful as a predictor for any given individual. This point is especially germane to evaluations of income-security programs at a time when income inequality in the United States has been increasing rapidly to unusually high levels. Evidence of that trend abounds. In 2005, the average chief executive officer (CEO) in the United States had an annual income that was 262 times the annual income of the typical U.S. worker, an inequality that was more than ten times greater than it had been in the mid-1960s. Given this trend, anyone concerned about his or her future income security should surely be interested in learning about the variance, not just the mean rate, of returns on alternative investment programs. As recent years have demonstrated repeatedly, it is entirely possible that even as mean rates of return increase, the likelihood that any person taken at random ends up in the low end of the distribution of returns also increases. That is part of what is meant by increasing inequality.[2]

How should people estimate and use information about variation in expected returns when trying to evaluate alternative programs? The standard quantitative approach is to estimate the variance or standard deviation of the distribution of returns. This number, when used in conjunction with the mean, summarizes most of the information contained in the distribution and thus is the most efficient method of evaluating variation around a mean rate of return. We should note, however, that this notion of efficiency is very similar to the notion of market efficiency just discussed: it is an efficiency purchased at the cost of summarizing by a single number what could in fact be a lot of difference of actual conditions. It can be a useful starting point, to be sure, but a mix of quantitative and qualitative approaches can yield a much more informative basis for comparing alternative income-security programs.

One could compare program outcomes for different profiles of investors and different sets of assumptions about investment conditions. For example, it would be very useful to know what proportion of people, and which categories of people, would do better under a program of private accounts relative to a repaired Social Security program. It also would be useful to know how the distribution of differences in quantitative outcomes correlates with other individual characteristics, such as earnings history, marital status, education, and health. To answer these and related questions, however, one would need the joint distribution of outcomes for individual participants, not just mean values for each group. An even better approach would enable us to generate the outcome distributions for alternative programs on both objective and subjective criteria (Heckman 2006), where subjective outcomes could include well-being experienced across the life course—that is, stresses and worries involved in consumption and investment decisions affecting future income streams, relative to present streams and demands (for example, security in present employment, housing, health care, children's schooling, and so forth). Granted, generating this type of joint distribution would be a complex task. In fact, it would rely on measurement technologies that presently yield only unreliable results, but even the former joint distribution is far more complex than simple comparisons of averages would suggest. This is in part because of differences in variances (shapes of the tails of the distributions) and in part because (as noted earlier) the future-period data for market-based outcomes would be more conjectural than the corresponding data for Social Security—again, assuming that Social Security survives the ongoing political threats and gains appropriate technical repair.

All these questions focus on individual outcomes, either in absolute or relative terms, and individual outcomes are important, but so are societal outcomes and trajectories. Questions addressing outcomes at the societal level are linked to outcomes for individuals, but this linkage can be quite complex. Which distribution of goods will take American society in the best direction, however citizens agree to define best?[3] How should we tailor a program that does most, if not all, of what we want it to do? When addressing the question of social welfare, many economists and policy analysts simply substitute "people" for the individual: thus, for instance, are people better off because of such-and-such? Here, people is typically intended as a straightforward aggregation of all individual members of a society, though issues of how that membership is defined are often involved in contentious ways (for example, where do illegal immigrants fit into the picture?), and welfare refers to the satisfaction of personal preferences individually and, within specified legal limits, freely. There is an inconsistency between the individualism of the latter (personal preference) and the aggregation or abstraction of the former (people).

This inconsistency highlights a major part of the difficulty in making the kinds of comparisons of program described in the preceding paragraph. Individual preferences are sentiments, as Adam Smith and countless others have recognized. As such, they can be assessed relative to one another by observing personal decisions and behaviors. If person A attends concerts of classical music more often than jazz concerts, and jazz concerts more often than R&B concerts, then person A has revealed accordingly her preference hierarchy for those three types of musical concert. Presumably, if one asked A to rank order the three types, she would rank them as just described. But if there is inconsistency between reports and behaviors, the tendency is strongly to rate actual behavior as more telling than verbal description. However, interpersonal comparisons of welfare cannot be made in terms of personal preference hierarchies. To see why, consider the following illustration. In contrast to person A, as just described, let's say that person B's preference hierarchy is jazz above both R&B and classical, and R&B above classical. The differences between those hierarchies are descriptively straightforward. Yet it would be perfectly coherent to learn that A would pay as much or more for a ticket to an R&B concert, for example, than person B would pay for the same ticket to the same concert, or, for that matter, a same-seat ticket to a jazz concert by B's favorite jazz musician. Are preference hierarchies thus of less relevance to personal welfare than is the pricing mechanism of market transaction? More important, is it acceptable to collapse the efficiency of social welfare (or social justice) into the efficiency of the pricing mechanism? Is the welfare of the average CEO worth 262 times the welfare of the average worker? Is the welfare of the average CEO ten times more important or valuable today, relatively speaking, than it was in the mid-1960s?

The general problem here is more than a technical matter of the correct weighting algorithm to apply when aggregating across individual preferences and circumstances to arrive at an assessment of social welfare. For instance, what really is meant by the word *social* in the phrase *social welfare?* What is a society if not the summation of its individual citizens, equally weighted as in one person, one vote? If questions of individual choice and personal liberty inevitably raise corresponding questions about the meaning of social and society—and thus inevitably the basic moral question of what, if any, obligations members of a society owe one another simply by virtue of that common membership— then why is the debate about Social Security and alternative programs of postemployment income provision being waged primarily in terms of financial accounting? Aside from or in addition to the individual-level cost-benefit analyses that have become so common in the debates, how should we judge the social costs of increased poverty in old age, or the social benefits of holding individuals accountable for their own economic security in old age? These are not the types of questions that either demographers or economists generally address, though their analytic frameworks and results certainly are relevant to, and hold implications for, the way the questions are heard as well as answered. Philosophers are the ones who dare to address those questions openly and robustly, but philosophers are rarely invited into boardrooms or congressional offices.

Solutions

No doubt some readers have persevered to this last chapter with the expectation that we would provide the answer. We do not. For reasons that should be clear by now, we cannot. All sorts of technical solutions to the technical problem have been offered by technical experts; we do not see a need for still another, different from those we already have. We will come back to this aspect of the expectation in a minute. More important than any of that, however, is the fact that any version of the answer must be an outcome of political process—whether insinuated through manipulations of an electorate by political operatives or negotiated openly among competing interests of a citizenry informed by whatever technicians, philosophers, moralists, and so forth, they choose to consult.

Our purpose in writing this book has not been to persuade our readers that this or that specific proposal, or general approach, for dealing with present problems of Social Security and future needs for postemployment income security is the correct solution. Rather, our purpose has been to place the debate in context and urge our readers to the view that their interests are best served if they demand a far more open, far less duplicitous political process, one that features more information-based, far less deceptive and manipulative discussions of the relevant issues, options, and ranges of consequences involved in the various options of proposed technical solutions. We do have a further suggestion, which we will come to shortly, but it is a suggestion of process, not of outcome.

A variety of technical solutions to the technical problems of Social Security in particular, and postemployment income provisions in general, have been proposed by various individuals and groups well versed in the technical dimensions. All of them would probably work, in some sense of that verb, but they would work differently with different results for different people, and probably with different new problems created in the process, to be faced down the road. Most of the proposals seem to be well intentioned. A few, however, seem to be efforts mainly to dissolve Social Security, with very little beyond generalities as proposed alternatives. One ellipsis concerns transition costs, how to pay for the shift from the current program to an alternative program, without robbing beneficiaries of the current program. Indeed, proposals of alternative programs tend to be rather short on specifics and fail to offer a detailed blueprint for getting from where we are to where we should be.[4] The proposals differ by assumptions of economic theory about how things work, by assumptions about present factual conditions, by assumptions of expected future conditions, and by assumptions of economic or political-economic ideology (insofar as that can be discriminated from economic theory), especially concerning the constitution of the good society (that is, the goals toward which an economic policy should work). Those differences alone are enough to virtually guarantee differences both in how the programs would work and in how well they would work, relative to present and near-future conditions of the problem or problems each would be addressing if enacted. There would likely be other differences that would emerge from the process of enactment itself, because though there is a strong tendency to believe that execution of plan can be a neutral event in a neutral medium, it never is, whether the execution is by market transaction or by government design.

There is also a strong tendency for proponents of a particular proposal or approach to oversell, especially with regard to effects. This is one indication that the motivating issues are ideological and moral, not simply technical, even though (or when) the proposal is presented as purely technical in nature. The fact of the matter is, despite such tendencies, no one does know how, or how well, any of the proposals would work if enacted, or what the various sets of consequences would be. This statement applies also, by the way, to the current implicit proposal of doing nothing and allowing Social Security to falter. The dynamics of the economic and demographic processes are complex; no one knows those processes well enough to predict with certainty what the consequences of any reasonably plausible intervention would be. Naiveté, inexperience, or disingenuousness might lead some to argue the contrary, but insofar as any proposal relies, at least in part and sometimes in large part, on behavioral change, it is very difficult to predict what the outcomes would be, and any such predictions are inherently probabilistic. This is especially the case to the extent that affected persons are ill informed as to what sorts of changes are expected of them and to the extent that they lack the skills or knowledge to implement such changes effectively. Furthermore, all of what has just been said was said as if the only relevant processes to be enacted were demographic and economic, without manipulation or amendment or distortion by political process, which returns us to the earlier point. However well conceived the complex economic and demographic processes of a plan might be, they will not be enacted as a neutral event in a neutral medium.

Any of the proposed solutions, including the implied proposal of doing nothing, is or will be an experiment, which implies an uncertain outcome. The proposals that led to the Social Security Act of 1935, and the compromised act itself, were experiments. Similarly, and as an example, any of the long sequence of labor-contract negotiations between automotive-manufacturing corporations and the United Auto Workers over the proper allocation of wages between present and future (deferred) compensation (that is, pension plans, health-care plans, and the like) also was experimental. Although it is probably true that some actors were more attentive than others to projections of long-term financial consequences of one or another arrangement, no one could be certain of outcomes. That has not changed.

That said, human beings, organized collectively in families, in cities, and in societies, engage in experiments with regularity. How can we motivate our children to take school seriously? How can we adopt a healthier lifestyle? How can we reduce our commute time to work? We try one thing, then another; sometimes we get it largely right the first time and need only tweak our approach; other times we get it largely wrong, and have to work to undo negative consequences before trying a different approach. And sometimes, we find an approach that works until conditions change. Our son makes a new best friend. We suffer an injury that makes sticking to our regimen difficult. The city begins extensive construction on the road we've been taking. We must rethink, reformulate a solution.

One of the advantages of human intelligence, at least in principle, is that experiments can be designed and conducted with more or less continual feedback about actual consequences relative to desired outcomes. Experiments on the general public have become a routine method of determining the effectiveness (and possible side effects) of new pharmaceuticals. Waiting for more controlled research projects to accumulate keeps potentially useful medicines out of the hands of people who might benefit. Further, the wide variation in individual biochemistry, comorbidities, and other health-related characteristics make it difficult and costly to determine how any particular patient will respond. The more complex the processes on which the experiment is conducted, the more difficult the monitoring, the more haphazard the awareness of what might be going wrong where, and so forth. Human beings, though, are learning creatures.

A Modest Suggestion

Why wait for another presidential commission or a new round of congressional hearings to choose a course of action? All too often those venues are now little more than stages for political maneuverings calculated with the next election in mind, at the cost of anything else. Given the increasingly bitter partisanship and declining civility in these formal circles, as well as the media-nurtured war of sound bites, why not try something different? Why not have a traveling panel of ideologically diverse demographers, economists, sociologists, public policy analysts, actuaries, philosophers, and perhaps others, conduct televised town meetings across the country, the principal intent being to educate, not persuade but inform, the electorate as to what is known and what is conjectured about the nature and conditions of the current and projected fiscal health of Social Security, the nature and conditions of alternative proposed responses to those technical problems, the range of probable and plausible consequences of those responses if enacted, and the underlying moral and ethical issues—all presented not as certain statements by some oracle but modestly, as best educated guesses, by informed persons who are not running for any public office and who will steadfastly attempt to maintain the venue as political in the sense of citizenship. Launching such an initiative would be an interesting experiment in itself.

Could it succeed? A pessimist (or should this be realist?) would argue that the odds are against it. Consider the possible reactions as depicted in table 8.1. Assume that two sets of competing interests must be addressed—those in favor of private accounts and those in favor of repairing and retaining Social Security as social insurance.[5] Presumably,

Table 8.1   Heuristic of Public Meeting Strategies

		Private Accounts	
		Nonpartisan	Partisan
Social Insurance	Nonpartisan	A	B
	Partisan	C	D

Source: Authors' compilations.

the citizenry in general has an interest in gaining access to information, having an opportunity to ask questions, receiving a balanced view of the issues, and arriving at some conclusions, tentative though they should be, about the next course of action. What of the two partisan camps? How might they approach the meetings?

The answer depends on whether they are willing to step back from the process—not that we would expect them to be uninvolved, but the least desirable approach, in our opinion, would be for one or both sides to approach these town meetings as if they were part of a general campaign. For example, trying to ensure that presenters would be loyal to the given side, trying to restrict who was allowed to attend the meetings, encouraging their members to attend and attempt to skew the discussion to one side, and to have their representatives available outside to provide ready reactions to the press about which side won that night would all be unwelcome interference.

In cells B and C, we would face situations in which one side decided to push partisanship, and the other side decided to cooperate with our goal. These situations are inherently unstable and would probably lead to a breakdown of the initiative. Of the remaining options, A and D, which would the general public prefer? Has a gladiator mentality infected the public to such an extent that most adults prefer the entertainment of a contest to the instruction of a schoolroom and the dialogue of a chautauqua? Would most adults see option A as too demanding of engagement, attention, and concentration? Would most adults prefer option D as another spectator sport, with carefully rehearsed performances and fans yelling at one another and for their choice of teams?

We do not know the answers to these questions. We do not know how to assess civic capacity in the many different communities across the country, nor are we in a position to judge the capacity of the many different members of our society for this type of public work. Perhaps it would be worth the effort of fielding such an initiative, just to learn that balance of public preference. But various foundations and nonprofit groups have been trying to stage meetings of this sort for at least the past decade. Attempts to spur civic engagement through public meetings or various reinventions of the chautauqua have engaged some people, though the people these projects tend to attract are already active in other types of local government pursuits and civic organizations. If a series of the proposed town meetings should actually be organized, what would be the likely result? Is it reasonable to expect citizens to engage in this type of long-term planning and execution? Is the expectation of this level of dedication to task, this level of responsibility for policy choices, less than or greater than asking citizens to take on the day-to-day responsibilities of learning, planning, staying informed, saving, investing, and performing the other myriad tasks involved in a completely individualized program of postemployment income insurance?

Let's think about the suggestion another way. If we fielded one of the proposed town meetings, we would hope to attract an audience as large as and perhaps larger than the number of citizens who attend local government meetings on particularly important and controversial issues of community policy—say, some type of general rezoning ordinance or changes to the level and structure of utility fees. A good number of those attending would be observers in the audience, but we would expect to see many people asking questions and speaking in favor of or opposed to the proposal at issue. Let's assume that the meeting did involve the activities of a collection of citizens who were especially thoughtful, eloquent, and good at explaining complex issues, with the result that the meeting concluded in a decision that had strong support from those in attendance. What of the interests of all those local citizens who did not (or could not) attend? Apparently, one could say, they did not feel sufficiently motivated by the issues to participate. In any case, they will live their lives after the policy change the way they lived their lives before the policy change. Perhaps a new shopping center is built at the edge of their community, or right in the middle of their community; perhaps they will pay higher (or lower) utility bills. What will be expected of them as a result of the policy change will usually be a matter of relatively small adjustments, on average. Now think about a proposal to substitute an individualized retirement-income program for Social Security (and ignore for the moment issues about transaction costs). If the policy change removes the social-insurance aspect of Social Security, thus diminishing earnings-replacement security for middle-class and working-class persons, the policy change will ask the majority of people—not just workers but nonworking spouses, not just the average citizen but all those not as skilled as the average, not just those with some affinity for issues of finance but those who have a glimmer of understanding and those who are clueless—to change fundamentally the way they approach their personal (or household) finances. Would that fact motivate them more energetically to attend the proposed town meeting, more likely than they now attend a local council meeting? If it did not, should they nonetheless be expected to muster the skills and vigilance required by successful management of their future-income accounts? Are they bad citizens (bad people) because of their absence? What would the local community be expected to do about the failures in that regard, about the people who are already dancing as fast as they can? Write them off as necessary casualties?

Holding all of that aside, the sad fact is that prospects for our suggested series of town meetings are not good, because by all evidence most U.S. citizens make very little effort to acquire new information, information that differs from what they already think, already know, or already think they know. This is not because they are incapable of the task. Several researchers have demonstrated that, as Bruce Ackerman and James Fishkin summarized the evidence, the general public "is more than capable of living up to demanding democratic expectations" (2004, 7). That is surely good news. But it puts in even starker relief the question recently asked by Alan Wolfe: why, then, do so many members of the electorate so frequently fail to acquire and effectively use new information, even when they are faced with electoral choices that have major impacts on their well-being?

> That question could not be more relevant than it is under conditions of the new politics of democracy. When ideologically driven elites are determined to substitute emotion for fact in the hopes of moving opinion in the directions they favor, the public's incentive to inform itself could not be greater. Yet at a time when Americans need information more, they evidently want it less. The most comprehensive examination of the knowledge Americans have about politics [reported in Delli Carpini and Keeter 1996] documented a level that by nearly all reasonable standards was shockingly low. (Wolfe 2006, 42–43)[6]

Where Do We Go from Here?

Were it not for the economic-demographic challenges currently facing Social Security and postemployment provisions more generally, would the question of how best to provide wage-replacement income be a focus of so much attention or stir such strong political passions? Probably not. But the basic issues would not thereby disappear. The technical problems facing Social Security are not newly recognized, and all along the path of repeated recognitions some rather simple solutions of those technical problems were at hand. That continues to be the case today. The fact that those solutions have not always been enacted, with the result that the technical problems of Social Security have worsened, leads one to question motivations. Has this failure been part of a much larger failure of governmental offices and political process, or has it been (either instead of or in addition to that) a failure specific to Social Security? This question, too, is difficult to answer, because there is so much evidence pointing each direction. For example, as Robert Kaiser recently pointed out in the *Washington Post* (August 13, 2006), the House of Representatives allocated most of its time during the month of July 2006 to these issues: flag burning, stem cell research, gay marriage, the Pledge of Allegiance, religion and gun control. Nothing much was accomplished beyond symbolic postures for the electorate, and most of the little bit that was otherwise accomplished had the look of a know-nothing endorsement of ignorance, intolerance, and irrelevance.

The problem of Social Security was no longer on the favored lists of talking points. On the other hand, a few months earlier, the problem of Social Security had been one of the hottest topics in town. Then it was remarkably easy to conclude—given the many unanswered questions and the general vagueness of the presidential administration's proposal to fix Social Security (the second G. W. Bush administration)—that the administration intended to simply abolish this governmental program, no matter how well it had been achieving its objectives, and despite the absence of an adequately specified alternative. We were reminded that the verb, *fix*, conventionally used to mean repair or restore, could also be used colloquially, meaning to neuter.

That modern societies need to support consumption by growing numbers of people who are no longer engaged in paid employment was a realization that surfaced late in the nineteenth century and increased in prominence during the twentieth. Decades were devoted to deciding how to define the proper categories into which such people should be sorted (unemployed, disabled, discouraged, retired, and so on), what specific criteria should be used to make those assignments and what behaviors or conditions should lead to reassignments, and whether—and if so, how—family members should be factored into a person's wage-replacement accounts. These decisions have been revisited and adjusted periodically as issues of contemporary work and family life that did not figure into the original blueprint have emerged. All along the way, the decisions have been guided by technical considerations (economic, demographic, and the like), but at root they began and remain as decisions about some rather fundamental moral-ethical issues. What sorts of persons should we aspire to be? Where should we, or must we, limit as well as require mutual obligations as members of the same society? Because of those issues, which, as discussed briefly in chapter 7, are seldom if ever simple binary choices between all this or all that, the decisions have always been contentious and, more often than not, contended.

Political process is supposed to negotiate between the technical and the moral-ethical as well as among different positions on the moral-ethical dimensions, so that members of society can achieve workable compromises toward effective decisions, effective executions of those decisions, effective monitoring of consequences of the decisions, and effective modifications as they agree are needed. The political process has been increasingly unable to serve that function, however, in this as in a growing array of other areas of the body politic. In place of effective governance, citizens are presented with entertainments of electoral politics and charades designed to mold and manipulate electoral sentiments in directions desired by political operatives (Brader 2006; Jacobs and Shapiro 2000; Manza, Cook, and Page 2002). Social Security, both the particular set of governmental income-insurance programs that come under that name and the general problem of postemployment income provision, has been often trivialized as a result of, and in the midst of, those failures of political process.

It bears repeating that the economic demography of the specific programs of Social Security would change, even in the absence of any unexpectedly large or small birth cohorts surviving to old age, has been known since the beginning of those programs. Moreover, the programs were designed not to be solely adequate to the consumption needs of the old-age population but to be minimal insurance as back-up to the other legs of a three-legged stool solution, occupationally based pensions and personal saving-and-investment behaviors. The expectation has been that a combination of those three avenues would function as a diversified portfolio of postemployment income sources. The programs of Social Security would be low-risk, guaranteed-eligibility, and a guaranteed-but-low-rate-of-return form of investment, the most conservative part of a portfolio. Occupational pensions were expected to provide better rates of return, with substantial collectivization of risk (though not as much as in Social Security) and with explicitly negotiated and designed rules to govern and assure (not simply promise) eligibility and payout. Considerably less conservative than Social Security, these private programs worked unless or until corporate management succeeded, with government approval, in redefining employment contracts after the fact, so as to use the pension funds for other purposes, change eligibility rules, and so forth. The third leg was left entirely up to the individual. That is, decisions about whether to engage in individual saving-and-investment behavior, what kind, how conservative or adventuresome to be in risk-taking, whether to leave proceeds untouched until retirement date, and so forth were left to each individual to make as he or she saw fit. Unless the individual invested in a group plan (for example, a mutual fund or unit-trust fund), there would be no pooling of risk. There would be no guarantees of eligibility beyond the individual's own willpower. Rates of return could be as high as the individual's market decisions made possible.

The three-legged stool solution was explicitly known by its designers to be experimental. They knew, for example, that the occupational-pension leg would work only insofar as negotiations of contract between management and labor enabled it to work. Indeed, business leaders (for example, Charles Wilson) and labor-union leaders (for example, Walter Reuther) did not see eye-to-eye on the proper organization of pension or health-care provisions for quite some time, and only after occupational provisions became a mandatory focus of collective bargaining did those differences have to be negotiated to mutually acceptable compromise (Klein 2003). Likewise, the designers knew that the personal-investment leg of the stool was experimental in several respects. For instance, would the average person have or acquire enough skill and self-discipline? Would the presence of Social Security and occupationally based pensions be treated as substitutes rather than supplements of personal saving and investment? More generally, there was an issue about the proper level of income (and wealth) inequality and whether progressive policies were good or bad. Is it more efficient for a society to concentrate private saving and investment in the hands of a relatively small number of persons, or is it better to disperse surplus income (income left over after basic consumption needs) more widely, believing that ordinary people will save and invest in promising future production factors rather than squander their surplus money on frivolous diversions?

As for the third leg, Social Security, the designers knew that it would be a target of critics of governmental action, that it would gain acceptance only if structured as an insurance program with universal (or near-universal) participation so that coverage in the risk pooling could extend to all, and that it would require periodic adjustments as demographic and economic facts changed. With respect to the last of these points, they believed that a seventy-five-year projection would be sufficiently forward-looking for the intended balance between revenues and benefits, and as a window within which phased adjustments could be modest. They were correct. Projections made decades ago have proven to be remarkably accurate. Indeed, Social Security has proven one of the great success stories of government action in the United States. This is not to say that better programs cannot now be designed. But the fact of that success, along with the fact that the successful record would continue if still relatively minor adjustments were made, suggests that the Social Security programs should not be dismissed until a carefully vetted, clearly superior alternative program has been designed in enough detail that one can have confidence that it is superior. Not, that is, unless the majority of citizens genuinely believe that they—and all others, too? or is that not part of the moral agreement?—can do without the low-cost, universally available risk pooling for their own future income security.

The apparent inability of political process to respond effectively, whether to the problem of Social Security or to any number of other serious matters (for example, affordable health care), has resulted in part from profound disagreements on some basic moral-ethical issues, as described in chapter 7. What sort of person, what sort of character, should public policy promote? Intelligent rather than ignorant? Capable rather than incapable? Self-disciplined rather than reliant on a paternalist guide and enforcer? Surely those are easy choices. They are also simplistic and unrealistic. It is not a matter of all this or all that. Intelligence and stupidity, for example, come in degrees. So, too, capability and incapability and all the other seemingly simple binary choices. If it is agreed that public policy should promote self-discipline rather than reliance on a paternalism, for example, what should then be done with regard to those persons who for whatever reason don't quite measure up to someone else's standard? Whatever the character trait, it will be arrayed along a dimension, a gradient, with most persons located in a broad middle and fewer persons located in either of the extremes (that is, extremely self-disciplined versus extremely not self-disciplined). What obligations, if any, do those in the middle range and those in the upper range have toward those in the lower range? Bear in mind that this is a question not only about those persons who are in the lower end of the distribution; it is also about all of those who might fall—and some will fall—to that location five, ten, twenty years down the road. It is also, however, a question about society as a whole. Recall that the problem of consumption in old age was addressed not only because there were too many old persons starving, dying of treatable illness, grappling with the despair and loneliness of poverty, but also because aggregate consumption in society was deemed too low. There was too little demand for goods and services that could be produced but were not being produced because too few persons could afford to buy them. A consumer society simply could not afford to have too many people who consumed too little. The recent epitome of recognition of this reality was the most prominent advice given after the most recent round of tax cuts: "Go shopping!"

The breakdown of political process has occurred also because, in their eagerness to manipulate public sentiments and opinions to their electoral advantage, too many politicians, and other political operatives, have engaged in the simplistic mentality of all this or all that. Consider, for example, the contrast of individual versus collective interest; much of the disagreement over basic moral-ethical issues can be, has been, summarized in those terms. The delusion of that otherwise useful contrast occurs when someone believes, or speaks as if he or she believes, that only individual interest is important or only collective interest is important—or even that one of these sides of the coin is always or uniformly more important than the other. As a long list of our predecessors understood, however, including such figures as James Madison and Alexander Hamilton, the individual and the collective really are two sides of the same coin. Each depends on the other. One side might become more prominent for a time and in certain venues, but the pendulum swings back and other venues counterbalance, precisely because each side cannot avoid calling forth the other. Political settlements that are effective are achieved as and through negotiations between these complementary sides. There have been periods of history, however, when that insight is lost, and the American public has fallen into one of those periods, a time of severe devolution of political process.

It is of course easy to blame the politicians. So many of them, it very often seems, are intent on making it so easy to blame them. A well-known journalist recently described the present devolution in the subtitle to his book, *Politics Lost*. It is a matter of "how American democracy was trivialized by people who think you're stupid," the you being any ordinary member of the electorate selected at random (Klein 2006; see also Jacobs and Shapiro 2000). The process of devolution has been more complex than that. Hunter Thompson and Richard Hofstadter would no doubt agree, were they living, that politics lost the battle when a morality of fear and loathing, a morality of paranoia, moved from the wings to center stage in the ongoing contest for the electorate's loyal attention. Political process has become fixated on efforts to mold and manipulate the loyalty and credulity of the electorate. The balance of the electorate has been complicit in that fixation.

At the grassroots level, the trivialization of political process has been manifest in a long-term dissolution of trust. There are many indicators of this dissolution. Repeated surveys of public opinion have shown, for example, that whereas about 80 percent of the public expressed trust in government during the mid-1960s, as few as 25 percent did by 2005. Cynicism has been a major beneficiary of that decline. Politicians reinforce public suspicion of governmental process. They fuel populist distrust in the very offices that they strive to win in electoral contests by proclaiming their own disdain of government. The electorate are not simply victims of that cynicism, however. They are full participants who know their roles in the charade. Alan Wolfe has aptly summarized the self-reinforcing circularity of this dance. Too many members of the electorate "feel no incentive to learn more about what is happening in Washington," or about issues that directly and indirectly affect their own present and future well-being, and this passivity

only encourages their leaders to take further advantage of their ignorance. When their leaders do exactly that, Americans could respond by blaming themselves for not paying attention and vowing to do better next time. But such introspection is unlikely to be present in a populistic politics committed to praising the common sense of ordinary people. And so Americans typically conclude that they were right to pay so little attention to politics because politicians are so self-interested and manipulative. A cycle in which ignorance breeds blame is thereby fueled by distrust. (2006, 43)

It has been common to point the finger especially at those members of the electorate who generally do not vote. These drop-outs are not, of course, the ones who positively elect the very politicians who both play them as pawns and become walking emblems of their distrust of politics and politicians. It should thus be no surprise that research has confirmed that it is generally the most committed and involved portion of the electorate who are most easily manipulated by political operatives (see, for example, Brader 2006).

As we have said more than once, it has been clear for some time that, though the problem of Social Security is technical (that is, economic-demographic) in the first instance, as a practical matter it has been and continues to be mainly a political problem, with moral-ethical basis and background. This same statement describes, we believe, the conditions of responding effectively to the technical problem. Recognizing that is not in and of itself a solution but is, we believe, an important step toward achieving a solution. The American public should realize that time is running short. The programs of Social Security can still be repaired and restored to fiscal integrity at relatively small cost, if the process is begun and completed soon. Before much more time has elapsed, the cost will become very large—both the direct cost of repair and the indirect costs of consequences down the road. At some point, delay will result in loss of the programs completely, which is no doubt what some partisans hope to see. It is of considerable interest in that regard, that once it became clear early in the second Bush administration that their preferred solution to the technical problem of Social Security did not have enough support, the problem of Social Security ceased to be a central topic of administration publicity. Apparently they saw no acceptable alternative. The relatively low-cost repairs that were still possible were apparently not an option. The electorate then saw apparently no reason to expect, much less demand, a continued and more effective response to the technical problem still troubling Social Security. This is presumably the same electorate that will be expected to manage its own future postemployment income security through private personal saving and investment plans, without the risk-pooling advantages of an insurance program such as Social Security and probably without occupationally based pension plans that involve any more risk-pooling than personal saving and investment plans.

= Notes =

Chapter 1

1. The technical issues of any proposed solution are quite complex. Some flavor of the challenge can be gained from a review of papers sponsored by the National Bureau of Economic Research (Campbell and Feldstein 2001). These papers are most convincing on precisely one point: the complexity of the task.

2. Hunter Thompson's *Fear and Loathing in Las Vegas* (1972) and "Fear and Loathing in Elko" (1992) remain two of the best diagnoses. Each in its own way is "a savage journey to the heart of the American dream" (the subtitle of his 1972 book, which first appeared the previous year in *Rolling Stone*).

3. Audience preference for negative over positive news, which media outlets reinforce because negative stories more easily lend themselves to dramatization, is in turn related to the fact that most people weigh losses of a given amount more heavily than they weigh gains of that amount (see, for example, Kahneman and Tversky 2000). This emphasis on loss aversion affects investment behaviors (see later chapters). Adam Smith glimpsed this asymmetry of valuation (see, for example, 1790/1976, 124–8, 157–8, 163, 164) and situated it directly within the self-interested actor's social network of moral sentiments.

4. Granted, the idea that this (or any) book can accomplish a clearing, rather than be sucked into the same morass it criticizes is ultimately a judgment readers will make. The cunning of unreason, to borrow the title of one of John Dunn's books, does not defeat hope but, ironically, somehow nurtures it.

5. It should also be noted that economists have been learning to relax several of the restrictive assumptions and thus making their models more powerful analytically as well as somewhat more realistic descriptively (see, for example, Loewenstein and Prelec 2000). Frank Hahn and Robert Solow give a powerful critique of neoclassical economics (1995). Wade Hands (2001) offers a good, generally accessible overview of the evolution of the methodology of economics, and where it stands today (see also White 2002, especially chapter 11).

6. Several of these technical terms (for example, FICA taxes) and competing preferences (for example, efficiency versus equity) will be discussed in chapter 2.

7. At the present time, for example, the U.S. monetary policy, as reflected in Treasury bills and bonds, is influenced as much by practices in Beijing and Seoul as in New York City and Washington, D.C. A number of top economists have been seriously assessing the likelihood that the U.S. dollar will cease to be the dominant reserve currency within the next few decades (see, for example, Eichengreen 2005).

8. A good, entry-level discussion, ending in brief discussions of alternative futures of U.S. society, is available in Beth Rubin's *Shifts in the Social Contract* (1996). Lest there be misunderstanding, we are not among those who decry globalization. Greater interdependence among the various cultures of the world is beneficial, on balance, to the whole, though we dislike the erasure or even diminution of differences that often comes with that interdependence. As one commentator recently noted, "The worldwide destruction of traditional cultures is just as much an uncontrolled experiment as global warming is" (Tripp 2005, 9). But a number of difficult adjustments and adaptations undoubtedly will be required, especially if we are to avoid the kinds of destructive reactions that have occurred in wake of previous episodes of rapid increase in the frequency and density of intercultural traffic.

9. The estimations were made within categories of the Standard Industrial Classification system and, for import and export data, the North American Industry Classification system; so the results are sensitive to composition of production and changes in that composition during the 1983 to 2003 period.

10. What most of the knee-jerk critiques of Marx and Engels forgot, or never knew, is that they were champions of capitalism—though not because they thought it was a preferred final end in itself, rather because they thought it was a necessary step, a means, to something even better.

Chapter 2

1. Comparing life expectancy for white men at birth, age twenty, and age sixty for 1940 and 2003, we see an increase from 62.8 to 75.4 at birth, from 47.8 to 56.3 at age twenty (that is, men surviving to age twenty in 1940 could expect to live to 67.8, on average, in 2003 to 76.3 on average), and from 15.1 to 20.6 at age sixty (that is, to 75.1 in 1940, to 80.6 in 2003).

2. Obviously there is some room for manipulation even with this simple measure, given that the age boundaries can be moved forward or backward. Decades ago, it was common for young men to enter the paid labor force at age sixteen, for example. More recently, the entry age is usually eighteen or even older, as larger proportions of men and women in their twenties delay entry into the paid labor force, a process some have called delayed maturation and others (for example, Nolte 2004) have called infantilization. Likewise, decades ago when old-age mortality was much higher, there were relatively few people older than sixty-five; but because of old-age morbidity and the rigors of labor in agrarian and early-industrial production, those people who did survive past sixty-five, or even past sixty, often had trouble remaining in the paid labor force.

3. These are, recall, age-eligible retirees who contributed through payroll taxes, plus their age-eligible spouses and dependent children; disabled workers and their families; and young survivor families.

4. The relevant literature in political and legal areas alone is truly enormous. The core and bulk of legal text in the Anglo American tradition is contract law, closely followed by tort law, both of which concern the regulation of liberties of agreement, property rights, and consequences thereof. One of the best overviews of the development of the underlying political theories is still C. B. Macpherson's (1962).

5. One of the most important ways in which actual markets differ from the ideal relates to the information function. Past and present cannot contain full information about any future, unless one's standard of knowledge assumes (as in some religious doctrines) that all future times have been ordained, in a humanly knowable way, and that there is a reliable way to discriminate the human claimants to that knowledge from the charlatans. There is therefore always the likelihood that some players will come to the market with privileged information gained externally (for example, awareness of this or that shock). Information itself tends to be strongly hierarchical.

6. Nor, of course, do actual hierarchies exactly fit the ideal of the hierarchical model. For example, because hierarchies generally manifest the descending thesis of authority, they tend to emphasize downward flows of information, thus ignoring or blocking upward flows especially from deviant sectors (for example, renegades, critics, and so on) within the organization, ultimately weakening the command and control leadership functions that are otherwise strengths of the hierarchical model.

7. This law was formulated from work in the seventeenth and eighteenth centuries on the theory of errors of measured observations. In more technical terms, it says that the arithmetic mean of the mean values of a very large number of pairwise independent random variables differs from the true arithmetic mean of those variables by less than a quantity ϵ with a probability that is arbitrarily close to one (that is, certainty). This is the basis of the statistical rule that the mean of a distribution of independent repeated measurements of an unknown quantity X is a better estimate of the true value of X than is any one of the measurements taken alone.

8. This is, granted, a very large if. Many people recoil from the notion of letting the market decide what value is, even though precisely that determination is made millions of time daily, even to the extent of measuring the value of this or that human life (as in, for example, setting premiums on life insurance policies). The question of what value is remains contentiously undecided in theory, however (see White 2002).

9. In fact, Smith used that phrase only a few times in all his writings, though it has become the emblem of Smithian theory. The insight behind the famous phrase was not original to him, but he did regard it as fundamentally important (see Smith 1776/1976, 456; 1790/1976, 181–3).

10. It was supposedly Abraham Lincoln who said (the attribution is traditional rather than documented), You may fool all of the people some of the time,

you can even fool some of the people all of the time, but you can not fool all of the people all of the time. Note that so many people, upon hearing that, take comfort in it.

11.   Another example is an efficient portfolio, a set of investment securities that, for any specified level of risk, yields the highest possible returns.

12.   Application of this efficiency framework extends also to production questions—not only what should be produced but also how that new product should be distributed to maximize gain and minimize loss.

13.   During the middle decades of the twentieth century, it also came to be used as a synonym for the value of investment securities, and then for the securities themselves, especially publicly issued corporate stocks. This elision of fairness with securities traded through market transaction established a specific notion of fairness in our common vocabulary. Within the specifics of the Social Security debate, this definition of fairness has been frequently used. A major friction between opposing camps has been the relative importance of two distributional principles—equity and adequacy—in the determination of benefits. In a debate that uses these terms, the equity principle defines benefit levels as a strict function of contributions, whereas the adequacy principle allows for redistribution to those with low earnings histories whose contributions would dictate a benefit too small to support a minimal standard of living. By implication, redistribution is viewed as unfair (inequitable) under the terms of the equity principle; on the other hand, an equitable determination of benefits leads to inadequacies. This type of framework establishes two points. First is that fairness or equity describes individual transactions and the process that governs them, not the outcome. Second is that to the extent that the outcome distribution requires some amendment, it should occur on the margin, by just enough to meet some minimal standard. We will discuss these issues again in later chapters.

14.   Meade's elegant work was a major stimulus for John Rawls's development of a theory of justice (1971; for a pertinent review of these extensive literatures, see Hausman and McPherson 1996).

15.   In fact, Paul Samuelson (1958) demonstrated that a perfectly competitive market is not necessarily efficient (see also Hausman and McPherson 1996, 206–7).

16.   A simple illustration is ticket scalping, often frowned on and in some jurisdictions illegal. Some people who won tickets to a 2005 musical concert organized by Bob Geldof for relief of world poverty (the Live8 concert) offered their tickets for sale through the eBay internet auction service. This action clearly qualifies as an instance of market efficiency. Geldof reportedly accused the sellers of sick profiteering, and a junior minister of the UK government urged eBay to remove the ticket offers (*The Economist*, June 18, 2005, p. 54).

17.   We use the qualifying phrase *narrowly defined* because externalities are themselves a source of inefficiency, given that the one gaining the benefit does not

pay full cost; instead, other actors must pay the difference when that additional cost can no longer be ignored. However, if an actor wants the balance of costs and benefits to appear more favorable, she or he could choose to omit any externalized costs from the balance sheet.

18.	We return to this difference momentarily, in the discussion of insurance functions, and then again later in the section on risk and uncertainty.

19.	Some analysts argue for a five period model, with the first and fifth periods being spent out of the labor force, the second entering employment too late, and the fourth leaving employment too soon.

20.	Indeed, as James Macdonald (2003, 481) has pointed out, the U.S. dollar has been a comparatively weak store of value. During the twentieth century it lost nearly 95 percent of its purchasing power. However, in the monetary system that was devised during that century (after the gold standard was abolished), stability of currency is conceived relative to an acceptable rate of inflation (the core task of the central bank being to keep to that rate). If that rate is defined as fluctuating between 2 and 2.5 percent, then the currency unit will necessarily lose (all else being equal) between 87 and 92 percent of its purchasing power during the course of 100 years.

21.	Because market is process, the dimension of time is critical to analyses of market phenomena, yet no existing treatment of the problem of time in economic theory has proved to be both workable and satisfying (for an introductory overview of major efforts, see Currie and Steedman 1990).

22.	We usually think about this from the other direction: a dollar's worth of goods today will cost more than one dollar in the future; but it is also true that, if I want to put money aside today so that I can purchase one dollar's worth of goods in the future, I needn't put aside one whole dollar, but something less than one dollar, assuming that by "putting it aside" I mean putting it in some interest bearing account. Perhaps the easier way to think about this is with savings bonds: to buy $100 savings bond as a gift, we pay less than $100, but the bond isn't worth the full $100 until some years in the future, depending on the rate of interest.

23.	There are many good lists of examples in the literature (see, for example, Loewenstein and Elster 1992; Loewenstein and Thaler 1989). A prime example of a negative discount rate is the willingness of "a large majority of US taxpayers [to] receive refunds every year from the Internal Revenue Service" (Loewenstein and Thaler 1989, 182). In other words, they do not refuse the investment option that pays at a rate below the prevailing interest rate. Their interest-free loan to the federal Treasury is the price they are willing to pay to have a government agency manage a substantial portion of their income accounts.

24.	Even Hegel, known to have been a great believer in the principle that most of what matters takes place "behind the back of consciousness," was quite willing to argue that the actual welfare of any given person is conditioned as much by that person's "caprices and particular endowment" as by any "objective system of needs," and that actualization of a person's right to welfare requires removal of "accidental hindrances"—which implies an ability to measure reliably where individual caprice and endowment each leave off and other factors begin (Hegel 1821/1942, 146–7).

25.   If I determine that risk pooling is not in my best interest, then I must commit to setting aside the amount of insurance I require. Otherwise, a decision to self insure degenerates into a decision to pretend my risk is zero.

26.   There is also the notion of generation in Karl Mannheim's sense, which began as more of a political-cultural than an economic-technical concept and is associated with the notion of historical period (see, for example, Hardy 1997). In that later guise it has relevance to the debate about Social Security (as briefly indicated below, and more extendedly in chapter 6).

27.   There are several unsettled issues involved in probability estimations—for instance, whether probability is objective or subjective, or "degree of belief," as Hirshleifer and Riley put it (1992, 10)—but we need not consider these here.

Chapter 3

1.   Here trust refers to a banking concept, a property interest controlled by the federal government for the purpose of paying future benefits. Within this framework, the Social Security Trust Fund is a capital sum which accrues interest and can be converted to currency under the terms of the purchase.

2.   Bear in mind that an actuary during the late 1930s would have been unlikely to foresee all the medical advances that would enable a thirty-year-old employee who was just beginning contributions to Social Security to live substantially longer than the then-current life expectancy tables indicated. Yet, for the population as a whole, their projections of the proportions aged sixty-five or older were remarkably accurate.

3.   Inequality can be measured in a variety of ways, all with certain advantages and disadvantages. The variance of a distribution, defined as the mean squared error (the calculated differences between each individual value and the mean, squared, summed and then divided by the number of cases less one), is one measure of the inequality of a distribution.

4.   Bismarck had introduced core ideas of social security decades earlier in Germany (for brief comparisons, see Blackburn 2002, 45–47; Borgmann 2005, 23–25).

5.   The 1983 amendments also made other changes in the program, which we discuss elsewhere.

6.   It was during this period that the famous notch issue emerged.

7.   Without the wage adjustment, two undesirable consequences would ensue. First, benefit levels would be influenced too much by end-of-career earnings, because these earnings are inflated relative to early-career earnings. Second, previous years of covered earnings were indexed to the average wage rate in effect at beneficiary's sixtieth birthday; this lessened the importance of the level of earnings during the year or years just prior to eligibil-

ity age and allowed workers at retirement to benefit from the economic growth that occurred during their working lives.

8. Until now we have ignored an important distinction, namely that two trust funds are attached to Social Security. One is dedicated to Old Age and Survivors Insurance (OASI); this is by far the largest and is normally referred to as Social Security (that is, retirement benefits). The second is dedicated to Disability Insurance (DI).

9. The letter to Livingston, dated November 17, 1998, can be found on the Concord Coalition's Web site (http://www.concordcoalition.org/press/1998/981117_livletter.html).

10. The numerical average of the monthly interest rates during 2005 was 4.312 percent, with an effective interest rate on all investments of 5.457 percent.

11. The separate trust fund for the Disability Insurance program of Social Security, also maintained by the Department of Treasury, held total assets of $195.6 billion at the end of 2005. It is projected to grow by a smaller amount (about $54 billion) because of projected annual surpluses each year through 2013, again assuming no change in tax rate or base.

12. U.S. companies with large defined benefit pension funds could invest without limitation until the passage of the Employee Retirement Income Security Act (ERISA of 1974), which regulated various aspects of employer-sponsored pension plans including vesting periods, fund investment, and accounting practices. The regulations on fund investment were designed to limit the risk and diversify holdings. Some large firms, such as General Motors, added in-house fund managers.

13. The G. W. Bush administration designed a version of such an account, which they called a Health Saving Account (see Office of Management and Budget 2004a, chapter 10).

14. One should also remember that for many new procedures, especially pharmaceuticals, only when masses of indicated patients have been treated do we have trials large enough to provide a statistically sound basis for estimating the physical or psychophysical costs (side effects) of using the new procedure or drug. This occurs for two reasons. One is the large variation in individual biochemistries, physiologies, behaviors, and environments, any of which can interact with the procedure or drug in unexpected and undesired ways. The other is that standards of safety are quite narrow: if a detrimental side effect in one of every thousand indicated patients were acceptable, trials could include fewer test cases. On the other hand, evidence that, contrary to the standard claim, pharmaceutical prices drive the cost of research and development, not the other way around, is strong (Scherer 2001).

15. We realize that this possibility also involves assumptions about the effectiveness of treatment at different stages of disease, and it is certainly not a general argument against early screening.

16. Bear in mind we were assuming no difference in appropriate treatment regime between patients correctly diagnosed by the new and patients

correctly diagnosed by the old technology. If earlier diagnosis permits a different and more effective treatment regime, the preference for the new technology would indeed be rational. We develop this point not to invite speculation about when early treatment is more effective than treatment at a later stage of the disease, but to emphasize the complexities involved in drawing conclusions on the basis of incomplete information.

17. This debate has continued since the oft-cited discrepancy (for example, Borgmann 2005, 16–17) between analytic findings by Martin Feldstein (1974) and contrary analytic findings by Alicia Munnell (1974).

18. There are so many different kinds of income sources, so many different ways in which incomes from different sources are taxed, eligible for use in saving and investment plans, and so forth, and so many different ways in which posttax income can be immediately consumed, that it is daunting for a person being interviewed to have to listen to all the categories, try to recall all the relevant information, and so on, before being asked about their saving and investment decisions and amounts. Asking about all the possible categories is important both because the interviewer does not know answers in advance (even when an answer to a prior question seems logically to suggest an answer to a later question) and because the interviewee will often forget categories without the probing. If anyone really imagines that the typical economic actor has full and accurate information about his or her own finances, that person needs experience as an interviewer.

19. Because the top-down method is residual, there are many places where measurement error occurs, so it is a tedious procedure. Although not widely noted, the residual category, personal saving, directly includes more than persons; nonprofit institutions that primarily serve households (for example, medical care, education, recreation, religious services), pension funds, private trust funds, certain kinds of insurance reserves, and unincorporated businesses are also included.

20. A more formal presentation follows. In the first period the person receives labor earnings and other income $Y_1 > 0$, which he must allocate between [immediate] consumption and retirement savings. Savings may be invested in part in a mutual fund, with an uncertain real rate of return, and in part in a risk-free asset. Let $S^m \geq 0$ denote savings in the mutual fund and $S^f \geq 0$ denote risk-free savings. In the second period, the person consumes her Social Security retirement benefit $Y_2 \geq 0$ and realized savings $(1 + r^m)S^m + (1 + r^f)S^f$, where r^m is the realized rate of return on the mutual fund and r^f is the risk-free rate of return. Thus, consumption in the two periods must satisfy the budget constraints

$$C_1 = Y_1 - S^m - S^f$$
$$C_2 = Y_2 + \left(1 + r^m\right)S^m + \left(1 + r^f\right)S^f.$$

The utility associated with consumption of the bundle (C_1, C_2) is $U(C_1) + \beta U(C_2)$, where β is the discount rate. Suppose that, when facing the consumption-savings decision in the first period, the person knows the amount of income he is currently receiving Y_1, but does not know either his future Social Security benefit Y_2 or the return r^m on the mutual fund. Suppose that she forms a subjective distribution $P(Y_2, r^m)$ and acts to maximize expected utility. Then, in the first period, the person chooses retirement savings to solve the problem

$$\max{}_s^m,{}_s^f U\left(Y_1 - S^m - S^f\right) + \beta \int U\left(Y_2 + \left(1 + r^m\right)S^m + \left(1 + r^f\right)S^f\right) dP\left(Y_2, r^m\right).$$

Thus, a person's retirement savings decision depends on his first-period income Y_1, his preferences [$U(\cdot)$, β), and his expectations $P(Y_2, r^m)$ of Social Security benefits and mutual fund returns. Our insertion of the word immediate is consonant with the authors' meaning; the insertion simply signifies that saving-investment is also a consumption, the only difference between it and immediate consumption being the period during which the consumption is realized. Some clarifications of vocabulary will be helpful to some readers. The two equations for budget constraint are definitional; for example, consumption in period 1 must be equal to the total of income during the period minus the total of saving/investment during the period. The phrase subjective distribution $P(Y_2, r^m)$ refers to a distribution of subjective probability values, here describing the person's best guess of the likelihood of each possible sum of that person's Social Security income (Y_2) and income from mutual-fund investments (r^m). The term dP means distribution of expectations or subjective probabilities (as just described). The mathematical operator $\int$ means that the second-period component of the utility function must be integrated across all of the person's subjective-probability distributions. The term $U(\cdot)$ is simply a shorthand wherein the ($\cdot$) refers to all of the parenthetical expression in the maximum utility equation above—that is, how a person prefers to distribute utility between immediate consumption and saving/investment during period 1, in order to achieve (assuming a distribution of subjective expectations and a preferred discount rate) a preferred second-period utility of income-consumption.

21.   As noted in chapter 1, Hahn and Solow were severely critical of the assumption that valid models of an economy as a whole could be achieved by simple aggregations of microeconomic models—that is, models of the behaviors of individual actors—when in fact the microeconomic models depend on such extreme simplifications. It is in part for just such reason that economists generally prefer to estimate rates of saving using the top down approach described above, despite its flaws, rather than by a bottom up approach that begins with individual behaviors.

Chapter 4

1.   The hospital insurance (HI) portion of Medicare is also funded through FICA taxation, but it is separate from the retirement provisions of OASI. Also, HI taxes are paid on total earnings.

2.   The 1935 Social Security Act covered most workers in commerce and industry, which included about 60 percent of the workforce at that time. In subse-

quent amendments, Congress expanded mandatory coverage to most remaining categories of workers, including state and local workers not covered by a public pension plan as well as offering voluntary coverage to state and local employees covered by public pension plans. Beginning in 1983, all newly hired federal workers were extended mandatory coverage; in addition, public employees may not withdraw from Social Security once they have accepted coverage. SSA estimated that 5.25 million state and local government employees (excluding students and election workers) are not covered by Social Security; however, employees who are not covered can still be eligible for benefits based on their spouses' earnings history or their own record of previous or subsequent covered employment. According to SSA estimates, 95 percent of state and local employees who are not covered receive Social Security benefits as workers, spouses, or dependents (GAO 2003).

3. Of course, we should note that a large proportion of the U.S. population continues to believe that Iraq did have weapons of mass destruction in spite of the subsequent reports that find to the contrary. An important aspect of the culture of us versus them involves the construction of realities: evidence contrary to one's reality can always be dismissed as propaganda.

4. The Social Security Trustees estimated this crossover date (the date when benefit payout would exceed program contributions) as 2016 in its 2001 report. Updated projections have tended to move the crossover date into the future, bit by bit. However, the exact date at which this occurs is not nearly as important as the fact that it will occur.

5. Privatization proposals, though often lacking in detail, generally limit the choices that can be made. For example, they usually propose a mandatory program rather than a voluntary one. In addition, they include limitations on the types of investments from which private account owners can choose, a restriction justified by the desire to limit the risk of loss in investment vehicles.

6. The initial attempt to legislate this approach produced a formula that adjusted each year's wages by the cumulative rate of inflation. But wage inflation was also increasing average monthly earnings, which meant that calculating original benefits for any given retiree extended through more of the earnings brackets defined by the formula. This double indexing—basing average monthly earnings on wage-inflated amounts and using inflation-indexed multipliers in the benefit formula—was adopted in 1972 and effective in 1975. This error was identified fairly quickly, and legislation to fix the error was passed in 1977. Nevertheless, the fix was not implemented until 1980. This five-year period of overly generous benefit levels created the notch in beneficiaries.

7. The ADR for 2005 is about .2, or 20 percent. In other words, changing this value into the number of retirees per worker tells us we have two retirees for every ten workers.

8. By 2020, the ADR is .35.

9. As the ADR moves toward .5, we approach two workers supporting each retiree.

Chapter 5

1. These effects are quite small, however, and would be offset by the transaction costs of trading in and out of the market in an attempt to benefit from them, although there have been some strategies that have succeeded handsomely (at least for a short period) trading on very small differences (see, for example, Dunbar 2000; for discussions of various other anomalies and limitations to the rational expectations model, see Kagel and Roth 1995; Kahneman and Tversky 2000; Loewenstein and Elster 1992; Hahn and Solow 1995; Hands 2001; Hausman and McPherson 1996).

2. Richard Thaler (1997, see also 2000) conducted an experiment with the aid of the *Financial Times*, a prominent newspaper, and found that the commonest choice was thirty-three, followed by twenty-two, with a distribution mean of 18.9, which implies that, on average, a little more than two iterations were made before players invoked their own individual stop signals.

3. One could become wealthy through stock investments even during the 1970s and 1980s, but it became easier during the 1990s using a technical-analysis approach, assuming that one could resist greed. Note that, except for already wealthy market players, this capability was significantly cohort-dependent. If one had been born too early (and thus had become very averse to downside risk) or if one had been born too late (and thus had not managed to accumulate enough liquid asset for investment in stocks), the likelihood of gaining great advantage during the stock-market boom of the late 1990s was relatively low.

4. An annuity is a contract sold by an insurance company; it is designed to provide payments to the beneficiary at specified intervals after retirement (or some alternative designated event). The beneficiary is taxed only when she or he begins taking distributions or withdraws funds from the account. Fixed annuities guarantee a certain payment amount; variable annuities do not specify an amount, because the amount depends on performance. Individual pension accounts would be annuitized to structure benefit payments.

5. The Dow Jones Industrial Average is the price-weighted average of thirty actively traded blue chip stocks that generally account for 15 to 20 percent of the market value of all stocks registered for trade on the New York Stock Exchange. The S&P 500 is an unmanaged index that generally represents the U.S. stock market without regard to company size. The Russell 2000 is a broader based index and includes many companies, including start-ups, that have small capitalizations. The Wilshire 5000 (which now includes about 6,700 companies) is the nearest to a total market index.

6. An index fund is one type of mutual fund that attempts to mimic the performance of a particular stock market index. The most common index fund attempts to track the S&P 500 by purchasing all 500 stocks in proportion to their contribution to the index. A mutual fund is an open-ended fund (the composition may change over time) that invests in a group of assets and is operated by an investment company. The choice of assets must be consistent with a stated set of objectives (for example, investments in southeast

Asia, investments in biotechnology). The public can buy shares of the mutual fund as they can buy shares in any publicly traded company that can sell stock in itself. In purchasing shares of a mutual fund, shareholders receive an equity position in the fund (in effect, in each of the securities that comprise the fund). The price of a share in a mutual fund will fluctuate daily, depending upon the performance of the securities held by the fund. Advantages of mutual funds include diversification and professional money management, but these funds often charge fees. A closed-end fund (the composition may not be altered) is actually an investment trust.

7. The easiest way to calculate the fifth root of 1.13373 is to convert that number to its natural logarithm (.125511428), divide that by five, which equals (.025102), and then take the antilog of that quotient, which gives 1.02542. In other words, the average multiplier for each of the five years is 1.02542, which is the same as saying that the average rate of change per year during the five-year investment period was 2.5 percent. For those still in doubt, inspect the following: $1000 \times 1.02542 = 1025.42$; $1025.42 \times 1.02542 = 1051.49$; $1051.49 \times 1.02542 = 1078.21$; $1078.21 \times 1.02542 = 1105.62$; $1105.62 \times 1.02542 = 1133.73$ (which is the same as 1133.71 but for rounding errors). Three technical points about the geometric mean should be noted. First, when the rate of change is constant, the geometric mean equals the arithmetic mean. (For example, if the annual rate of change is exactly 5 percent each year, the geometric mean and the arithmetic mean each equal 5 percent.) Second, the greater the variation in the rate of change from year to year, the larger the discrepancy between the arithmetic mean and the geometric mean, the latter always being the smaller of the two. Third, as should be evident from inspection of the formula for the geometric mean (as given with specific annual values), the order of the annual rates of change, whether positive or negative, makes no difference.

8. Note that the preceding illustration was nothing more than the application of a compound interest rate (2.542 percent) with compounding occurring only at the end of each year. The formula for calculating the accumulated value of an initial investment for some number of years at a specified rate (with annual compounding) is:

Total Accumulation = Initial Principal $\times$ (1 + rate)^{years}

So the initial investment of $1,000 at 2.542 annual interest (annual compounding) for twenty years is given as:

$1000 \times (1.02542)^{20} = 1000 \times 1.6521 = 1652.10$.

9. According to Thomas MaCurdy and John Shoven (2001, 28), for example, "the average real rate of return on stocks [for the period] 1954–97 was 9.7 percent." Their reference was to the S&P500 collection of stocks. Their wording was technically correct: they said "average real rate of return" and not "annualized real rate of return"; the former is an arithmetic average, while the latter is the geometric average. While one might assume that professional economists will understand the difference in wording, other readers probably will not.

10. Although usually attributed to Barnum, the statement was apparently made by George Hull, who, as inventor of the Cardiff Giant hoax, became Barnum's competitor.

11. The annualized real rate is calculated as the geometric mean of the series of 101 years, with adjustment for inflation. The arithmetic mean of that same series is 8.7 percent.

12. The standard deviation is a statistical measure of variability. It is based on the variance, which is sometimes referred to as the mean squared error, which translates into the average (arithmetic mean) of the deviations (the difference between any particular value and the mean), squared. The standard deviation is the square root of the variance.

13. Probability statements describing a range of possible outcomes are far better than claims of certainty for point estimates (again, the law of large numbers). But the presumed precision of 65 percent chance, and the like, as opposed to, say, 50 percent chance, is usually false in the context of stock markets, insofar as the presumption is that one can have confidence in the precision of those numerical differences.

14. We used the phrase, superficially simple reason, because the description that follows seems to refer to a simple process; but it is actually quite complex and not yet well understood. If someone did well understand how traders succeed when they succeed and fail when they fail, that understanding would presumably be put to good profit-making use in the market. But this sun would rise only once, so to speak, as other traders would soon catch on and join the club—with the result that the market process itself would adjust, and the understanding would no longer be adequate.

15. A random walk is a theory of investment claiming that market prices follow a random path up and down, without being influenced by past price movements. Under these conditions, it is impossible to predict with any accuracy the direction in which the market will move at any point in time and particularly over the short term.

16. We are mindful of controversy about whether this premium really exists. Some analysts believe stocks are not more risky than bonds. The issue is unsettled and will not be pursued here.

17. Undoubtedly with that in mind, as Edmund Andrews reported in the *New York Times*, Alan Greenspan, late in his long tenure as chairman of the FRB, chided investors for their lax attitudes toward market risk. An unexpected "negative event" that results in "increased investor caution elevates risk premiums and, as a consequence, lowers asset values and promotes the liquidation of the debt that supported higher prices," he explained. "This is the reason that history has not dealt kindly with the aftermath of protracted periods of low risk premiums" ("Greenspan Chides Investors," August 27, 2005).

18. As with many other measured quantities, people disagree about how inflation should be defined and calculated (for example, Baker 1997). Some of those differences are important in specific contexts, but here we are simply

illustrating the effect of inflation, using the standard CPI-U measure for all time periods.

19. In a highly popular paper Robert Haugen and Nardin Baker (1996) claimed to have devised a strategy that would give market returns as much as 36 percent higher than the market average. Doug Hanna and Mark Ready (2005) later demonstrated that the strategy did not work as advertised when applied to a different sample of data, and once transaction costs were taken into account the claimed advantage diminished to zero. The Haugen-Baker strategy involved unusually high transactions costs because of frequent trading.

20. There was also considerable variance in what funds counted as management expenses, but the SEC study attempted to standardize for those differences.

21. Based on information provided by the Investment Company Institute, Alicia Munnell and her colleagues (2006) estimated aggregate average return (not adjusted for inflation or fees) for IRAs, defined benefit plans, and 401(k)s for the 1998 to 2003 period. Defined benefit plans fared best, with an annualized return of 5.96 percent. The 401(k)s came in a full percentage lower at 4.91. IRAs were the lowest at 3.29 percent. These figures are geometric means constructed from the information contained in (2006, table 7). The amount of diversification in 401(k) plans is also problematic. Sarah Holden and Jack VanDerhei (2006) show that one-third of 401(k) participants have none of their account invested in equities; almost 16 percent had all of their account in equities.

22. Notice that markets in air pollution were not voluntarily built by polluting firms (hierarchical organizations) but were introduced (where they were) by governments (hierarchical organizations) and can be ignored, or used to specific advantage, far more easily by the more than by the less powerful firms.

23. Transaction costs are very low. In 2004, for instance, the cost for OASI was slightly greater than one-half of one percent (that is, 0.6 percent), for DI, it was 2.7 percent. By comparison, the Hospital Insurance portion of Medicare had costs of 1.8 percent, and the Supplemental Medical Insurance portion, costs of 2.1 percent. In general, the costs of administering health care are higher than the costs of administering postemployment income insurance.

24. The situation was worse for retired women (one in four), retired African American men and women (one in three), and unmarried Hispanic or Latina women (one in two). Further, among those sixty-five or older, 65 percent of all people, 75 percent of Hispanics, 75 percent of unmarried women, and 80 percent of African Americans obtained at least half of their total income from Social Security (Office of the Actuary 2005, tables 677, 685, and 687).

25. This standard deviation is based on data for end of year 2003, the latest available data for calculating variance. (The mean payout was $922; $797.62 for women.) It is a very close estimate of the September 2005 standard deviation.

26. Again, there is some disagreement about the size of the equity risk premium. John Geanakoplos, Olivia Mitchell, and Stephen Zeldes (1998), for instance, assume that it is about 2.3 percent. The 5.5 percent estimate, however, is the usual best estimate and is agreed to by supporters of a PRA system (for example, Feldstein, Ranguelova, and Samwick 2001).

27. Obviously we are ignoring the fact that for earlier periods the real rate of return for Social Security was much higher than 2 percent.

28. Annualized and cumulative rates of return would vary by individual according to date of entry into the labor force, number and length of periods of unemployment, and similar factors—some of which could result in high correlations for specific groups (for example, African American men, because of high rates of imprisonment). Julia Coronado, Don Fullerton, and Thomas Glass (2000) demonstrate that though Social Security is indeed progressive-redistributive, it is only mildly so, and that most of the reform proposals would be regressive-redistributive, though only mildly so. Angus Deaton, Pierre-Olivier Gourinchas, and Christina Paxson (2000) note similar findings.

29. Note also that we are here ignoring the fact that Social Security includes Disability Insurance, which presumably would have to be covered separately from the PRA program, perhaps by a surcharge on the PRA payroll tax.

30. In fact, economic growth in the United States slowed considerably after early 1970s. Growth in GDP and in employment earnings were slower than expected; tax revenues did not keep pace with earlier projections; and thus spending on public welfare was increasingly constrained during the latter years of the twentieth century, even before politicians began their campaign to starve government of revenue by cutting taxes. Contrary to their chant, analysis of relevant data for several rich countries including the United States reveals no evidence of a relationship between economic growth and either the size of government or the level of taxes (see, for example, Slemrod and Bakija 2004, 114–20).

31. If the growth rate proves to be greater than the assumed rate, then the Trust Fund survives that much longer. In fact, if the growth rate is much above the assumed 1.9 percent, the Trust Fund remains solvent throughout the period of projections to 2079.

32. John Geanakoplos, Olivia Mitchell, and Stephen Zeldes (1998) estimate the cost at about 3 percent for an indefinitely longer period.

33. On the other side of the coin, Feldstein and his colleagues were probably overly generous in their assumption that the increase in national saving due to addition of a PRA system to supplement and then replace Social Security would generate a very large volume of new capital formation and a commensurate increase in corporate-tax revenues, which would then underwrite a huge transfer into the Trust Fund during a long period of transition. The chain of reasoning from their initial assumptions is quite complex in political as well as economic terms. Much could go wrong with their scenario. One possible impression is that they began with their conclusion, which was (is) that a PRA system should replace Social Security, and then

sought a set of assumptions that would generate the required fiscal substitutions. Even so, then, it is all the more remarkable that their scenario needed the supplement of a government-funded social insurance program.

34. Their book, announcing a coming generational storm, attempts to paint Social Security with the same brush of red ink that will indeed characterize the impending fiscal disaster of health care in the United States.

35. In general, tax rate and tax base are not independent; a rise in rate tends to diminish the size of the base. As employers' wage bills increase, they tend to look for cheaper labor, assuming equivalent quality and quantity of output. However, the FICA base could be expanded both by expanding the list of covered workers and by removing the ceiling. High-earnings workers in the United States are unlikely to find equal or better wage rates in other countries any time soon. Indeed, for these workers the problem will increasingly be that their jobs will be supplied by labor from lower-wage countries, which (as we saw in chapter 1) is already occurring.

Chapter 6

1. Athenian citizens were only a small proportion of the residents of Athens, thus their direct democracy was restricted in ways comparable to the restrictions of representative democracy in the United States. Within those restrictions, their democracy was far more a rule by the people. Athenian proponents of democracy, too, however, also had to contend with a "fear of the individual" sentiment and distrust of the common people (or rabble, to use the late eighteenth-century American idiom).

2. For example, Indiana University's Center for Survey Research asked a battery of questions during the 2002 congressional elections. This and other survey results reported in this paragraph are from that study. Whereas the study used Likert scale categories (such as strongly agree, somewhat agree, and so on) and tabulated results in percentages, we pool to a simpler agree versus disagree format and use more approximate values (for example, 83 percent becomes more than four of five). Other studies have reported broadly similar results.

3. An instance can be seen in the Pew Center data analyzed in the next section (see figure 6.2).

4. Gerrymandering has made the large majority of House districts virtually automatic for one party. Incumbents have an almost insurmountable advantage. The large majority of elected officials come from the top 20 percent of the income distribution and usually have never experienced life in the bottom half, let alone the bottom fifth, of the distribution.

5. The allusion is to the middle, or electrically charged, rail of an electric train: "Touch it and you die!"

6. The mean balance was about $27,000. The difference between median and mean indicates that a relatively small number of IRA owners had very large account balances.

7. This fact has important implications for the thrust of an argument that will be considered in chapter 7—namely, that the typical adult, if given enough autonomy and the correct incentives, is knowledgeable enough and disciplined enough to develop the requisite skills to manage his or her own postemployment income insurance program.

8. The percentage of undecided respondents was at least twice as high for this proposal as for any other; it was the same across all three political groups; and it had been as large in the September and December 2004 surveys. As will become clear in a moment, it was sensitive to respondents' perceptions of how much they knew about the proposal.

9. Logistic regression is a standard technique of analyzing the simultaneous relationships of many predictor variables to a dependent variable that contains only two possible states (we are ignoring the 6 percent of the respondents who did not choose between the two options). In this context, simultaneous means that the effect of each predictor variable is net of the effect of all other predictor variables in the given combination (that is, columns of the table). The tabular entry for each predictor variable consists of three numbers. Using the entry for Age in column 1 as illustration, the first number (–.017) means that the net relationship of age on choice of options is negative and of modest strength (the larger the absolute value of the number, the stronger the relationship). The second number (.003) is analogous to a standard deviation and estimates variability in the strength of that net relationship. It can also be used to construct an interval estimate that gives us the range of likely values for this relationship. In this case, the calculation would be $-.017 \pm 2(.003) = -.023$ to $-.011$. The third number is the result of a test of the ratio of the first to the second number (a t test), which yields an estimate of the probability that the $-.017$ value reflects something other than sampling error. The smaller this third number (for example, .0001), the more confident we are that $-.017$ is a reasonably good estimate of the true strength of the relationship in the population. In general, with a sample size of about 1,400 cases, we prefer the third number to be at least as small as .05, though no magical threshold attaches to that (or any other) number (for a brief but more detailed introduction to logistic regression, see Long and Cheng 2004).

10. It is more realistic in the sense that a person is never just a gender or just a married (or divorced or widowed, and so on) person, and so on, but instead has all of those various characteristics at once; and whereas some characteristics reinforce each other, certain other characteristics can counteract each other, and still others can be relatively neutral to one another. By analyzing all of the variables in relation to the choice of options at the same time, we gain a more realistic picture of how much the likelihood of choosing the PRA option is influenced by each variable relative to all others.

11. That the programs of Social Security are only mildly progressive is hardly accidental. They were designed as a response to crisis—severe economic depression—at a time when, despite increasing labor strife as workers struggled to assert their rights to their own labor, prevailing sentiment among the political leadership of the country was staunchly opposed to redistribution away from the rich to the poor through any means other than charity.

Interests in the accumulation of capital dictated just the reverse, a distribution of resource away from the poor, near-poor, and middle classes (chiefly in the form of products of their labor) to a relatively small pool of industrialists who supposedly knew what to do with large sums of capital, for the good of the country. As Christopher Jencks points out, Social Security, like private insurance, "reinforced the existing social and moral order" (1992, 1–2). This was the vital condition for business support of the proposed legislation.

12.   It is also relevant, however, that low-income workers have had little experience with private (or employer sponsored) pensions. Of the bottom fifth of workers (measured in terms of employment earnings), only one in six have pension benefits, and one in four have health benefits. This contrasts with about seven of ten workers who are in the top fifth, and over half of those in the middle fifth, of employment earnings.

13.   Manichaeism was one of the ancient religions, originating in what is now Iran and thought to have been developed from Zoroastrianism. It was based on the teachings of Mani, who gave central attention to the principle of dualism. Some scholars argue that it was imported into Christianity through Saint Augustine of Hippo. Manichees reduced all distinctions to the cosmic struggle between two rival powers, alternatively known as Good and Evil, Spirit and Matter, the Kingdom of Light and the Kingdom of Darkness.

14.   This question came after one that introduced the topic of the earthquake and tsunami in the Indian Ocean, and asked whether the respondent had made a donation, was planning to do so, and if so when. Responses were distributed roughly in thirds, with a small plurality saying no, not right now. These respondents were more likely (by about 10 percentage points) to say that Washington had donated more than its share. Perhaps this view was at least in part a justification of or rationalization for the lack of a personal donation, but it could also mean simply a consistency in underlying attitude.

15.   This proportion did not vary according to geographic area (using Census Bureau categories). One might expect people in the western states, most of them on the Pacific Rim, would be more alert to the tsunami threat than people in the midwestern states, and perhaps they were, but they were not less likely to say they didn't know as their answer to the survey question. There was also no significant correlation between region and the other response categories to this question.

16.   The self-described very liberal respondents were consistently the most atypical across all five of the institutional arenas. But note that they were also few in number ($n = 58$), which means that their percentage distributions are the least reliable of the five political ideology categories.

17.   It is difficult to be precise about these matters because conditions and strategies can change from year to year. Until 2003, GM Asset Management (GMAM) had allocated funds to alternative investments such as hedge funds, but primarily to more typical investment vehicles, such as large-capitalization equities and high-grade bonds. After 2000, the fund suffered two losing years. Even so, pensioners were due more than $6 billion a year

in benefits. By the end of 2002, the GM pension plan was underfunded (assets were less than liabilities) by about $19 billion. In 2003, GM borrowed $18 billion and changed to a much riskier investment philosophy—concentrating on hedge funds, emerging markets, junk bonds, and derivatives. In retrospect, their timing was exceptionally good. Interest rates were low and the stock market was ready to move up. The two-year experience using this strategy has been quite positive. In 2005, for example, GM's pension fund had a return of 13 percent (compared to a total S&P return of 4.9 percent) and is now overfunded by $6 billion, or what is needed to pay one year's pension benefits. This is in contrast to the company's U.S. health-care plans, which were underfunded by $61 billion in 2005, as reporter Carol Loomis points out in a *Fortune* magazine article ("GM beats the market!" May 1, 2006). Several points are worth emphasizing. This was a high risk strategy using only the borrowed money. The performance over two years was impressive. The types of investments yielding this return are not investments that average workers understand. Last, the advisability of this approach for the long term remains to be seen. As always, risk attaches to an enterprise's ability to forecast its own future conditions, and that ability has been much reduced for old-line firms in conditions of globalized competition. Neither private firms nor the markets in which they raise money can control exogenous factors, and often not endogenous factors such as return on own investments, to an extent that "insures" favorable outcomes. Employees past and present, as well as stockholders and both upstream and downstream partners (for example, suppliers) suffer the consequences.

18. The premiums are paid from assets of the corporate pension plans. In 2005 the premium for single-employer plans was $19 per worker or retiree plus $9 for each $1,000 of unfunded vested benefits. The premium in multi-employer players was a flat $2.60 per worker or retiree. The premium rate is set by congressional legislation; PBGC management has no control over revenues and little over outlays.

19. Defined-benefit pension plans offered by states and local governments to their employees are also heavily underfunded—though no one knows exactly how much across all states, because bookkeeping and reporting rules for these pension plans are even less adequate than those for corporate pensions. By some estimates, the shortfall across all state plans is nearly $500 billion.

20. By the end of 2005, the PBGC covered 44.1 million workers in more than 30,000 active plans; it was directly responsible for the future benefits of 1.3 million active and retired workers whose plans had failed.

21. The PBGC estimates its future exposure to new probable terminations as high, with approximately $108 billion in underfunding exposure to plan sponsors they considered reasonably possible (*PBGC Annual Report 2005*, 4).

22. The issue became a controversy in the campaign leading up to Chile's presidential election in December 2005. The six pension-fund management firms argued that their fees accounted for only a 2 percentage point difference in

total payout, but at least one Chilean economist estimated their real annual
return on operating assets in recent years to be greater than 50 percent.
Between the deduction of management fees and the fact that some workers,
especially the self-employed, have evaded paying the 12.4 percent tax on
earnings, Chile's PRA system could fail more than half of the eligible workers, leaving the difference to be paid by other government revenues (*The
Economist*, November 12, 2005, p. 40).

23. The funding of SMI is different. As the Social Security Administration
describes it, "the financing of [the Part B and Part D] accounts is provided
by beneficiary premiums and Federal general fund revenue payments automatically adjusted each year to meet expected costs. Thus, under current law
both SMI accounts are fully financed throughout the 75-year projection
period no matter what the costs may be" (Office of the Actuary 2005, 14).

24. This figure demonstrates the misleading character of arguments such as
Laurence Kotlikoff's and Scott Burns's generational warfare (2004), which
lumps both Social Security and health care together as if they faced uniform
problems and would have to be addressed by the same set of solutions.

25. This document presented by the Social Security and Medicare Boards
of Trustees, and probably prepared for news media and related uses, is entitled "Status of the Social Security and Medicare Programs: A Summary
of the 2006 Annual Reports." It is dated May 2, 2006. As of March 15, 2007,
the complete document was still available on SSA's website as www.ss.
gov/PACY/TRSUM/trsummary.html. Because some concern has been
expressed that the website posting is temporary, we have downloaded the
complete document and will make it available upon request to either author.

Chapter 7

1. The life of the city, as place of residence, as economic engine, and as center of political authority, collapsed throughout Europe after the fall of the
Roman Empire, and it remained virtually nonexistent (for most Europeans
by the seventh or eighth century not even a distant memory) throughout the period popularly known as Europe's Dark Age. With the re-
establishment of long-distance trading and differentiation of that activity
from the local merchant function, city life recovered with and after the
twelfth-century renaissance.

2. The notion is famously depicted in the frontispiece to Thomas Hobbes'
Leviathan (1651): the human figure of monarch is graphically composed of
a multitude of small human figures, the subjects, and as one scans down the
monarch's body, the figures of the monarch's subjects spill out as the population of the totality of the monarch's realm, evoking both the shepherd's
flock and the cornucopia of a land's wealth.

3. Diary keeping was one recommended means of that practice, a conscience-
enforced surveillance of self in the world. Puritans, especially men, were
great diarists, in diligence if not style or expansiveness. Because they were
intensely private, most of these documents were destroyed after the person's

death. Most of the surviving diaries seem rather pedestrian today, for all the freight they carried for the writers. The few exceptions are extraordinary documents of self-on-self scrutiny, reproach, and project of betterment.

4.   Elizabethans who had benefit of personal education, and Puritans placed high value on it, learned Latin to the extent of being able to read even the complexities of Cicero and Horace. The latter's *Odes* gave great weight to sober, very measured harnessing of sensible pleasures lest the violent energies of the ecstatic individual (literally, an individual out of place), no less than those of a dictatorial body, deliver all to havoc. Horace wrote from experiences of his time, and the Elizabethan English understood his message.

5.   Try to imagine Cervantes' great novel, *Don Quixote de la Mancha*, without the dual counterparts (one old, the other new) against which Don Quixote's romantic passions gained distinction. The first part of Cervantes' novel was written at about the same time as Shakespeare's *Hamlet* (1601).

6.   Generally credited to the work of Charles Horton Cooley, the term looking-glass self illustrates how we develop a self-image on the basis of the re-actions of others, as we understand them. We imagine how we appear to others, imagine their judgments of us, and based on those judgments, re-spond with feelings of pride or shame. Through our imagining, we share the judgment of the other.

7.   Developments toward the idea of the corporation as a legal subject on a par with the human person had begun, however, in France, not Britain.

8.   Smith's reasoning strikes us today as reminiscent of Darwin's, when in fact it is the other way around: Darwin's reasoning in *On the Origin of the Species* was modeled after the reasoning of late eighteenth- and early nineteenth-century political economists such as Adam Smith.

9.   See Charles Taylor (1989) for a social history of particular relevance here.

10.   Of the many references to Mammon, a few selections are enough. During the Middle Ages, for example, Mammon was typically personified as the demon of avarice, wealth, and injustice. In literature, Mammon's identifi-cation as a god of covetousness or avarice has been linked to Spenser and Milton and to later sources as a metaphor for the materialist spirit of the nineteenth century.

11.   Nugatory means ineffective or futile.

12.   A chautauqua refers to a meeting, usually held outdoors during the sum-mer months in tents, which featured public lectures and entertainment (for example, magicians, concerts and plays). Said to originate in the village of Chautauqua, New York, in 1874, it became popular during the late nine-teenth and early twentieth centuries. The Chautauqua Movement is a term that's been applied to the early adult education movement in the United States. The circuit of chautauquas that traveled from town to town con-tributed significantly to the education of adults and spurred interest in pub-lic institutions such as libraries, museums, universities and other cultural programs (local symphonies, theater groups, art exhibits, and the like).

13. Self-help books were highly successful publishing ventures. The same year that Darwin published *On the Origin of Species* and John Stuart Mill published *On Liberty*, 1859, a fellow countryman by the name of Samuel Smiles published a book that outsold each of those classics. The message of his *Self-Help* was not so different: life is a struggle, filled with challenges that are to be overcome by pushing character or, if not, to be filters that weed out the weak. Too much government robs people of resilience and conviction. Being born to silver plate is just as erosive, a view but for which Smiles might have been adopted as pet sloganeer by persons who profit from running against government. Smiles's book was a great success and is still in print, primarily because its message can easily be read as validation that one's success has been due to hard work and right living.

14. Perhaps the most famous remembrance is a brief address Hand delivered May 21, 1944, in Central Park, New York City, in which he said, "The spirit of liberty is the spirit which is not too sure that it is right; the spirit of liberty is the spirit which seeks to understand the minds of other men and women; the spirit of liberty is the spirit which weighs their interests alongside its own without bias" (1974, 190).

15. It is also, as Quentin Skinner recently pointed out, an invitation to tyranny—as when "in time of emergency civil liberties must bow to national security," because (by this view) "liberties are held not as rights but by grace of rulers, and it is for them to tell [the ruled] what counts as an emergency" (2002, 18).

16. Recall from popular culture the success of works such as William H. Whyte's *The Organization Man* (1956) and Sloan Wilson's *Man in the Grey Flannel Suit* (1955), or, a generation later, Terry Gilliam and Tom Stoppard's cinematic statement in *Brazil* (1985). One of the oddities of some recent political commentary, including that having to do with Social Security, is that critics who rail against government bureaucracy are silent about, or (even more oddly) enthusiasts of, bureaucracy in its corporate commercial forms.

17. Although both the mean and median are measures of central tendency—average or typical values—of a distribution of observed amounts, they can give very different results. In a normal, or bell-shaped distribution, these averages are the same; the fiftieth percentile (the value in the distribution that splits the distribution, half of the observations falling below this value and half above it) and the arithmetic mean (the center of gravity of a distribution) are the same. When a distribution is positively skewed, with a small percentage of cases with very high values, the arithmetic mean registers a higher value than the median. The greater the difference between the median and the arithmetic mean, the more skewed the distribution. Noting this difference is particularly important when examining monetary distributions, because the more skewed the distribution, the more the arithmetic mean distorts the notion of typical.

18. The Dow Jones Industrial Average declined 95 points on Wednesday, October 14, another 58 points on Thursday, and another 108 points on Friday. As might be expected, that Monday morning was greeted with great nervousness, which only increased as trading hours continued and was satis-

fied, as it were, with the whopping 508 point (22.6 percent) decline, by far the largest one-day drop in history.

19.   The equity class is the least and the guaranteed class the most conservative of the three classes, in the sense that equity is the most volatile and carries the greatest likelihood of either a gain (at any given rate) on the invested principal or of a loss (at any given rate) of principal, whereas guaranteed is the least volatile and has strong protection against loss of principal but at the cost of a low rate of potential gain.

20.   Rugh also found evidence of what Shlomo Benartzi and Richard Thaler (2001) call naïve diversification—that is, a smorgasbord approach (a little of this, a little of that, and so on) rather than a calculated and often reassessed diversity of investment portfolio designed to maximize long-term accumulation of assets.

21.   Unfortunately, these analyses are based on group averages (typical behaviors of the several age groups), not on the measured changes of behavior of specific individuals, and thus are subject to bias due to aggregation effects. Note that the composition of the age groups changes during the thirty-nine months (only some of the members of the group of participants aged thirty-five to forty-four on December 31, 2000, are in that same age group on March 30, 2004). Some of the observed difference in group averages is due to cohort effects, and some is due to change in individual behavior during the period.

Chapter 8

1.   We are excluding here the political threats to Social Security programs, given that this uncertainty is a matter of political will.

2.   However, the electorate has repeatedly declared that it supports a high degree of inequality. Recent polls have shown, for instance, that as much as 70 percent of the public have declared in favor of repealing the estate tax, a tax that affects the wealthiest 1 percent of households. At the same time, the balance of the electorate seems to believe that the United States is exceptional in having high rates of upward mobility, when in fact studies comparing incomes of fathers and sons at equivalent stages of career have shown that sons born to low-income fathers are less likely to move up in the United States than in other countries such as Denmark, Norway, and the United Kingdom (see, for example, Solon 2002; Corak 2004; Lee and Solon 2006).

3.   Again, a major issue is whether and how our current political process can both educate and produce agreements.

4.   A proposal from Robert Ball, former commissioner of Social Security (also deputy director, acting director, and assistant director of the Bureau of Old Age and Survivor's Insurance) is different in that it suggests three specific steps: first, gradually raise the earnings ceiling on which FICA taxes are paid until taxes are being paid on about 94 percent of earnings, as originally designed; second, designate collections from the federal estate tax to be

credited to the Social Security program; and third, gradually diversify trust fund investments beyond Treasury bills until we have roughly 20 percent of assets invested in alternative products, using a board similar to that of the Federal Reserve to make these decisions. A second proposal is to shift from wage indexing to price indexing in determining benefits, which improves the financial profile of the program solely by reducing benefits. A third is to adopt a version of progressive price indexing, which would apply wage indexing to those with low earnings histories and price indexing to those with high earnings histories, thereby reducing benefit growth only for high earnings workers (personal communication; also see www.robertmball.org).

5. We understand that the two sides we have presented to this debate are not homogeneous in all features. Those who favor private accounts do not have one specific program in mind; rather, they support in principle the notion of moving to some system of private accounts. Likewise, those who defend Social Security differ in how they believe the program should be revised to address not only its financial shortfall, but also to address other aspects of the benefit structure that they feel are less well suited to contemporary behavior.

6. It does not appear that the citizenry's relevant knowledge has improved since 1996. A Zogby poll of a sample of 1,213 American adults in August 2006 found that, where 74 percent could name the members of the *Three Stooges* comedy act (Larry, Curly, Moe), only 42 percent could name the three branches of government (legislative, executive, judicial). Thomas Mann, of the Brookings Institution, and Norman Ornstein, of the American Enterprise Institute, liberal and conservative think tanks, respectively, have collaborated in a diagnosis of the enfeeblement of the legislative branch, its failure to uphold its constitutional role as first branch of government (2006). Perhaps on balance the electorate simply does not care.

References

Aaron, Henry J. 1966. "The Social Insurance Paradox." *Canadian Journal of Economics and Political Science* 33: 371–4.

Aaron, Henry J., and Robert D. Reischauer. 1998a. *Countdown to Reform: The Great Social Security Debate.* New York: Century Foundation Press.

———. 1998b. *There When You Need It: Saving Social Security for Future Generations of Americans.* New York: Century Foundation Press.

Abramson, John D. 2004. *Overdosed America: The Broken Promise of American Medicine.* New York: HarperCollins.

Ackerman, Bruce, and James S. Fishkin. 2004. *Deliberation Day.* New Haven, Conn.: Yale University Press.

Advisory Council on Social Security. 1938. *Final Report.* S. Doc. 4. 76th Cong., 1st sess. Washington: U.S. Government Printing Office. Available at http://www.ssa.gov/history/reports/38advise.html.

———. 1949. *Final Report.* S. Doc. 208. 80th Cong., 2nd sess. Washington: U.S. Government Printing Office.

———. 1958. "Misunderstandings of Social Security Financing." Report. Washington: U.S. Government Printing Office. Available at http://www.ssa.gov/history/reports/58advise4.html.

———. 1964. *The Status of Social Security Program and Recommendations for Its Improvement.* Washington: U.S. Government Printing Office.

Ameriks, John, Andrew Caplin, and John V. Leahy. 2002. "Wealth Accumulation and the Propensity to Plan." NBER Working Paper 8920. Cambridge, Mass.: National Bureau of Economic Research.

Andrews, Edmund L. 2004. "Economic View: Social Security Reform, with One Big Catch." *New York Times,* December 12, 2004.

Appelbaum, Eileen, Annette Bernhardt, and Richard J. Murnane, eds. 2003. *Low-Wage America.* New York: Russell Sage Foundation.

Arias, Elizabeth. 2006. "United States Life Tables, 2003." National Vital Statistics Reports 54. (April 19). Washington: U.S. Government Printing Office.

Arrow, Kenneth J. 1974. *The Limits of Organization.* New York: W. W. Norton.

———. 1986. "Rationality of Self and Others in an Economic System." In *Rational Choice,* edited by Robin Hogarth and Melvin W. Reder. Chicago, Ill.: University of Chicago Press.

Baker, Dean, ed. 1997. *Getting Prices Right: The Battle over the Consumer Price Index.* Armonk, N.Y.: M. E. Sharpe.

Baker, Dean, and Mark Weisbrot. 1999. *Social Security: The Phony Crisis.* Chicago, Ill.: University of Chicago Press.

Ball, Robert. 1985. "The 1939 Amendments to the Social Security Act and What Followed." In *50th Anniversary Edition, Report of the Committee on Economic Security of 1935 and Other Basic Documents Relating to the Development of the Social Security Act*. Washington: National Conference on Social Welfare.

Barkun, Michael. 2003. *A Culture of Conspiracy*. Berkeley, Calif.: University of California Press.

Baumol, William J., Alan S. Blinder, and Edward N. Wolff. 2003. *Downsizing in America*. New York: Russell Sage Foundation.

Beach, William W., and Gareth E. Davis. 1998. "Social Security's Rate of Return." Report. Washington: The Heritage Foundation. Available at: http://www.heritage.org/Research/SocialSecurity/CDA98—01.cfm.

Bellah, Robert N., Richard Madsen, William M. Sullivan, Ann Swidler, and Steven M. Tipton. 1985. *Habits of the Heart*. Berkeley, Calif.: University of California Press.

Benartzi, Shlomo, and Richard H. Thaler. 2001. "Naïve Diversification Strategies in Defined Contribution Savings Plans." *American Economic Review* 91(1): 79–98.

Berkowitz, Edward O. 1991. *America's Welfare State: From Roosevelt to Reagan*. Baltimore, Md.: Johns Hopkins University Press.

Berlin, Isaiah. 1958. *Two Concepts of Liberty*. Oxford: Clarendon.

Bernheim, B. Douglas, Jonathan Skinner, and Steven Weinberg. 2001. "What Accounts for the Variation in Retirement Wealth Among US Households?" *American Economic Review* 91(4): 832–57.

Blackburn, Robin. 2002. *Banking on Death*. London: Verso.

Block, James E. 2002. *A Nation of Agents*. Cambridge, Mass.: Belknap.

Bohn, Henning. 1997. "Social Security Reform and Financial Markets." In *Social Security Reform*, edited by Steven A. Sass and Robert Triest. Boston, Mass.: Federal Reserve Bank of Boston.

Borgmann, Christoph. 2005. *Social Security, Demographics, and Risk*. Berlin: Springer.

Brader, Ted. 2006. *Campaigning for Hearts and Minds: How Emotional Appeals in Political Ads Work*. Chicago, Ill.: University of Chicago Press.

Burke, Edmund. 1989. *The Writings and Speeches of Edmund Burke*. vol. 8, *The French Revolution 1790–1794*, edited by L. G. Mitchell. Oxford: Oxford University Press.

Campbell, John Y., and Martin Feldstein, eds. 2001. *Risk Aspects of Investment-Based Social Security Reform*. Chicago, Ill.: University of Chicago Press.

Campbell, John Y., Martin Lettau, Burton G. Malkiel, and Yexiao Xu. 2001. "Have Individual Stocks Become More Volatile?" *Journal of Finance* 56: 1–43.

Cohen, Wilbur J., and Robert J. Myers. 1950. "Social Security Act Amendments of 1950: A Summary and Legislative History." *Social Security Bulletin* 13(10) (October): 3–14.

Congressional Budget Office. 2002. *The Long-Term Budget Outlook*. Washington: U.S. Government Printing Office.

Converse, Philip E. 1964. "The Nature of Belief Systems in Mass Publics." In *Ideology and Discontent*, edited by David E. Apter. New York: Free Press.

Corak, Miles, ed. 2004. *Generational Income Mobility in North America and Europe*. Cambridge: Cambridge University Press.

Coronado, Julia Lynn, Don Fullerton, and Thomas Glass. 2000. "Long-Run Effects of Social Security Reform Proposals on Lifetime Progressivity." NBER Working Paper 7568. Cambridge, Mass.: National Bureau of Economic Research.

Currie, Martin, and Ian Steedman. 1990. *Wrestling with Time*. Ann Arbor, Mich.: University of Michigan Press.

Deaton, Angus, Pierre-Olivier Gourinchas, and Christina Paxson. 2000. "Social Security and Inequality over the Life Cycle." NBER Working Paper 7570. Cambridge, Mass.: National Bureau of Economic Research.

Delli Carpini, Michael X., and Scott Keeter. 1996. *What Americans Know About Politics and Why It Matters*. New Haven, Conn.: Yale University Press.

DeLong, J. Bradford, Andrei Shleifer, Lawrence Summers, and Robert Waldmann. 1990. "Noise Trader Risk in Financial Markets." *Journal of Political Economy* 98(4): 703–38.

Denton, Barry. 1997. *Only in Heaven*. Sheffield, UK: Sheffield Academic Press.

Derthick, Martha. 1979. *Policymaking for Social Security*. Washington: Brookings Institution Press.

Dimson, Elroy, Paul Marsh, and Mike Staunton. 2002. *The Triumph of the Optimists*. Princeton, N.J.: Princeton University Press.

Dionne, E. J., Jr. 1999. "Why Social Insurance?" *Social Security Brief* No. 6. Washington: National Academy of Social Insurance.

Dodds, Eric R. 1951. *The Greeks and the Irrational*. Berkeley, Calif.: University of California Press.

Dominitz, Jeff, Charles F. Manski, and Jordan Heinz. 2003. "Will Social Security Be There for You?" NBER Working Paper 9798. Cambridge, Mass.: National Bureau of Economic Research.

Duggan, James E., Robert Gillingham, and John S. Greenlees. 1993. "The Returns Paid to Early Social Security Cohorts." *U.S. Treasury Research Paper Series*. Washington: U.S. Treasury Department, Office of the Assistant Secretary for Economic Policy.

Dunbar, Nicholas. 2000. *Inventing Money: The Story of Long-Term Capital Management and the Legends Behind It*. New York: John Wiley & Sons.

Dunn, John. 2000. *The Cunning of Unreason*. London: HarperCollins.

———. 2005. *Setting the People Free*. London: Atlantic.

Durkheim, Emile. 1902/1984. *The Division of Labor in Society*, 2nd ed, trans. by W. D. Halls. New York: Free Press.

Eichengreen, Barry. 2005. "Sterling's Past, Dollar's Future: Historical Perspectives on Reserve Currency Competition." NBER Working Paper 11336. Cambridge, Mass.: National Bureau of Economic Research.

Emerson, Ralph Waldo. 1841/1968. "Self-Reliance." In *The Selected Writings of Ralph Waldo Emerson*, edited by Brooks Atkinson. New York: Modern Library.

Fama, Eugene F., and Kenneth R. French. 2002. "The Equity Premium." *Journal of Finance* 57: 637–59.

Farmer, J. Doyle, Paolo Patelli, and Ilija I. Zovko. 2005. "The Predictive Power of Zero Intelligence in Financial Markets." *Proceedings of the National Academy of Sciences* 102(8 February): 2254–9.

Federal Old-Age and Survivors Insurance and Federal Disability Insurance Trust Funds, Board of Trustees. 2006. "The 2006 Annual Report of the Board of

Trustees of the Federal Old-Age and Survivors Insurance and Federal Disability Insurance Trust Funds." Annual report, House document 109–103. Washington: U.S. Government Printing Office.

Feldstein, Martin S. 1974. "Social Security, Induced Retirement, and Aggregate Capital Accumulation." *Journal of Political Economy* 82: 905–26.

———. 1998a. "Is Income Inequality Really a Problem?" In *Income Inequality: Issues and Policy Options*. Kansas City: Federal Reserve Bank of Kansas City.

———. ed. 1998b. *Privatizing Social Security.* Chicago, Ill.: University of Chicago Press.

Feldstein, Martin S., Elena Ranguelova, and Andrew Samwick. 2001. "The Transition to Investment-Based Social Security When Portfolio Returns and Capital Profitability Are Uncertain." In *Risk Aspects of Investment-Based Social Security Reform*, edited by John Y. Campbell and Martin Feldstein. Chicago, Ill.: University of Chicago Press.

Frankfurt, Harry G. 2005. *On Bullshit.* Princeton, N.J.: Princeton University Press.

Fuchs, Victor R., Alan B. Krueger, and James M. Poterba. 1998. "Economists' Views about Parameters, Values, and Policy." *Journal of Economic Literature* 36: 1387–425.

Geanakoplos, John, Olivia S. Mitchell, and Stephen P. Zeldes. 1998. "Social Security Money's Worth." NBER Working Paper 6722. Cambridge, Mass.: National Bureau of Economic Research.

Gottschalk, Peter, and Timothy M. Smeeding. 2000. "Empirical Evidence on Income Inequality in Industrialized Countries." In *Handbook of Income Distribution*, edited by A. B. Atkinson and F. Bourguignon. Amsterdam: North-Holland.

Graetz, Michael J., and Jerry L. Mashaw. 1999. *True Security: Rethinking American Social Insurance.* New Haven, Conn.: Yale University Press.

Groshen, Erica L., Bart Hobijn, and Margaret M. McConnell. 2005. "U.S. Jobs Gained and Lost through Trade." *Current Issues in Economics and Finance* 11(August): 1–7.

Grund, Francis J. 1837. *The Americans in Their Moral, Social and Political Relations.* Boston, Mass.: Marsh, Capen, and Lyon.

Gustman, Alan, and Thomas Steinmeier. 1999. "What People Don't Know About Their Pensions and Social Security." NBER Working Paper 7368. Cambridge, Mass.: National Bureau of Economic Research.

Hahn, Frank, and Robert Solow. 1995. *A Critical Essay on Modern Macroeconomic Theory.* Cambridge, Mass.: MIT Press.

Hand, Learned. 1974. *The Spirit of Liberty*, 3rd ed. New York: Alfred A. Knopf.

Hands, D. Wade. 2001. *Reflection Without Rules.* Cambridge: Cambridge University Press.

Hanna, Doug, and Mark Ready. 2005. "Profitable Predictability in the Cross Section of Stock Returns." *Journal of Financial Economics* 78(3): 463–505.

Harder, Ben. 2005. "Pushing Drugs: How Medical Marketing Influences Doctors and Patients." *Science News* 168(30 July): 75–76.

Hardy, Melissa A., ed. 1997. *Studying Aging and Social Change.* Thousand Oaks, Calif.: Sage Publications.

Hardy, Melissa A., Lawrence Hazelrigg, and Jill Quadagno. 1996. *Ending a Career in the Auto Industry.* New York: Plenum.

Harsanyi, John C. 1955. "Cardinal Welfare, Individualistic Ethics, and Interpersonal Comparisons of Utility." *Journal of Political Economy* 63(4): 309–21.

Haugen, Robert A., and Nardin L. Baker. 1996. "Commonality in the Determinants of Expected Stock Returns." *Journal of Financial Economics*, 41(3): 401–39.

Hausman, Daniel M., and Michael S. McPherson. 1996. *Economic Analysis and Moral Philosophy*. Cambridge: Cambridge University Press.

Heckman, James R. 2006. "The Scientific Model of Causality." *Sociological Methodology* 35(1): 1–97.

Hegel, Georg W. F. 1821/1942. *The Philosophy of Right*, trans. T. M. Knox. New York: Oxford University Press.

Hibbing, John R., and Elizabeth Theiss-Morse. 1995. *Congress as Public Enemy: Public Attitudes Toward American Political Institutions*. Cambridge: Cambridge University Press.

Hirshleifer, Jack, and John G. Riley. 1992. *The Analytics of Uncertainty and Information*. Cambridge: Cambridge University Press.

Hofstadter, Richard. 1965. *The Paranoid Style in American Politics*. New York: Alfred A. Knopf.

Holden, Sarah, and Jack VanDerhei. 2006. "Additional Figures for the EBRI/ICI Participant-Directed Retirement Plan Data Collection Project." *Perspective* 12(1A). Washington: Investment Company Statistics.

Howard, Christopher. 1997. *The Hidden Welfare State: Tax Incentives and Social Policy in the United States*. Princeton, N.J.: Princeton University Press.

Ibbotson and Associates. 2004. *Stocks, Bonds, and Inflation: 2004 Yearbook*. Chicago: Ibbotson and Associates.

Jacobs, Lawrence R., and Robert Y. Shapiro. 1998. "Myths and Misunderstandings about Pubic Opinion Toward Social Security." In *Framing the Social Security Debate*, edited by R. Douglas Arnold, Michael J. Graetz, and Alicia H. Munnell. Washington, D.C.: National Academy of Social Insurance/Brookings Institution.

———. 2000. *Politicians Don't Pander: Political Manipulation and the Loss of Democratic Responsiveness*. Chicago, Ill.: University of Chicago Press.

Jencks, Christopher. 1992. *Rethinking Social Policy*. New York: HarperCollins.

Kagel, John H., and Alvin E. Roth, eds. 1995. *The Handbook of Experimental Economics*. Princeton, N.J.: Princeton University Press.

Kahneman, Daniel, and Amos Tversky, eds. 2000. *Choices, Values, and Frames*. New York and Cambridge: Russell Sage Foundation and Cambridge University Press.

Kant, Immanuel. 1784/1983. "An Answer to the Question: What is Enlightenment?" In *Perpetual Peace and Other Essays*, translated and edited by Ted Humphrey. Indianapolis, Ind.: Hackett.

Katzner, Donald W. 1998. *Time, Ignorance, and Uncertainty in Economic Models*. Ann Arbor: University of Michigan Press.

Keister, Lisa A. 2000. *Wealth in America*. Cambridge: Cambridge University Press.

Klein, Jennifer. 2003. *For All These Rights*. Princeton, N.J.: Princeton University Press.

Klein, Joe. 2006. *Politics Lost: How American Democracy Was Trivialized by People Who Think You're Stupid*. New York: Doubleday.

Kollmann, Geoffrey, and Carmen Solomon-Fears. 2001. *Major Decisions in the House and Senate on Social Security: 1935–2000.* CRS Legislative Histories, RL30920. Washington: U.S. Social Security Administration. http://www.ssa.gov/history/reports/crsleghist3.html.

Kotlikoff, Laurence J., and Scott Burns. 2004. *The Coming Generational Storm.* Cambridge, Mass.: MIT Press.

Laffont, Jean-Jacques. 1986/1989. *The Economics of Uncertainty and Information,* translated by J. P. Bonin and H. Bonin. Cambridge, Mass.: MIT Press.

Lee, Chul-In, and Gary Solon. 2006. "Trends in Intergenerational Income Inequality." NBER Working Paper 12007. Cambridge, Mass.: National Bureau of Economic Research.

Leimer, Dean R. 1994. "Cohort-Specific Measures of Lifetime Net Social Security Transfers." ORS Working Paper 59. Washington: Office of Research and Statistics, Social Security Administration.

Levy, Haim, and Deborah Gunthorpe. 1993. "Optimal Investment Proportions in Senior Securities and Equities under Alternative Holding Periods." *Journal of Portfolio Management* 19(Summer): 30–36.

Light, Paul. 1995. *Artful Work: The Politics of Social Security Reform.* New York: Random House.

Lipset, Seymour Martin, and William Schneider. 1987. *The Confidence Gap.* Baltimore, Md.: Johns Hopkins University Press.

Loewenstein, George, and Jon Elster, eds. 1992. *Choice Over Time.* New York: Russell Sage Foundation.

Loewenstein, George, and Dražen Prelec. 2000. "Anomalies in Intertemporal Choice." In *Choices, Values, and Frames,* edited by Daniel Kahneman and Amos Tversky. New York: Russell Sage Foundation.

Loewenstein, George, and Richard H. Thaler. 1989. "Anomalies: Intertemporal Choice." *Journal of Economic Perspectives* 3(4): 181–93.

Long, J. Scott, and Simon Cheng. 2004. "Regression Models for Categorical Outcomes." In *Handbook of Data Analysis,* edited by Melissa Hardy and Alan Bryman. London: Sage Publications.

Lowi, Theodore J. 1990. "Risks and Rights in the History of American Governments." In *Risk,* edited by Edward J. Burger. Ann Arbor: University of Michigan Press.

Lubove, Roy. 1968. *The Struggle for Social Security, 1900–1935.* Cambridge, Mass.: Harvard University Press.

Luhmann, Niklas. 1979. *Trust and Power.* New York: John Wiley & Sons.

Lusardi, Annamaria. 1999. "Information, Expectations, and Saving for Retirement." In *Behavioral Dimensions of Retirement Economics,* edited by Henry J. Aaron. Washington: Brookings Institution Press.

Macdonald, James. 2003. *A Free Nation Deep in Debt.* New York: Farrar, Straus & Giroux.

Machen, J. Gresham. 1923. *Christianity and Liberalism.* New York: Macmillan.

Macpherson, Crawford B. 1962. *The Political Theory of Possessive Individualism.* Oxford: Oxford University Press.

MaCurdy, Thomas E., and John B. Shoven. 2001. "Asset Allocation and Risk Allocation." In *Risk Aspects of Investment-Based Social Security Reform,* edited by John Y. Campbell and Martin Feldstein. Chicago, Ill.: University of Chicago Press.

Madrian, Brigitte, and Dennis F. Shea. 2001. "The Power of Suggestion: Inertia in 401(k) Participation and Savings Behavior." *Quarterly Journal of Economics* 116(4): 1149–525.

Malthus, Thomas R. 1798/1890. *Essay on the Principle of Population*. New York: Ward, Locke.

Mann, Bruce H. 2002. *Republic of Debtors*. Cambridge, Mass.: Harvard University Press.

Mann, Thomas E., and Norman J. Ornstein. 2006. *The Broken Branch*. New York: Oxford University Press.

Manza, Jeff, Fay Lomax Cook, and Benjamin I. Page, eds. 2002. *Navigating Public Opinion*. Chicago, Ill.: University of Chicago Press.

Mares, Isabela. 2003. *The Politics of Social Risk*. Cambridge: Cambridge University Press.

Marx, Karl, and Friedrich Engels. 1848/1976. *Manifesto of the Communist Party*. In *Collected Works, Vol. 6*. New York: International Publishers.

Matthews, George T. 1958. *The Royal General Farms in Eighteenth-Century France*. New York: Columbia University Press.

McHale, John. 2001. "The Risk of Social Security Benefit-Rule Changes." In *Risk Aspects of Investment-Based Social Security Reform*, edited by John Y. Campbell and Martin Feldstein. Chicago, Ill.: University of Chicago Press.

Meade, James E. 1964. *Efficiency, Equality, and the Ownership of Property*. London: Allen & Unwin.

Mitchell, Olivia S., Robert J. Myers, and Howard Young. 1998. *Prospects for Social Security Reform*. Philadelphia, Pa.: University of Pennsylvania Press.

Munnell, Alicia H. 1974. "The Impact of Social Security on Personal Savings." *National Tax Journal* 27(4): 553–67.

———. 2004a. "Population Aging: It's Not Just the Baby Boom." *Issue in Brief* No. 16. Boston, Mass.: Center for Retirement Research at Boston College.

———. 2004b. "A Bird's Eye View of the Social Security Debate." *Issue in Brief* No. 25. Boston, Mass.: Center for Retirement Research at Boston College.

———. 2005. "Are the Social Security Trust Funds Meaningful?" *Issue in Brief* No. 30. Boston, Mass.: Center for Retirement Research at Boston College.

Munnell, Alicia H., Francesca Golub-Sass, and Andrew Varani. 2005. "How Much Are Workers Saving?" *Issue in Brief* No. 34. Boston, Mass.: Center for Retirement Research at Boston College.

Munnell, Alicia H., James G. Lee, and Kevin B. Meme. 2004. "An Update on Pension Data." *Issue in Brief* No. 20. Boston, Mass.: Center for Retirement Research at Boston College.

Munnell, Alicia H. and Mauricio Soto. 2005. "What Does Price Indexing Mean for Social Security Benefits?" *Just the Facts on Retirement Issues*, No. 14. Boston, Mass.: Center for Retirement Research at Boston College.

Munnell, Alicia H., Mauricio Soto, Jerilyn Libby, and John Prinzivalli. 2006. "Investment Returns: Defined Benefit vs. 401(K) Plans." *Issue in Brief* No. 52. Boston: Center for Retirement Research.

Myers, Robert. 1998. "A Glaring Error: Why One Study of Social Security Misstates Returns." *The Actuary* (September).

Nagel, Rosemarie. 1995. "Unraveling in Guessing Games." *American Economic Review* 85(5): 1313–26.

National Center for Education Statistics. 2005. *A Profile of the American High School Senior in 2004: A First Look*. Washington: U.S. Department of Education.

Nolte, Paul. 2004. *Generation Reform*. Munich: Verlag C. H. Beck.

Nyman, John A. 2002. *The Theory of the Demand for Health Insurance*. Stanford, Calif.: Stanford University Press.

Office of the Actuary. 2005. *The 2005 Annual OASDI Trustees Report*. Washington: U.S. Social Security Administration.

———. 2006. *The 2006 Annual OASDI Trustees Report*. Washington: U.S. Social Security Administration.

Office of Management and Budget. 2004a. *Economic Report of the President, 2004*. Washington: Executive Office of the President.

———. 2004b. *Historical Tables, Budget of the United States Government, Fiscal Year 2004*. Washington: Executive Office of the President.

Office of Policy. 2004. *Annual Statistics Supplemental to the Social Security Bulletin, 2003*. Washington: U.S. Social Security Administration.

———. 2005. *Annual Statistics Supplemental to the Social Security Bulletin, 2004*. Washington: U.S. Social Security Administration.

O'Rourke, P. J. 2005. "Freedom, Responsibility . . . And What? Social Security Reform—An Explanation." *The Atlantic* 295: 42.

Orszag, Peter, and Joseph Stiglitz. 2001. "Rethinking Pension Reform." In *New Ideas About Old Age Security*, edited by Robert Holzmann and Joseph Stiglitz. Washington: The World Bank.

Peck, Jamie. 2001. *Workfare States*. New York: Guilford.

Pension Benefit Guaranty Corporation. 2005. *Annual Report*. Washington: Pension Benefit Guaranty Corporation.

Peterson, Peter G. 1996. *Will America Grow Up Before It Grows Old? How the Coming Social Security Crisis Threatens You, Your Family, and Your Country*. New York: Random House.

Pew Research Center for the People and the Press. 2005. "Bush Failing in Social Security Push." Pew Report #236. Washington: Pew Research Center. http://people-press.org/reports/display.php3?ReportID=238.

Pfaff, William. 2005. *The Bullet's Song*. New York: Simon & Schuster.

Poterba, James M. 2000. "Stock Market Wealth and Consumption." *Journal of Economic Perspectives* 14(2): 99–118.

Rabin, Matthew. 1993. "Incorporating Fairness into Game Theory and Economics." *American Economic Review* 83(5): 1281–302.

Rangel, Antonio. 2003. "Forward and Backward Intergenerational Goods: Why Is Social Security Good for the Environment?" *American Economic Review* 93(3): 813–34.

Rangel, Antonio, and Richard Zeckhauser. 2001. "Can Market and Voting Institutions Generate Optimal Intergenerational Risk Sharing?" In *Risk Aspects of Investment-Based Social Security Reform*, edited by John Y. Campbell and Martin Feldstein. Chicago, Ill.: University of Chicago Press.

Rawls, John. 1971. *A Theory of Justice*. Cambridge, Mass.: Harvard University Press.

Reinsdorf, Marshall B. 2004. "Alternative Measures of Personal Scoring." *Survey of Current Business* 84(September): 17–27.

Reno, Virginia, and Anita Cardwell. 2005. "Social Security Finances: Findings of the 2005 Trustees Report." *Social Security Brief* No. 20. Washington: National Academy of Social Insurance.

Reno, Virginia, and Joni Lavery. 2005. "Options to Balance Social Security Funds over the Next 75 Years." *Social Security Brief* No. 18. Washington: National Academy of Social Insurance.

Reno, Virginia, and Kathryn Olson. 1998. "Can We Afford Social Security when Baby Boomers Retire?" *Social Security Brief* No. 4. Washington: National Academy of Social Insurance.

Rohter, Larry. 2005. "Chile's Retirees Find Shortfall in Private Plan." *New York Times*, January 27, 2005, p. A1.

Rothschild, Emma. 1995. "Social Security and Laissez Faire in Eighteenth-Century Political Economy." *Population and Development Review* 21(4): 711–44.

Rubin, Beth. 1996. *Shifts in the Social Contract*. Thousand Oaks, Calif.: Pineforge.

Rugh, Jacob S. 2004. "What Happened to TIAA-CREF Participant Premium and Asset Allocations from 2000 to 2004?" *Research Dialogue* No. 80. New York: TIAA-CREF Institute.

Samuelson, Paul A. 1947. *The Foundation of Economic Analysis*. Cambridge, Mass.: Harvard University Press.

———. 1958. "An Exact Consumption-Loan Model of Interest With or Without the Social Contrivance of Money." *Journal of Political Economy* 66(6): 467–82.

Sandage, Scott. 2005. *Born Losers*. Cambridge, Mass.: Harvard University Press.

Sargent, Thomas J. 1999. *The Conquest of American Inflation*. Princeton, N.J.: Princeton University Press.

Scherer, Frederic M. 2001. "The Link Between Gross Profitability and Pharmaceutical R&D Spending." *Health Affairs* 20(5): 216–20.

Schieber, Sylvester J., and John B. Shoven. 1999. *The Real Deal: The History and Future of Social Security*. New Haven, Conn.: Yale University Press.

Schram, Sanford. 1995. *Words of Welfare: The Poverty of Social Science and the Social Science of Poverty*. Minneapolis, Minn.: University of Minnesota Press.

Seabright, Paul. 2005. *The Company of Strangers*. Princeton, N.J.: Princeton University Press.

Sen, Amartya. 1970. "The Impossibility of a Paretian Liberal." *Journal of Political Economy*, 78: 152–7.

Sered, Susan Starr, and Rushika Fernandopulle. 2005. *Uninsured in America: Life and Death in the Land of Opportunity*. Berkeley, Calif.: University of California Press.

Sheffrin, Steven M. 1996. *Rational Expectations*, 2nd ed. Cambridge: Cambridge University Press.

Shiller, Robert J. 1989. *Market Volatility*. Cambridge, Mass.: MIT Press.

Skidmore, Max J. 1999. *Social Security and Its Enemies*. Boulder, Colo.: Westview Press.

Skinner, Quentin. 2002. "A Third Concept of Liberty." *London Review of Books* 24 (April 4, 2002): 18.

Sklansky, Jeffrey. 2002. *The Soul's Economy*. Chapel Hill, N.C.: University of North Carolina Press.

Slemrod, Joel, and Jon Bakija. 2004. *Taxing Ourselves*, 3rd ed. Cambridge, Mass: MIT Press.

Smith, Adam. 1776/1976. *The Wealth of Nations*, edited by R. H. Campbell and A. S. Skinner. Oxford: Oxford University Press.

———. 1790/1976. *The Theory of Moral Sentiments*, 6th ed, edited by A. L. Macfie and D. D. Raphael. New York: Oxford University Press.

Snee, John, and Mary Ross. 1978. "Social Security Amendments of 1977: Legislative History and Summary of Provisions." *Social Security Bulletin* 41(3): 3–20.

Social Security Act of 1935. Public Law 74-271. HR 7260. 74th Cong., 1st sess. (August 14, 1935). As emended, 42 U.S.C. §§ 301–1397.

Solon, Gary. 2002. "Cross-Country Differences in Intergenerational Earnings Mobility." *Journal of Economic Perspectives* 16: 59–66.

Steuerle, C. Eugene, and Jon M. Bakija. 1994. *Retooling Social Security for the 21st Century: Right & Wrong Approaches to Reform*. Washington: Urban Institute Press.

Stockton, David. 1990. *The Classical Athenian Democracy*. Oxford: Oxford University Press.

Summers, Lawrence H. 2004. "The United States and the Global Adjustment Process." Speech at the Stavros S. Niarchos Lecture. March 23, 2004. Washington: Institute for International Economics.

Surowiecki, James. 2004. *The Wisdom of Crowds*. New York: Doubleday.

Swenson, Peter. 1997. "Arranged Alliance: Business Interests in the New Deal." *Politics and Society* 25(1): 66–116.

Taylor, Charles. 1989. *Sources of the Self*. Cambridge: Cambridge University Press.

Thaler, Richard H. 1997. "Giving Markets a Human Dimension." *Financial Times*, June 16, 1997, p.6.

———. 2000. "From Homo Economicus to Homo Sapiens." *Journal of Economic Perspectives* 14(1): 133–41.

Thaler, Richard H., and Shlomo Benartzi. 2004. "Save More Tomorrow." *Journal of Political Economy* 112(S1): S164–87.

Thompson, Hunter S. 1972. *Fear and Loathing in Las Vegas: A Savage Journey to the Heart of the American Dream*. New York: Random House.

———. 1992. "Fear and Loathing in Elko." *Rolling Stone* 622, January 23, 1992, p. 1.

Thompson, Lawrence. 1998. "The Predictability of Retirement Income." *Social Security Brief* No. 3. Washington: National Academy of Social Insurance.

Tripp, Nathaniel. 2005. *Confluence*. Hanover, N. H.: Steerforth Press.

U.S. General Accounting Office (GAO). 1999. *Social Security: Issues in Comparing Rates of Return with Market Investments*. Report to the Chairman, Special Committee on Aging. Washington: U.S. Government Printing Office.

———. 2003. *Social Security Issues Relating to Noncoverage of Public Employees*. Testimony Before the Subcommittee on Social Security, Committee on Ways and Means, House of Representatives. Washington: U.S. Government Printing Office.

U.S. Security Exchange Commission. 2000. *Report on Mutual Fund Fees and Expenses*. Washington: Security Exchange Commission, Division of Investment Management.

Venti, Steven F., and David A. Wise. 2000. "Choice, Chance and Wealth Dispersion at Retirement." NBER Working Paper 7521. Cambridge, Mass.: National Bureau of Economic Research.

Wallis, John Joseph, and Douglass North. 1986. "Measuring the Transaction Sector in the American Economy, 1870–1970." In *Long-Term Factors in American Economic Growth*. Chicago, Ill.: University of Chicago Press.

Washington, George. 1786/1997. *Writings*, compiled by John Rhodehamel. New York: Library of America.

Weber, Max. 1904/2002. *The Protestant Ethic and the Spirit of Capitalism*, translated by P. Baehr and G. C. Wells. New York: Penguin.

———. 1909/1956. "Address to the Verein für Sozialpolitik." In *Max Weber and German Politics, 2d.*, edited by J. P. Mayer. London: Faber & Faber.

Wermers, Russ. 2000. "Mutual Fund Performance." *Journal of Finance* 55: 1655–703.

White, Harrison. 2002. *Markets from Networks*. Princeton, N.J.: Princeton University Press.

Whitgift, John. 1851–1853. *The Works of John Whitgift*, 3 vols. Cambridge: Cambridge University Press.

Whitman, Walt. 1871/1982. *Democratic Vistas*. In *Complete Poetry and Collected Prose*, compiled by Justin Kaplan. New York: Library of America.

Williamson, Oliver. 1975. *Markets and Hierarchies*. New York: Free Press.

Wolfe, Alan. 2006. *Does American Democracy Still Work?* New Haven, Conn.: Yale University Press.

Zaret, David. 1985. *The Heavenly Contract*. Chicago, Ill.: University of Chicago Press.

Index

Boldface numbers refer to figures and tables.

one-earner couples, IRR for, **108,** 110–11

On Liberty (Mill), 192

optimism, economic: in stock market, 123–31; and support for PRAs, **152,** 161–62

O'Rourke, P. J., 2

outsourcing of PRA management, 171

ownership principle, 88, 163–67

parent and children cohorts, 39

Pareto, Vilfredo, 29

Pareto efficiency, 29, 30–31

Pareto optimality, 29, 30–31

Patelli, Paolo, 128

PAYG (pay-as-you-go) program: failure in late 1970s economy, 50; historical shifts to, 47, 81–82, 94; inequalities in, 104; privatization position's criticism of, 88–89; rates of return, 94–95; unsustainability of, 111

Pension Benefit Guaranty Corporation (PBGC), 169–71, 251*n*20–21

pension plans: contribution rates to voluntary plans, 200–201; contributions as self-tax mechanism, 48; and investment in public debt instruments, 54; IRAs, 147–48; state and local government, 23, 75, 81, 83–84, 94, 251*n*19. *See also* employer-sponsored pension plans; private retirement accounts (PRAs); Social Security

perfect competition and efficiency vs. fairness, 31

personal interest rate, 34–36, 63–64, 118, 201

Pew Research Center for the People and the Press, 148, 160, 162–63

polarization in political ideologies, lack of, 157–58

political affiliation variable, 149, 150, 158

politics: and adjustments to Social Security, 1, 10, 84; and appeal to ideology, 220–21, 225; civic engagement, 212–13, 223–25, 230–31; as context for Social Security, 9; and culture of fear and loathing, 3–5, 158, 181, 193–95, 230; devolution of American, 229–31; diminishing ability to control events, 14, 16; and efficiency distortions, 215–16; failure of moral leadership, 226–27, 228–29; and fairness, 32; and governmental incapacity-incompetence, 174–79; and health care debate, 55; impact on market model, 26, 182, 189; and information manipulation, 22, 48, 122, 135–36, 215–16; negotiation of individual and collective views, 230; overview of issues, 143–44; and ownership society, 163–67; polarization issue, 157–58; and preservation vs. privatization, 65, 140, 147–63; Social Security as demonstration project for, 2–3; and terminology manipulation, 17–18; trust and risk, 167–74; and Trust Fund, 48–49, 51, 53–54, 83, 95–96; and undermining of Social Security, 5–6, 43–46, 80–81, 95, 225–26. *See also* Congress, U. S.; democracy

Politics Lost (Klein), 230

Ponzi scheme, 105

pooling of risks, 36–37, 42, 45, 71–73, 176

population categories and projections, 18–19

postemployment income insurance: and manufacturing workers, 164–65; and moral hazard, 3, 58–59, 138, 167; prediction challenges, 33–34, 221; saving and investing role in, 227–28. *See also* pension plans

Poterba, James, 8, 28

poverty: and fairness, 97; and inability to invest for retirement, 138, 250*n*12; Social Security's role in mitigating, 74–77, 83–84, 136–37